"As a high school principal, one of my goals for all students is equipping them with knowledge to make the right decisions about college. Understanding which direction will provide the best education for the money is a hard road to navigate. *OnToCollege* has assembled a clear path to better prepare students and families when faced with the daunting task of college decision making."

—Matt Blomenkamp

Principal, Bennington High School

On
To
College
with John Baylor

(402) 475-7737

www.OnToCollege.com

On
To
College
with John Baylor

Platinum Guide
for College

Finding Your Best-Fit
College at the Lowest Cost

On To College with John Baylor

PLATINUM GUIDE FOR COLLEGE

FINDING YOUR BEST-FIT COLLEGE AT THE LOWEST COST

ISBN: 978-1-942412-14-4

Cataloging in Publication Data on file with the publisher.

www.OnToCollege.com

Publishing and production: Concierge Marketing Inc.

Revised for 2018-2020

10 9 8 7 6 5 4 3 2 1

CONTENTS

INTRODUCTION

You've just opened the *OTC Platinum Guide*, a treasure trove for schools and families.

Scholars, it is a time to be excited and focused. This is a precious time, when opportunities are boundless and knowledge is critical. Any instincts to be a passive couch slug should be vigorously resisted. Attitude determines altitude.

You, your parents, and your counselor have just become sales executives, selling a worthy product: You! The goal is to accentuate the product for the customers: admissions and financial aid folks.

Everything here supports your hard-working college counselor: a dream catcher in a student's life. Your counselor may write you a college recommendation, approve your final college list, and help you negotiate those final financial aid offers.

We want you to have many college options at a variety of costs. Then you and your parents can head off on that fun trip to visit your final college choices.

So commit to becoming a two- or four-year college graduate with minimal debt. Step one: get into your 'best-fit' college at the lowest cost.

NOTES

Part 1

Where do you start?

On To College

with John Baylor

WELCOME TO THE *ONTOCOLLEGE*™ *PLATINUM GUIDE*!

HOW TO GET INTO YOUR BEST-FIT COLLEGE AND SPEND LESS.™

This book is different than all the other guides out there. We've been where you are, so we founded OnToCollege™ on the premise that you might need a guide through the maze of education, career, and life. I devoted my own career to helping young people improve their test scores, craft the most effective applications, and gain access to a two- or four-year degree at minimal cost. OnToCollege™ has worked with thousands of families doing just what you are doing—figuring out your future.

We've compiled the knowledge we gained from working with students and their families, and I've organized it in a way that I know will make a difference.

- First, you'll learn essential information about what schools are looking for in today's applicants.

- Second, you'll sort out your own hopes, dreams, special skills, and realities.

- Third, you'll find valuable resources that help you set an objective, develop a strategy, create your tactical plan, and ultimately, realize your goals.

I know it's hard to sit down and read a book in the midst of the busiest, scariest, and most important years of your life: high school. I have bundled information into this book in an easy-to-read, no-fluff package that tells you what to do now and what to do next. You don't have to read it front to back to get great information that will make a difference, but I know that if you apply the information provided, you'll win this college admissions game.

When you see these icons, you'll find information on
topics that we think are particularly important.

 This icon features hot tips we know you'll want to look out for.

 This icon indicates budget items of particular importance.

 This icon represents *OTC* Recommended items.

 This icon is for Important Insider Info for making your summers count.

Get a notepad and jot important notes,
tips that you think will help you, and your goals.

Highlight tips you like, write in the margins—whatever it is that makes you go for it!

OnToCollege with John Baylor urges students to borrow annually no more than $5,000 and to earn annually at least $3,500, primarily during breaks. Thus, the student can handle about $8,500 of the net cost each year. So if a college has a $16,500 Net Cost annually, the student can handle $8,500 of that amount. $8,000, or $667 a month, is the difference, the responsibility of the parents or guardian — an amount that may be comparable to rent on an apartment. College can be affordable. Use this book to become a smart college shopper.

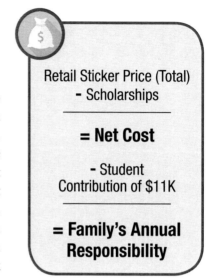

Retail Sticker Price (Total)
- Scholarships
──────────────────
= Net Cost

- Student
Contribution of $11K
──────────────────
= Family's Annual Responsibility

Plus, a family with an adjusted gross income (AGI) of under $160,000 should qualify for an annual $2,500 federal tax credit: the American Opportunity Tax Credit. Partial tax credits are available for families with an AGI between $160,000 and $180,000. Single parent families must have an AGI of less than $80,000 for the full $2,500 tax credit. So the student and tax credit together can offset as much as $11,000 of the net cost. **$11K Paves the Way!**

STUDENT'S ANNUAL CONTRIBUTION
(IF FAMILY HOUSEHOLD INCOME IS LESS THAN $160,000)

(Borrow) $5,000

(Earn during breaks) $3,500

+ (American Opportunity Tax Credit) $2,500

(Savings) $11,000

So subtract at least $8,500 from your family's obligation annually. If your family's income falls below $160,000 a year, subtract $11,000 from your net cost. **$11K paves the way!**

Borrowing $5,000 a year over four years is $20,000, an amount that will result in about $225 monthly loan payments until age 31, a responsibility that should not limit life choices. Borrowing much more probably will. Unless you'll definitely be earning a lot after college, *OTC* discourages borrowing more than $20,000 total—or $5,000 a year.

So think about real value when choosing schools. Blind hope is not a strategy to pay for college. Naïve college shopping can lead to suffocating indebtedness and real regret.

CHAPTER 1

WHERE DO YOU START?

 ## THE 2-2-2-1 RULE

Setting a goal at the beginning of a project is the same as setting your intention. It gives you a destination for a journey. Knowing what outcome you are shooting for can motivate you to keep going, and give you something to measure to prove you made it! We want to help you become a college graduate with minimal debt. If you're blessed to live with affluence, you need to focus on the right college. If your ability to pay for college is limited, we need to find the right college at the right price.

Especially for those of you on a budget, *OTC* suggests a simple approach. It's called the 2-2-2-1 Rule. By the end of the first part of this book, we want you to have the following actions decided and ready to accomplish:

> ### Again, if you're on a budget, apply to at least 2 in-state universities, 2 state colleges, 2 private colleges, and 1 community college.

The 2-2-2-1 Rule maximizes aid regardless of your ultimate GPA, class rank, or ACT or SAT score. For example, in our state, an ACT score of 26 gets no money at any of our in-state public universities, but can garner a full four-year tuition scholarship at a public state college.

The 2-2-2-1 Rule usually triggers maximum choices at multiple cost levels no matter what state you call home.

It's a simple equation, but we know it's not quite so simple: you still need to identify the right 7 colleges (and often a few more, as we recommend that all students apply to 7 to 16 colleges).

DECIDING WHAT SCHOOLS TO CONSIDER FOR YOUR 2-2-2-1 LIST

All students should seek to go to the right college—those on a budget also need the right price. Some believe they can only afford to go to the college close to home—one reason to start your journey with the 2-2-2-1 rule.

Talk to People You Know

Your teachers, counselor, parents, teachers, relatives, family, and friends want to help you achieve your goals. Ask them to suggest colleges that may be a good fit for you.

Do Your Homework

Research the colleges you're considering. Ask your counselor for resources, consult *OTC's America's Most Affordable Colleges: Our Definitive List of the Best, Lowest-Cost Schools*. Finalize your 2-2-2-1 list, and then add to it.

Wayne Gretzky said that he never scored on any of the shots he didn't take. If you don't apply, you won't learn what your cost would be. Any school that could be your right college at the right price needs to be on your list.

The more information you gather from as many resources as possible, the better your college choices will be:

- Attend your school's College Night

- Consult with your school counselor and teachers

- Follow student blogs at the colleges you are considering

- Talk to college admission staff

- Visit college campuses, if possible

- Ask college representatives to recommend current students or recent graduates to talk to

Maintain Perspective

During your search, hone your preferences and goals. Everyone changes throughout high school; your preferences and goals may change and grow as you do.

NOTES

CHAPTER 2

WHERE DO YOU WANT TO GO?

 ## QUESTIONS TO ASK YOURSELF

To maximize your chances of going to your 'best fit' for less, apply to a minimum of seven and no more than sixteen schools. Nine questions to ask yourself:

1. In what area of the country do you want to go to school? Prioritize your choices geographically: local, regional, or national. I believe that New England, the east coast, the Rust Belt, the Pacific Northwest, and the Midwest have the majority of the nation's rigorous schools. There are plenty of exceptions: Pomona, Emory, Rice, and more. Considering international colleges? Google "Scottish Ivies" and check out our list of Canadian colleges in Appendix F. You can get a solid college degree for $20k to $30k a year in Canada—sometimes less.

2. What is the extracurricular activity in college that you will participate in meaningfully: an instrument, sport, school newspaper, debate, chorus, volunteer work, theater, student government? Search your heart. Every college student needs a productive extracurricular passion. Why? You're about to have more free time than you realize. Your high school classes and activities probably amount to forty to seventy hours of regimented time weekly. A normal college course load is just fifteen hours a week in class, plus your study time (and this after your lazy summer following graduation)! Unless you must earn money for 20-plus hours of free time each week, have a passion to fill that time, or you'll regret how you wasted it. Students engaged in an extracurricular are less likely to feel disconnected and more likely to graduate.

3. What will my cost probably be? The best way to determine how home equity and your other financial assets will influence your financial aid package is to use each school's net price calculator. Plug in your figures into each school's net price calculator, found on the school's web site. You might avoid schools that will be too expensive even after need-based aid (and those that don't offer significant merit-based aid—see Appendix D). For example, one of my recent students wanted to go to Boston University. Her family made about $200,000 a year. Unless she won merit-based scholarships, BU would have cost her about $70k a year. She settled on a less expensive choice, opting for financial freedom rather than committing to loans that would crush her in her twenties.

4. How much money is the family prepared to spend for that undergraduate degree— not borrow—spend? Divide by four, and then add $8,500 per year to that budget because the student should be able to contribute $3,500 annually from earnings during school breaks and $5,000 from borrowing. There should be plenty of choices beyond that budget thanks to need-based and merit-based aid, but applicants need at least two financial safety schools that will fit within the budget. I rarely recommend borrowing beyond $5,000 per year for four years because $20,000 of debt can be paid off by age 31 for only about $215 per month—a manageable amount that shouldn't alter important life choices. College should create financial freedom, not indebtedness.

5. What major? STEM majors (science, technology, engineering, and math) typically get paid more in the near term. Engineering, architecture, and a specialized science (oceanography, botany, entomology) might limit your choices to big universities, while pre-med, marketing, business, history, and nearly everything else shouldn't. Choose what you love. Vocational majors, sometimes called "career majors" (marketing, nursing, journalism, etc.) usually are helpful for that entry-level job because they prepare you for a specific job. Liberal arts majors concentrate on teaching the ability to critically reason and communicate well, which can add job security throughout your life. Try to choose small, scintillating seminars; stay away from large lazy lecture halls. Before choosing a major, do some job shadowing and personal inventory. If you don't like details, forget pre-law or pre-med. Your future career should ultimately be the intersection of what you love to do, what you're good at, and what people will pay you to do.

6. How important is climate? Do you equate warm weather with joy? If so, it may be more difficult to find a college with a rigorous, well-regarded education because hot temperatures and academic rigor often do not go together.

7. What percent of the students have cars on campus? If you'll need a car, expect about $2,000 more in annual costs. Plus, a campus filled with cars means:

- lots of parking lots and parking hassles

- a campus with students looking to get away

- a spread out campus, which dilutes the sense of community and common purpose

  Some colleges prohibit freshmen from bringing cars because of these drawbacks. They know that the new-found freedom can distract young students; and their job is to get you through to graduation.

8. What is the ideal number of students in your freshman English course?

- Fewer than 20 students—then you'll want a school of 2,000 students or fewer. This type of school is where undergrads typically take priority.

- 21-45 students—then you can handle a school of 2,000 to 4,500.

- If more than 45 students is okay with you, you can go for a big school of more than 4,500 students: a university sometimes filled with 'lecture hall' educations.

9. Would you consider an all-female or all-male school? Single gender colleges can be great options because they're often prestigious, rigorous, buttressed by great alumni networks, and easier to gain admission. Every good all-women's school is either affiliated with or near a coed-college. Biggest difference: no coed dorms, no coed bathrooms, and classes and meals with less than 10 percent men. Sociological studies strongly suggest that women perform better academically without men around. Fewer distractions lead to greater productivity. There are few men's schools. Wabash College in Indiana (excellent!), Hampton-Sydney in Virginia, and Deep Springs in California (tops) are examples.

# BUILDING YOUR COLLEGE LIST

Classify your choices into four types: A, B, and C list schools, plus Money Schools (schools that offer significant merit-based aid—see Appendix D)

A List (dream schools)

Top schools, many of which might reject you. "If you don't have dreams, you've got nightmares." Chase dreams. The worst they can do is reject you or not offer enough scholarship money.

B list (good-match schools)

Solid schools you'd like to attend, many of which you should get into, and are also a decent financial match.

C list (safety schools)

These are schools that fit your budget and avoid more than $20,000 in debt for the degree. A back up or two you'd like to attend that will definitely accept you and fit your budget.

Money Schools

Colleges that offer generous merit-based aid that you can win: see Appendix D, as well as the list of Canadian Colleges in Appendix F, and our book *America's Most Affordable Colleges*.

Those seeking financial aid need to be strategic. There are plenty of excellent B and C and even A list schools that dole out merit-based scholarships to entice top applicants.

The cost of each application will be about $50 (with exemptions often granted to students who apply online or show financial hardship).

RESOURCES (WEBSITES THAT CAN HELP WHITTLE DOWN YOUR LIST):

- American Universities: www.clas.ufl.edu/au/

  Offers a direct link to the website of every American university or college. It also has links to Canadian and international universities.

- College Board: www.collegeboard.com

  You can register for the SAT and SAT Subject Tests. Also access the CSS PROFILE financial aid application, explore their college search engine, and search for scholarship dollars.

- Financial aid site: www.finaid.org

  This is a good website for specific financial aid questions and links to other useful websites. You can also find a practice FAFSA here.

- Free Application for Federal Student Aid (FAFSA): www.fafsa.gov

  Every American citizen or permanent resident applying for financial aid has to submit this form. Never pay to file your FAFSA. File in October each year, beginning senior year, because scholarships are often awarded on a first-come, first-served basis.

- NCAA: www.ncaa.org/about/student-athlete-eligibility

  Future college athletes should review this website for regulations and forms for the athletic recruiting process.

LESS SELECTIVE COLLEGES

Don't be fooled by the term "Less Selective"—quality and selectivity don't always go together. Less selective just means that this school is not one of the sixty or so that rejects the majority of its applicants. There are excellent colleges that are less selective, focused on undergraduate education, and effective at changing lives.

SELECTIVE COLLEGES

At selective schools, admissions committees get to be choosy. Yale, Princeton, Harvard, and Stanford routinely reject 92-94 percent of their applicants.

Remain calm—these are some of the nation's most selective colleges (and brand-name, designer-label schools do not necessarily provide the nation's finest undergraduate experiences).

Inform yourself and pick the best school for you that provides the best value. Many colleges offer a good education. But with sticker prices often above $40,000/year, many offer suspect value, if you're on a budget.

Grades, rigor within the curriculum, and test scores are very important, but there are more top applicants than there are dorm beds at selective schools. Admissions committees have to look for attributes beyond The Big 3. Volunteering will help differentiate you and should pay you more (scholarship) dollars than most jobs ever will. Your application essays and recommendation letters are also increasingly important.

Choosing schools that are popular among your peers is rarely the right choice: the herd mentality can lead to poor decisions that may not fit your career objectives, and worse, may provide distractions that make it more difficult to succeed.

NOTES

NOTES

CHAPTER 3

THE BIG 3

If you're interested in finding your best-fit college at the lowest cost, here are The Big 3 (these will really help):

1. GPA during grades 9-11 and the first semester of grade 12 (class rank),

2. ACT or SAT score (take your preferred test at least four times), and

3. one extracurricular (prioritize one—be the best you can be, and market that skill).

 ### GPA - BUT WHAT IF YOU DON'T HAVE A 4.0?

Work hard to ensure your GPA reflects your potential. When you have good grades and challenging classes, selective colleges should reward you. It's not about acing every basket-weaving or photography class—it's about taking courses that further your knowledge and interest in a subject. Many selective schools are looking for a composite of factors:

1. Rigor in the transcript: if offered, try to take AP courses and AP tests (or IB courses & IB tests) without over-burdening yourself.

2. Test scores: take the ACT or SAT four (or more) times

Rigor vs. Class Rank

Rigor means "demanding and challenging." Difficult courses show colleges that you embrace challenges. Find the best teachers and the best classes. Plus demanding core classes are likely to translate into solid ACT and SAT scores.

However, some scholarships are based on class rank. Learn how your high school determines class rank, and make course choices that demonstrate rigor without jeopardizing class rank.

 ## ACT AND SAT SCORES

The best paying job you'll ever have in high school is improving your ACT or SAT score. Improving your GPA should also pay well in future scholarships. Excellence at one extracurricular skill can also enhance your scholarships.

And college is inclusive: there is typically need-based aid for residents with incomes of $150,000 a year or lower and significant need-based aid for those making less than $75,000 a year.

 ## EXTRACURRICULAR ACTIVITIES

Achievement in one extracurricular in high school means participating in ways that matter, both to you and to the group to which you belong. Signing up for something means showing up. Participate as much as you can, and it will make a difference for your college prospects too. You'll develop leadership skills, learn new skills not taught in a regular classroom setting, and maybe even have fun and make lasting friendships.

Significant achievement in one extracurricular area will make you more marketable to selective schools. College admissions committees look for quality, not quantity. Listing nine different clubs and organizations may hurt your chances. Achieving excellence in at least one activity will be most valuable, as it highlights your strengths rather than just showing how busy you can be.

Extracurricular activities don't all have to take place during the school year. Participating in purposeful summer programs can offer you an immersive learning experience, as well as show your drive and determination to succeed. Champions are made during the off-season.

 The best paying job you'll ever have in high school is improving your ACT or SAT score.

It's during the quiet times without an audience that one builds the foundation for greatness. Larry Bird practiced basketball in the rain. Mia Hamm did wind sprints on her own in a park. Good musicians practice every day. Vacations are not only an ideal time to dedicate yourself to extracurricular achievement—they can also lay the foundation for improved school performance. My worst high school grade was in Latin. The summer after my sophomore year I dedicated myself to mastering Latin vocabulary. After buying a Latin vocabulary book, I proceeded to write out my own vocabulary sheets. I taped them next to my bed and next to my bathroom mirror—places where I could incorporate them into my daily routine. Just ten minutes a day for about six weeks solved my Latin struggles. Vocabulary was holding me back, so I attacked it without consuming much of any one day.

Use your summers and vacations to have fun and be with your family, but find time for focused skill-building. If you need to shore up your math, foreign language, or science foundation, find the right book and spend small amounts of every day ensuring a foundation for success. A tutor can help as well, but the resolve to be your best, armed with a game-plan, may be sufficient.

Furthermore, applications ask for your summer activities. So be sure to have productive skill-building summers. A summer job helps as well since many admissions folks do not come from affluence. But don't let a job keep you from improving an extracurricular skill or your academic foundation. Consider a reasonably-priced college summer academic camp (See Appendix B). Work in a science lab. And don't forget to read at least one book a month.

NOTES

CHAPTER 4

WHAT ELSE MATTERS?

Life is more than grades and test scores. A vibrant campus environment is built with engaged students, and admissions pros know that students who volunteer regularly and excel at an extracurricular are more engaged in their communities.

It's important to note that this chapter could make the difference in you being accepted over someone else who has similar academic credentials. The Big 3 are huge, but these additional attributes can seal the deal:

- Volunteerism

- Revealing personal essays filled with specifics

- Meaningful teacher (2) and college counselor (1) recommendations filled with specifics (Choose one humanities and one STEM teacher from junior or senior year.)

- Having a job during breaks and summer vacations

 ## VOLUNTEERISM

Schools are looking for self-assured, creative, compassionate leaders; volunteerism can demonstrate all these qualities. Volunteering in a hospital, soup kitchen, or the local YMCA are all good choices. Even better might be a volunteer activity that you create. Schools (and many private scholarships) seek volunteers and leaders. Creating your own volunteer activity demonstrates that you are both.

Go with a friend to teach basketball, English, or swimming to underprivileged kids each week. Identify something that your school needs, and, with a friend, embark on a year-long fund-raising campaign by starting a student committee to raise the necessary money. Be creative, have fun, and make a difference.

Whatever you decide to do, show commitment. At the very latest, start your activity halfway through your junior year. Starting early also allows you to switch activities, if necessary. Ideally, volunteer at least once a week during the school year and twice a week during the summer.

The right volunteer project can be another well-paying job—think college scholarships—all while making you a better person. Volunteering is food for the soul.

PERSONAL ESSAYS

In addition to outside activities, admissions counselors want to know if you will fit in well at their school, so they look to personal essays to discover your interests, values, habits, passions and views about life. Writing an essay that truly reflects YOU will help match you with your best-fit college. See Chapter 14 to learn how to do it well.

TEACHER AND COUNSELOR RECOMMENDATIONS

Essays reveal your perception of yourself and your interests, but obtaining meaningful teacher and counselor recommendations shout how others see you.

Most selective schools require three recommendations: two from junior or senior year teachers in core academic subjects (English or History, and Math or Science) and one from your senior year college counselor. Less selective colleges rarely require recommendations for admission, but scholarships or exclusive academic programs might.

It is important for you to…

- get to know a few teachers well from junior or senior year;

- get to know your senior year college counselor well.

These recommendations can be important because they reinforce the rest of the information within the application.

For months, admissions folks read applications 12-15 hours a day to understand and the applicant pool. Compelling recommendations help when they are filled with specifi recommendations, filled with generalizations, don't.

For your recommendations, choose your teachers wisely: someone who likes you, knows you're smart and hard-working, happily gave you a great grade, and is familiar with your character and passions. A teacher who also is your extracurricular coach could be doubly helpful.

Since you often cannot choose your counselor, visit her early in high school and include her in your big decisions: course choices, summer plans, hopes and dreams, and the college application process. The better your counselor knows you and your family, the more specifically she can write about you.

None of these good people get paid anything extra for writing recommendations.

1. Be sure to ask them nicely if they'd feel comfortable writing you a recommendation, and give them plenty of advance notice before the recommendation is due. September or October of senior year is a good time to ask.

2. Get them all necessary papers and addressed, stamped envelopes (or website information).

3. Since teachers and counselors may not remember all of your scintillating attributes, be sure to offer your counselor and teachers a brief resume showing your character and personality.

4. Get each a nice gift after your recommendations are in: a $25 gift certificate to a restaurant plus a hand-written thank you note, for example.

Check the box that waives your right to read the recommendation (though some teachers will give you a copy). Typically, each teacher will only need to write one recommendation for you, which all your colleges will then receive.

Deadlines for college applications vary. Teacher recommendations do not need to be in by the deadline, although you should try to get them submitted within two weeks after the application deadline at the latest.

In summary, Teacher and Counselor Recommendations can benefit you in many ways.

- Get 3 recommendations.

- Choose teachers from junior and senior year only, an English or History teacher and a Math or Science teacher.

- Get to know your senior year counselor early.

- Recommendations need specifics about you.

- Ask well ahead of time.

- Get a brief resume to them well ahead of time.

- The recommendations can arrive after the application deadline.

- It's your responsibility afterwards to ensure that everything arrived at the admissions office—this typically can be accomplished online.

- Lots of 'thank yous' and a gift (after the recommendations are in) also help.

Remember that these dedicated adults get paid nothing extra for their essays written solely on your behalf and for your benefit. After the recommendations have been sent, be sure to give the teachers and counselors a thank you gift. A restaurant or sports store gift certificate is a nice touch, along with a handwritten note.

What about an extra recommendation?

- Admissions folks are swamped and usually don't like extra recommendations from pastors, US Senators, Mayors, or other individuals. It is rarely advisable to send anything unsolicited. In fact, some schools strictly forbid extra recommendations. Possible exceptions:

    - A recommendation from a college donor or board member who truly knows you and your family well should help.

- If you are a tireless volunteer with a long history of selfless acts, a brief recommendation attesting to your selflessness by someone you worked for could reinforce the compelling essay you wrote about your volunteer efforts.

- Lately, some schools are allowing more than three recommendations. Stanford and Swarthmore are two such examples. Inquire by phone or email to learn how each of your schools feel about unsolicited recommendations.

Bottom line: If you seek an extra recommendation, choose only people who truly know you well.

 ## DOES MY JOB ADD TO MY CHANCES?

Job hours during the school year will usually come at the expense of The Big 3—grades, scores, and one extracurricular—skills that are proven to improve your ability to win admission and financial aid. So unless you're feeding your family or helping pay the mortgage, try not to work Sunday nights through Thursday nights during the school year. If you are helping to feed your family, be sure to write about it in your application essays.

Summer and weekend jobs do provide a picture of achievement and drive. Most admissions folks do not come from affluent families themselves. Thus, showing your job experience suggests that you share a similar background, which may help create a connection between you and your admissions judges.

NOTES

CHAPTER 5

GETTING INTO YOUR BEST-FIT COLLEGE AT THE LOWEST COST

 ## THE STRATEGY

After many years of working with students and their families, I've found that the following strategy will net you the most reward for your effort. The more effort you put in early, the better for your future, and the more likely you are going to land in your best-fit college at the lowest cost.

1. Get your maximum GPA. Typically grades 9, 10, 11, and the first semester of grade 12 are the ones that count.

2. Get your maximum ACT or SAT score. Prepare for and take that test at least 4 times (twice junior spring and twice senior fall). Particularly talented test takers might start with the sophomore year, June ACT or SAT to learn if becoming a National Merit Semi-finalist on the October, junior year PSAT is plausible. A 27 on the ACT or 1250 on the SAT late sophomore year portends a possible top one percent score on the October, junior year PSAT and a national merit award—with much preparation during the summer and fall.

3. Excel at one (or more) extracurricular(s)

    a. Champions are made during the off-season.

    b. Colleges look for the Big 3: GPA (class rank), the Test Score(s), and one extracurricular skill.

4. You and your parents should determine your annual budget. Scrutinize your current expenditures–what can be cut? Don't forget to subtract the savings your departure for college might create at your household, so you aren't doubling certain expenses. Add about $8,500 per year to that budget because you, the student, should be able to earn $3,500 and borrow $5,000 annually. And remember, families with an adjusted gross income (AGI) of less than $160,000 (and who pay at least $2,500 in Federal Income Tax) receive a tax credit of $2,500 annually: The American Opportunity Tax Credit

(see Chapter 9). A tax credit is a dollar-for-dollar reduction in your federal taxes, so add that amount to what you can pay. Partial tax credits are available for families with an AGI between $160,000 and $180,000. Single parent families must have an AGI of less than $80,000 for full $2,500 tax credit, $80,000-$90,000 for partial tax credit. So the student and tax credit together can offset as much as $11,000 of the net cost.

 IF YOUR FAMILY HOUSEHOLD INCOME IS LESS THAN $160,000:

(Borrow) $5,000
(Earn) $3,500
+ (American Opportunity Tax Credit) $2,500
─────────────────────
(Savings) $11,000

So if your family's income falls below $160,000 a year, subtract $11,000 from your net cost to understand what the parents or guardians are responsible for.

---

5. Be sure to have at least one financial safety school on your college list that fit your budget. Private colleges offering merit-based aid, in-state non-flagship public colleges, and community colleges often end up with lower net costs.

6. Apply to 7 to 16 colleges (maximize competition and scholarships). Yes, you might have to spend $40 to $80 per application, so be strategic.

7. Only work at a job during vacations or Friday nights or Saturdays.

   a. Work 60-plus hours a week in the summer, if necessary.

8. Apply for privately-offered, merit-based aid at...

   a. fastaid.com;

   b. educationquest.org (or your state's equivalent);

   c. your school's counseling site (mom or dad should oversee this effort)

9. If you're ready for a productive life adventure or are academically fatigued, apply for a challenging gap-year (see Chapter 15).

   a. Apply to colleges as you would normally.

   b. Also apply for gap-year experiences, ideally abroad.

   c. Accept your best college admissions offer.

According to a Gallup poll, a full 71 percent of Americans watch the clock at work: i.e. 71 percent of adults dislike their job. One reason to become a two- or four-year college graduate with minimal debt is to improve your chances of joining the 29 percent!

    d.   Defer admission one year.

    e.   Have a one-year experience mastering a foreign language and/or an extracurricular skill.

10. Have your parents fill out the FAFSA (FAFSA.gov) each October beginning senior year.

    a.   Have them fill out a practice FAFSA as soon as possible at finaid.org.

    b.   Have them meet with a financial advisor knowledgeable in college finance to maximize your eligibility for need-based aid.

YOU SHOULD BE ASKING: WHY APPLY TO SEVEN TO SIXTEEN SCHOOLS?

Competition for admission is greater than ever. The ease of the Common Application contributes to the increased competition. Plus, with many private universities hanging out $250,000 retail sticker prices for a degree, many students should foster healthy competition for their services. The more schools bidding for you, the more leverage mom and dad will have when they negotiate your financial aid package with your favorite two or three colleges. *Hello better scholarships and lower costs!*

NOTES

CHAPTER 6

MAKING APPLICATIONS WORK HARDER FOR YOU

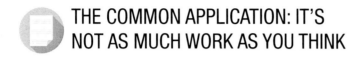

THE COMMON APPLICATION: IT'S NOT AS MUCH WORK AS YOU THINK

In an effort to simplify the task of applying to multiple colleges, most schools requiring essays accept the Common Application (CA). Now you can apply to ten schools for about the same effort required to apply to one. Of course, hundreds of thousands of your peers across the country are also taking advantage of the CA, explaining one reason that applications to top schools have jumped significantly since the late 1990s. Many schools, such as Yale and Allegheny, also require an essay or two in their supplement to the CA, but the CA still makes applying dramatically less burdensome.

More than 500 colleges accept the CA. Just go to www.CommonApp.org to begin your secure, online Common Application.

There you will also find links to each school's supplement to the CA, if it requires one. Do not send anything to an admissions office until you are certain that everything on the online application is perfect. Make sure your grammar and spelling are correct. Proof it. Ask someone you trust to proof it as well.

The Common Application now asks for a 650-word essay.

See Chapter 14 and Appendix A for additional help on your essays. Try to get your essay started in the summer before senior year and finished well before November.

Appendix C in this Guide shows a list of the more than 500 colleges that accept the CA. The website www.CommonApp.org will contain the most up-to-date list.

Nearly every college allows you to fill out and transmit your application online. Still, if you're a throw-back, you can fill out your application the old-fashioned way—with a typewriter or exquisite penmanship. If you decide to apply online, acquaint yourself in early fall with the online Common Application and begin filling it out. You'll have a password, and no school will see your efforts until you click 'send.'

APPLYING EARLY

Early Decision

ED is an application option that allows students to make binding commitments to their first-choice school. An ED application signals that you have weighed your options and that if accepted, you will attend. Due to its binding nature, you can only apply to one school ED.

- Benefits of ED

    - It's easier to get in ED. The regular-decision 2013 admit rate at Williams was less than 15 percent. Williams' early-admit rate for 2013 was 43 percent.

        - ED increases a college's yield, and national school rankings (*US News & World Report*, etc.) use 'yield' as one criterion for ranking colleges. Yield is the number of students admitted who accept, divided by the total number of students admitted. A higher yield means a higher ranking. Since every ED student attends, ED students increase the yield.

        - ED lowers a college's admit rate (the number of students admitted, divided by the total number applying). Rankings also use the admit rate as a measure of selectivity—the lower the admit rate, the better the ranking.

    - You're done with the process sooner. However, you'll need to prepare those other applications because they'll be due January 1 or January 15, and you won't learn of the outcome of your ED application until around December 15.

- Drawbacks of ED

  - You typically won't learn of your financial aid offer until spring, probably April. Hopefully your ED school will meet all of your financial needs, but if not, you won't be able to create competition for you by playing schools against each other. If your decision is contingent on financial aid, ED is rarely advisable. Some schools, though, are now providing ED and Early Action applicants with their financial aid offer in December: Swarthmore, for example.

Early Decision 2

Although it is offered by a limited number of colleges, ED 2 operates exactly the same as the first round of ED, except with a later deadline. ED 2 gives students, who didn't get into their ED school, a second chance at an early admission somewhere else, with all of the ED benefits and drawbacks. The ED 2 deadline is usually identical to the Regular Decision deadline (typically January 1 or 15).

Early Action

Early Action (EA) is non-binding. You may still apply to other schools regular decision, and you will not be required to make a final choice until May 1. You can apply Early Action to more than one school.

- Benefits of EA

  - It may be slightly easier to get in EA. Usually, though, the EA applicant pool is higher quality, which might explain the higher acceptance rate for EA applicants over Regular Decision applicants.

  - You get organized sooner. Students unburdened by an October application deadline often leave all the work for the end of December.

Deadlines for both Early Decision (ED) and Early Action (EA) applications are usually October 15, November 1, or November 15. On December 15, just weeks before most of your other application deadlines, you'll find out if you're...

- accepted

- deferred to the regular application pool, or

- rejected

NOTES

CHAPTER 7

THE ACT®, SAT®, SAT SUBJECT TESTS, & AP® TESTS

 TESTING YOUR BOUNDARIES

THE ACT

The ACT consists of four sections: English, Math, Reading, and Science. Each subtest has a maximum score of 36. The final score is the average of the four sub-scores, although many colleges super-score the ACT: taking your highest sub-scores from all of your ACT tests. The ACT is accepted by all colleges for admission.

The ACT includes an optional 40-minute Writing Test, which we recommend taking twice if you're applying to selective colleges. Good diagnostic test scores help with admission at selective colleges. On occasion the Writing Test may also be relevant to less-selective schools, depending on the major. Check the admissions tab on each college's website to see if your target schools and/or programs value the extra effort.

To sign up to take an ACT, go to www.ACTstudent.org.

> Increasing your test score is the best paying job a high school student will have.

Many less-selective colleges will accept applicants with a 20 or higher on the ACT, but just 3 more points will cause many private colleges to add at least $1500 a year to the financial aid offer—over 4 years, that's $6,000. Five more points can mean $2,500 a year or more. Apply to a selective college, and the test score becomes even more important, affecting not just aid but admission itself. Jump to a 30 or higher, and you're eligible for bigger scholarships. Jumping that test score is the best paying job a high school student will have. Check out Appendix D and *OTC's America's Most Affordable Colleges* to learn more about the potential huge financial impact of higher ACT or SAT scores.

The SAT

Historically, the SAT has been preferred by colleges on the coasts. Today, all colleges will accept either the ACT or SAT, so you get to choose. The SAT has two Math sections, a Reading section, and a Writing and Language section (very similar to the ACT's English section). The two math sections together amount to 800 points as do the Reading and Writing and Language sections. The maximum score possible is 1600.

The SAT includes an optional 50-minute Writing Test, which we recommend taking twice if you're applying to selective colleges. Good diagnostic test scores help with admission at selective colleges. On occasion the Writing Test may also be relevant to less-selective schools, depending on the major. Check the admissions tab on each college's website to see if your target schools and/or programs value the extra effort.

To sign up to take an SAT, go to www.CollegeBoard.com. If you do decide to submit an SAT score, many colleges also want three SAT 2 Subject Test scores (see next page).

Comparing the SAT and the ACT

- The ACT consists of English (2/3 grammar), Reading, Math, and Science.

- The SAT consists of Writing & Language (2/3 grammar), Reading, Math, and Math.

- The ACT has math and science sections, while the SAT has two math sections (one allows you to use a calculator and one doesn't).

- The ACT's Science section primarily tests your ability to assess charts, tables, and graphs. Science skill and knowledge is not necessarily critical for success.

- Both the ACT and the SAT have an optional writing section.

- The SAT is more generous with time allowed. But students can learn to work faster, turning the ACT's shorter time allowances to a competitive advantage.

OTC's ACT Prep course targets speed and accuracy.

 TESTING SCHEDULES

ACT Testing Schedule: 6 test dates

Registration Deadline	Late Registration Deadline*	Test Date
$46.00 or $62.50 with Essay**	add $29.50 to your fee	
early-August	mid-August	early-September
mid-September	late-September	late-October
early-November	mid-November	early-December
early-January	mid-January	early-February
early-March	mid-March	early-April
early-May	mid-May	early-June
early-June	late-June	mid-July

If you missed the late registration deadline, you may take the ACT on standby, which adds $53 to the original fees of $46.00 and $62.50. Sign up at www.ACTStudent.org and contact your test-site high school ahead of time for details.

**Take ACT Plus Writing if applying to selective colleges.*

SAT and SAT Subject Tests Testing Schedule: 7 test dates

Registration Deadline	Test Date	Tests Offered
early-September	early-October	SAT and SAT Subject Tests
early-October	early-November	SAT and SAT Subject Tests
early-November	early-December	SAT and SAT Subject Tests
early-February	mid-March	SAT only
late-March	early-May	SAT and SAT Subject Tests
late-April	early-June	SAT and SAT Subject Tests
late-July	late-August	SAT and SAT Subject Tests

Cost to take the SAT: $47.50. Cost to take the SAT with Essay: $64.50. You may register up to two weeks late—add $29 to your cost.

(Stand-by or wait list fee: add about $51)

THE SAT SUBJECT TESTS

An SAT Subject Test is a one-hour, subject-specific diagnostic test. Subjects include math, foreign languages, history, and sciences. Many colleges require 3 Subject Tests if you submit SAT scores (typically colleges require zero Subject Tests if you submit ACT scores—but check the college's website to confirm).

The best time to take SAT Subject tests is just after your final exam in that topic, usually June of your junior year. Cost to take the SAT Subject Tests: $26, plus $18 per additional test taken (up to two additional Subject tests—or three total—per test day). Language with listening tests cost $26 each.

Each test—the ACT, SAT, and SAT Subject Tests—will send out scores to four colleges for free. Choose four each time you take a test. You might withhold scores if you have a huge score already with little upside, and you fear this next test score could drop. Then wait to see the score before releasing it.

ADVANCED PLACEMENT AND INTERNATIONAL BACCALAUREATE TESTS

Schools want reassurance that courses taken are rigorous. AP tests mean academic rigor. Differentiated and advanced classes are great, but an AP course, when coupled with a 4 or 5 on the corresponding AP test, is gold. A 5 is considered equivalent to an "A" in a college-level course, a four equivalent to a "B." Most colleges grant college credit for a score of 4 or 5. Get a 4 or 5 on an AP test sophomore and/or junior year, and you have college credit along with a much more appealing application. If you take an AP course, always take the AP test in May. The AP test is true opportunity—colleges won't see a score of 3 or lower. If your high school does not offer AP courses, try to take the most rigorous courses available. You can also take an AP test without having taken that AP course—a bold move that shows real scholarship. Just take the AP test at the nearest school that offers it. Always use a prep book to prepare for your AP tests, and take lots of sample tests!

International Baccalaureate (IB) courses followed by IB exams are at least as impressive as AP courses.

ADVANCED PLACEMENT TEST DEADLINES

Early January	Deadline for home-schooled students and students whose schools do not offer AP courses to contact AP Services for a list of local AP Coordinators at whose school they could arrange to test. Or just ask your high school.
May	Testing dates
Mid June	Deadline for receipt of requests for grade withholding, grade cancellation, or a change in college grade report recipient.
Early July	AP grade report released to students, high schools, and designated colleges.

Advanced Placement Testing Schedule: First Week, early May*

Week 1**		
Test Date	**Morning (8 AM)**	**Afternoon (12 PM)**
Monday **First Week of May**	AP Chemistry AP Environmental Science	AP Psychology
Tuesday **First week of May**	AP Computer Science A AP Spanish Language and Culture	AP Art History AP Physics 1: Algebra-based
Wednesday **First week of May**	AP English Literature and Composition	AP Japanese Language and Culture AP Physics 2: Algebra-Based
Thursday **First week of May**	AP Calculus AB AP Calculus BC	AP Chinese Language and Culture AP Seminar
Friday **First week of May**	AP German Language and Culture AP United States History	AP European History
Studio Art: Last day for your school to submit digital portfolios and to gather 2-D Design and Drawing students for the physical portfolio assembly. Students should have forwarded their completed digital portfolios to their teachers well before this date.		
Week 2**		
Test Date	**Morning (8 AM)**	**Afternoon (12 PM)**
Monday **Second week of May**	AP Biology AP Music Theory	AP Physics C: Mechanics
IMPORTANT ALERT AFTERNOON (2 p.m.) Special Exam time. **AP Physics C: Electricity and Magnetism is the only exam given at 2 p.m.**		
Tuesday **Second week of May**	AP United States Government and Politics	AP French Language and Culture AP Spanish Literature and Culture
Wednesday **Second week of May**	AP English Language and Composition	AP Italian Language and Culture AP Macroeconomics
Thursday **Second week of May**	AP Comparative Government and Politics AP World History	AP Statistics
Friday **Second week of May**	AP Human Geography AP Microeconomics	AP Latin

*Check with school counselors for exact schedule.

**Students wishing to take the exams that are scheduled for the same time slot should ask their AP Coordinator to contact AP Services.

 TESTING FEES

ACT	ACT + Essay	SAT	SAT + Essay	SAT Subject Test	AP Tests
$39.50	$56.50	$43	$54.50	$26 + $18/test	$92* each

Though currently accurate, these prices may have inched upward. Sadly, don't expect them to decrease.

To sign up for an AP test, talk to your AP teacher or counselor. If you are home-schooled, find a local high school that offers AP tests and sign up.

*For each AP Exam taken by students from low-income families, the College Board will provide a $30 fee reduction per exam.

Motivated students should consider getting an AP Test Prep book for their better courses and then prepare for and take the AP tests in those subjects. You can take an AP test even if you haven't taken that AP course—a bold choice that shows real scholarship. Be bold. Prepare, and go for it.

On To College

with John Baylor

Part 2

How do you afford all this?

NOTES

Don't forget to subtract the student's annual contribution of $11K (or at least $8,500) from your family's Net Cost. See pages 3 and 4.

Yes, college can be affordable. **$11K Paves The Way.** Your eventual annual Net Cost equals the college's Retail Sticker Price minus your student's Scholarships. But the family's actual annual cost is Net Cost minus $11,000—the student's yearly contribution. **$11K Paves The Way!**

So, subtract $11,000 from your expected annual Net Cost—the student can borrow up to $5,000 a year, earn at least $3,500 during breaks each year, and possibly qualify for $2,500 each year thanks to the American Opportunity Tax Credit. **$11K Paves The Way!** As for the student's pizza and laundry costs, they can earn that working at most ten hours per week on campus while at school.

CHAPTER 8

COLLEGES AND COSTS: TIME TO GET SERIOUS

The retail sticker price for college has risen at a rate higher than inflation for years. Thankfully, few students pay retail sticker price.

The keys are to accentuate the Big 3—GPA, Test Scores, and One Extracurricular skill—and to create competition for your enrollment! Hello scholarships!

So, what is the annual retail cost of college (everything included except travel and pizza money)?

- In-state, public (Nebraska colleges are listed; your in-state public colleges may be more expensive.)

  - Wayne, Peru, and Chadron: about $15,000 (for Nebraska and non-residents)

  - UNL, UNO, and UNK: about $19,500 (for NE residents)

- In-state, private (Nebraska colleges are listed; your state's private colleges may be more expensive. Nebraska private colleges offer a free application process and lots of merit-based aid.)

  - Wesleyan, Doane, Hastings, St. Mary's, Concordia, Midland, York: about $37,000

  - Creighton: about $46,000

- Out-of-state, public (Always strive to gain admission to their Honors Program, which can provide the attention and rigor common at schools with fewer students.)

  - The most prestigious—Michigan, Cal-Berkeley, Virginia, UVM…—exceed $50,000.

- KU, K-State, Colorado State, Iowa State, Iowa, Minnesota, Purdue, UNC, Michigan State, UMass, Oklahoma, UNH, URI... $28,000 to $48,000.

- Truman State (MO), SUNY-Geneseo (NY), Castleton State (VT), Evergreen State (WA), Alabama State Universities, New College (FL)...$25,000-$38,000.

  - Plus non-flagship public universities often use more merit-aid than their larger public university peers to lure students.

- Private

  - The majority of private, selective schools will have a total retail sticker price of between $42,000 and $68,000 a year. Some are still less than $56,000—William & Mary, Baylor, Centre, etc.

  - Religious schools can be less than $45,000: Brigham Young, Wheaton, Franciscan University of Steubenville, etc.

  - Community Colleges typically cost about $5,000 a year for tuition and fees, but you'll also need to pay for food and housing.

Many schools have generous merit-based aid packages to lure top applicants. 'Money Schools' turn good high school grades, scores, and an extracurricular into big scholarships.

Our list of such schools and scholarships for you in Appendix D will reduce your annual retail cost to $30,000 or less. Use Appendix D to enhance your final college list, which should consist of A, B, and C list colleges (see Chapter 2), at least one financial safety school, plus "Money Schools."

Access *OTC's America's Most Affordable Colleges* as well to learn about the dozens of four-year colleges for less than $24,000 a year—many under $16,000 a year. Ultimately apply to seven to sixteen colleges.

- Other options

  - Service Academies have superb reputations and pay students to attend —they are rigorous both physically and academically. Students commit to a prescribed period of paid work with the military after graduation (generally four to six years). Check Appendix G for more information on the Service Academies. **Or go to a non-military university, and let ROTC pay tuition!**

  - Canadian schools typically cost between $20,000 and $30,000 US, though aid is rare. McGill (Montreal—the 'Harvard of Canada') and many others are worthy of your exploration. See Appendix F for a comprehensive list of Canadian College profiles; a 26 or higher on the ACT should get you in, though McGill will probably require at least a 29.

  - Scottish Ivies: University of Edinburgh, Aberdeen, Glasgow, and St. Andrews all use the US college lecture-based format and will probably cost between $40,000 and $50,000 a year; a 28 on the ACT should get you in. Aid is limited.

"One Rate, Any State": Peru State and Chadron State are available to non-Nebraskans for about $15,000 total cost per year. Everyone can be a college graduate with minimal debt.

NOTES

CHAPTER 9

FINANCIAL AID

TERMINOLOGY

Understanding the various categories of financial aid and what types of aid are accessible to you and your family starts with understanding what the terms actually mean. Here, you'll find common terms that are used by counselors, parents, financial aid staff, and your fellow students. Be sure you understand how they work and what they mean to your own goals.

NEED-BASED AID

Need-based financial aid is awarded through the following process:

1. Free Application for Federal Student Aid (FAFSA)

    Most families with college students should fill out a FAFSA because the FAFSA may trigger eligibility for need-based aid and federally subsidized loans.

    Parents: complete the FAFSA and send it in to the Federal Government in October senior year. Fill out the FAFSA online at www.fafsa.gov. Never pay for the FAFSA forms.

2. Student Aid Report (SAR)

    Using the information supplied on the FAFSA, the government calculates the Expected Family Contribution (EFC) for the coming school year. The EFC is reported on the SAR and sent to the student's family. The EFC is also sent to the financial aid offices of the colleges the student listed on the FAFSA.

3. Financial Aid Profile (CSS Profile)

   About 300 colleges, most private and/or selective, will also require the student to complete another financial questionnaire known as the CSS Profile, which is more involved than the FAFSA. Register and file the CSS Profile online at www.CollegeBoard.com. While the FAFSA does not ask for home equity, the CSS Profile does. While the FAFSA does not look at the non-custodial parent's income, the CSS Profile does. Thus, if you are seeking need-based aid and have a lot of home equity, or your parents are divorced and only one has a large income, you may want to apply to non-CSS Profile schools. For the latest list of schools that require the CSS Profile in addition to the FAFSA, go to profileonline.collegeboard.org.

4. Your financial aid award: Retail College Cost minus EFC = Need

   To calculate financial need, each college will take its retail cost of attendance (everything: tuition, books, room, board, fees, transportation, etc.) and subtract the EFC. Financial need may be offered in 3 forms: grants or scholarships, work-study, and loans. Schools rarely offer a financial aid package that meets the financial need fully. The more appealing the applicant, the better the aid package: more grants and less loans and work-study. Thus, your merit (the Big 3) enhances your need-based aid, as well as your merit-based aid.

If your family makes less than $75,000 a year, you'll qualify for plenty of need-based aid. If your family makes up to $225,000 a year, you may still qualify for need-based aid. So fill out the FAFSA at FAFSA.gov and submit it in October, senior year!

A Step-by-step Strategy for Maximizing Need-Based Aid

One: Take care of the Big 3: GPA, ACT or SAT, and one extracurricular skill. This will maximize merit-based aid and improve the composition of your ultimate need-based aid award—more grants and scholarships and less loans and work study.

Two: Have your parents fill out a trial FAFSA online ASAP at www.finaid.org/calculators/

Three: Have your parents meet with a qualified financial advisor ASAP to explore all methods for reducing your EFC (Expected Family Contribution) and thus maximizing your eligibility for aid. Here are some ideas that should serve this goal.

1. Minimize the money in a student's name. Since the government's EFC formula takes only 5 percent of the parents' non-retirement assets into consideration, as opposed to 20 percent of the student's non-retirement assets, nearly all available funds should be in the parents' (or grandparents') names. Shifting funds from a student's account to the parents' account is the opposite of what you would do to minimize taxes, but is helpful for need-based financial aid eligibility.

2. All retirement assets, whole life insurance policies, and annuities accumulated before January of the student's high school sophomore year are NOT considered in government's calculation of your EFC. So put all funds possible into retirement accounts.

3. Similarly, if you plan to sell investments, do so prior to January of the student's sophomore year in high school, as any capital gains will be applied as income if realized during the year considered for financial aid. Any capital gains or accumulated retirement assets prior to January of the student's high school sophomore year will be ignored.

4. Home equity is not considered in the government's formula (though it is revealed in the CSS/Profile Application). Thus, any college not using the CSS/Profile will ignore home equity (and a wealthy non-custodial parent's income, if divorced). So to maximize need-based eligibility at non-CSS Profile schools, plow whatever non-retirement assets you can into home equity and automobile equity.

5. Medical and dental expenses not covered by insurance are typically deducted from your income by colleges requiring the CSS/Profile Application. Thus, pay all medical expenses possible during the year applying—after December of the high school sophomore year.

6. For self-employed parents, make large, business-related purchases after December 31 sophomore year.

Four: Apply to at least seven colleges—and as many as sixteen—to create healthy competition. Apply to the rival schools of your top college choices, a strategy that can help your leverage in the spring should your parents try to negotiate more generous aid. And apply to plenty of local schools—their sticker prices are often lower and financial aid more generous. They often can become great values to attend or good bargaining chips with which to negotiate. On a budget? You might apply to Nebraska's private colleges—it's free to apply and Nebraska Wesleyan, Doane, Hastings, etc. grant plenty of merit-based aid. Bonus: they provide rigorous educations.

Five: Have your parents fill out the FAFSA at FAFSA.gov and submit it in October of each year that precedes a year when you'll be in college. Financial aid is often rewarded on a first-come, first-served basis. Be sure to indicate all the colleges that you want to receive the government's response to your FAFSA.

Six: Most selective colleges also require the CSS/Financial Aid Profile Application in addition to the FAFSA. Determine if any of your college choices require it, and, if so, have your parents also fill it out very soon after the FAFSA. The CSS/Financial Aid Profile Application asks the same questions as the FAFSA but goes into detail regarding items such as home equity, insurance policies, non-custodial parent income, and retirement accounts when determining financial aid eligibility. If you are seeking need-based aid and you have a lot of home equity, or your parents are divorced and one has a high income, you may want to apply to many non-CSS Profile schools. The latest list of CSS Profile schools is at profileonline.collegeboard.org. The CSS Profile requires $25 to set up an account and $16 per school sent.

Seven: Within weeks, the federal government will issue your SAR (Student Aid Report), which states your EFC (Expected Family Contribution). Have your parents review it to ensure it reflects accurate information.

Eight: Send copies of both the student's and family's Federal Tax Return, along with attached W-2 forms to each of your colleges' financial aid offices

Nine: If the government issues a second SAR, be sure to send a copy to each of your colleges' financial aid offices.

ELIGIBLE NEED-BASED AID = TOTAL ANNUAL COST OF COLLEGE minus EFC

Ten: In April senior year, at the latest, colleges will tell you whether you're admitted and will send you your Financial Aid Award Letter. You have until May 1, senior year to decide.

Eleven: Have a parent respectfully request additional aid if, in fact, there is still unmet need. You'll be asked for additional documentation if there has been a change in the family's financial circumstances, but explaining your other college offers and their price points also can persuade the financial aid office to be more generous. Begin this process of renegotiating the offer by calling your admissions contact to ask whom dad or mom should contact regarding the financial aid offer.

MERIT-BASED AID

Grants

- This is the best kind of aid, since you don't pay it back. Major federally-financed grants include...

    - Federal Pell Grants: designed to assist very low-income undergrads and are awarded based on low EFCs.

    - Federal Supplemental Educational Opportunity Grants: like Pell grants, FSEOGs are awarded only to students with great financial need.

    - Many additional college-offered or state-sponsored, need-based grants are available for residents who are Pell-eligible or nearly Pell-eligible. For example, *CollegeBound Nebraska* covers 15 credits of free tuition for Nebraska residents at UNL, UNO, and UNK. *Access NWU* is Nebraska Wesleyan's free tuition scholarship offered to fifty Nebraska Residents a year with an EFC below $1000.

Scholarships: another example of aid you don't pay back.

- Some college-offered merit-based scholarships are not renewable, so maximize aid freshman year. Some colleges reduce aid after freshman year—**ask to what extent you can expect the first year aid to increase annually with college costs.**

- The National Merit Scholarship is $2,500, but it's also a trigger to a windfall of additional money. To win, you need to be in the top 1 percent of test-takers in your state on the PSAT junior year: the required minimum score varies by state.

    Thus, sophomore year, if you earn at least a 1200 on the PSAT or a 27 on an ACT, take SAT/PSAT Prep before your October, Junior year PSAT. *OTC* offers online SAT/PSAT Prep for the SAT at www.OnToCollege.com.

- Privately offered scholarships

    - Local: For example, EducationQuest.org has a great list for Nebraska students. Your state should have an equivalent site for in-state aid. Also regularly check your high school's website for local scholarships.

- National: these are very competitive. Search our list of the most generous national, privately offered scholarships in Appendix E as well as FastAid.com and target 30 to 90 scholarships. If paying for college is no challenge, allow other students to win these merit-based, privately offered scholarships.

We recommend that mom and dad lead the private scholarship search. They will choose the scholarships they think you can win, fill out all the forms, and ask you for essays. And stay vigilant at school for scholarship opportunities by asking counselors and teachers for ideas. The motivated applicant applies for at least 30 and as many as 90 privately-offered scholarships.

1. See our selections of generous national, privately-offered scholarships in Appendix E.

2. Others can be found at www.fastaid.com.

3. Your state may have a site for in-state, privately-offered scholarships.

4. For local scholarships, visit your own high school's website.

If you need financial aid, *OTC* recommends that you apply for 30 to 90 privately-offered scholarships.

 LOANS

Be careful to actually read the information about the type of loan you are considering prior to signing. Loans have to be paid back, and there is little to no consideration later in life if you should run into financial challenges.

These 7 tips include ideas from a WealthManagement.com article, June, 2012.

1. The best college loan for students is the Stafford Loan.

   You must attend college at least halftime to qualify for a Stafford. Regardless of credit scores, all students receive the same fixed rate and protections.

There is a limit on the amount of money that students can borrow each year through the Stafford Loan program. Here are the current maximum amounts:

Freshmen: $5,500   Sophomore: $6,500

Juniors: $7,500   Seniors: $7,500

There are two types of Stafford Loans—a subsidized and unsubsidized version. The subsidized loan is the more valuable one because students with these will not be responsible for the interest that accrues while in school (The federal government covers the interest payments).

Students will learn if they qualify for a subsidized Stafford when they receive their financial aid packages in the spring. The decision depends on the family's financial wherewithal and the cost of the school: the greater the cost, the more likely a student will qualify for the subsidized loan. Six percent of subsidized Stafford borrowers come from households with incomes in excess of $100,000, and 24 percent have family incomes between $50,000 and $100,000.

2. Look for borrower protection.

Paying back the Stafford will be more manageable as long as students apply for the federal Income-Based Repayment Plan or IBRP, which allows qualified students to repay their loan based on what they can afford, not what they owe.

3. If a life-changing college opportunity warrants, parents might consider borrowing options.

Students should be the only ones borrowing for college—and no more than $5,000 per year. However, sometimes MIT, Cal Tech, or a similar life-changing, albeit expensive, option warrants consideration of additional loans. While the Stafford is a no brainer for students, parents' choices are more complicated and less desirable. Parents can borrow through a home equity line, the federal PLUS Loan for Parents, or cosign a private student loan for their child. Some parents also dip into their retirement accounts, which is not recommended.

The PLUS Loan currently offers parents a fixed interest rate of 6.84 percent and charges a fee based on the loan amount. Parents can begin paying 60 days after the loan is disbursed or wait until six months after the child graduates, stops attending school, or drops below half-time status.

Because the PLUS interest rate is high, using a home equity line of credit will probably be cheaper.

For those who itemize, the interest on equity lines is tax deductible. You might also take out a line of credit—sometimes as low as 4 percent.

4. Check out credit unions.

   Credit unions are newer players in the private loan marketplace and are well worth trolling. Non-profit credit unions can be a less expensive alternative. While rates can change, the rates on private loan rates through credit unions have been as low as 3.5 percent. A good place to look for college credit union loans is cuStudentLoans.org.

5. Check out school credit unions.

   Some colleges and universities maintain their own credit unions to tap for student loans. Institutions with credit unions include Harvard, University of Chicago, Amherst, Mount Holyoke, Smith, Princeton, MIT, and the California State University system.

6. Apply for multiple loans.

   Unfortunately, you won't know what private loan rate you will qualify for if you don't actually go through the process of applying.

   If you're interested in comparing private college loans, try these three comparison sites: Alltuition.com, SimpleTuition.com, eStudentLoan.com

7. Don't over-borrow; seek financial freedom in your twenties.

   We say borrow no more than $5,000 a year, which will result in loan payments of about $215 a month through age 31. You don't want to be paying college debt in your thirties. Of course, if you're studying engineering, you might borrow more.

 # WORK STUDY

Work study is an on-campus job. Employment may be government subsidized. If you want to work on Friday nights or part-time on the weekends, fine. Anything more may compromise the precious education you're spending so much to receive. If at all feasible, try to work no more than twelve hours per week during the weeks at school. (Work sixty hours a week during vacations.)

ROTC

- See Appendix G

FINANCIAL PHILOSOPHIES FROM FAMILY TO FAMILY VARY

- Let the student contribute at least $3,500 in earnings each year to the cost of college. This can be earned during breaks and summer vacations, with any excess providing pizza and gas money at school. Try to maximize student earnings during vacations and minimize the need for work while at school.

- Let the student be responsible for all loans. Our thought is that any loan principal beyond $20,000 after graduation will probably require more than 8 years to pay back. So $5,000 a year in loans ought to be about the limit. Of course, these numbers can vary based on the student's expected earnings, reliability with money, shopping habits, and the family's financial situation. So the student's earnings and loan contributions end up adding about $8,500 a year to the family's contribution (but don't tell anyone—get your official EFC as low as possible to maximize financial aid).

- Work with a trusted financial planner knowledgeable in college finance. You want the lowest EFC possible so as to maximize your financial need and ultimate need-based Financial Aid Package. Make yourself appear as poor as possible—well before October of your student's senior year of high school (and each October thereafter until the middle of Junior year in college, as your EFC is determined annually). There are ethical ways to do this (make anticipated large purchases before then, pay down principal on your mortgage, maximize money in your retirement funds, etc.). Work closely with a financial planner well before senior year.

- And remember, families with an adjusted gross income (AGI) of less than $160,000 receive a full tax credit of $2,500 annually: the American Opportunity Tax Credit. A tax credit is a dollar for dollar reduction in your federal taxes, so add that amount to what you can pay. Partial tax credits are available for families with an AGI between $160,000 and $180,000; $80,000-$90,000 for single parents. Single parent families must have an AGI of less than $80,000 for the full $2,500 tax credit.

RESOURCES—FREE WEBSITES THAT CAN HELP:

- BigFuture.org: a College Board site packed with information about expected costs for all colleges.

- EducationQuest.org (for Nebraska students): great free local resource filled with great college application information including a database of local scholarships. Find your state's equivalent website.

- Fastaid.com: lots of privately-offered scholarships

- SchoolSoup.com: lots of privately-offered scholarships

- CollegeAnswer.com

- CollegeScholarships.com: another large matching private scholarship database that provides a scholarship package built for you as well as a personalized letter with your information to each of the scholarship sponsors.

- WealthManagement.com—solid college-planning financial advice.

- CollegeResults.org—each college's graduation rates, average net cost, loan default rates, female-to-male ratio, endowment size, and more.

Don't forget to scour our list of generous school-offered, merit-based scholarships in Appendix D and national private scholarships in Appendix E. *OTC's America's Most Affordable Colleges* will also help minimize your costs.

Have mom or dad sign up at fastaid.com right now: it's free. Fill out a profile, and the site will offer plenty of merit-based scholarship opportunities.

NOTES

NOTES

Don't forget to subtract the student's annual contribution of $11K (or at least $8,500) from your family's Net Cost. See pages 3 and 4.

CHAPTER 10

BUDGETING FOR COLLEGE

> Remember: apply to many colleges–ideally seven to sixteen total, including two financial safety schools. Competition can make financial aid folks more generous. Then, senior spring, use diplomacy and tact when negotiating your aid package with the financial aid office. Also, apply for as many private scholarships as possible–at least thirty–see Appendix E and fastaid.com.

You might now be more knowledgeable but probably still skeptical about how you might actually pay college bills for four years. Here are a few ideas that may lower your cost. Every family's financial situation is different. Before doing any of the following, be sure to consult a qualified financial consultant to confirm which of these strategies make sense for you.

1. One great way for parents to put aside money for college is with 529 savings accounts. Money goes in pre-tax and can be used for educational purposes. Go to www.planforcollegenow.com for more information.

2. A student is expected to supply 50 percent of her income to college expenses, after a $3,500 exemption. So again, don't earn much more than $3,500 a year unless you're feeding your family. If you do earn much more than $3,500 annually, and you're looking for need-based aid, open up a retirement account and plow as much as possible into it. Retirement account money will not be assessed for EFC purposes.

    So dedicate as much income as possible to retirement accounts, money neither considered income nor assets for EFC purposes.

3. Grandparents can contribute to college costs, and their participation does not show up on the FAFSA. So, one option is to move student's assets into a grandparent's college or 529 account.

4. If grandparents wish to contribute to a student's college costs, they should pay the school directly, instead of giving the money to the student, which would add to the EFC. Also, it would be best not to use the grandparents' 529 account money until later years of college, because then you will drain EFC-assessed money sooner, while the grandparents' 529 account only grows.

5. The sooner you finish the FAFSA (Free Application for Student Aid), the better your chance to receive college grants and scholarships, which are generally distributed on a first-come, first-serve basis. Also you don't want to be late for a college's aid priority date, which is usually in early March. The FAFSA also qualifies you for subsidized loans should you later choose to take any out. So ethically make yourself appear as poor as possible by December 31 of the student's sophomore year.

6. Led by Harvard's 2004 Financial Aid Initiative, about twelve highly selective colleges now require little more than 10 percent of the family's pre-tax income per year for families earning $150,000 or less, and families making less than $65,000 a year pay nothing. Thus, if you get into Swarthmore, and your parents make $150,000 a year, your maximum cost should be $15,000 per year. To get the latest list of schools using this generous formula, google "Harvard Financial Aid Initiative," an attempt to help the middle and upper-middle classes afford selective private colleges.

NOTES

CHAPTER 11

WHAT TO DO WHEN:
THE CALENDAR

 FRESHMAN YEAR

Fall:

- Take as rigorous a course load as you can happily manage. Challenging courses will be healthy for you and impressive on your college applications. They'll also lead to higher ACT & SAT scores.

- Choose extracurricular activities that you love and will probably pursue all four years, so that come senior year you'll likely excel at one. If you do what you love, you'll excel at it.

Winter & Spring:

- Menial jobs may help you with some expenses, but they may not help your admission chances much. So only work a job for essential money—a higher GPA or an extracurricular school activity can pay more eventually in scholarships than a job pays short term after-tax. For example, doing well in science can help earn a college scholarship that will bring you more money than most high school jobs ever will. And doing well in school will probably require much less time than a job.

- Work during vacations, but avoid working Sunday night through Thursday night during the school year, if at all feasible. Of course, if you're feeding your family or helping pay the mortgage, lengthy hours at a job may make sense.

Summer:

- Have productive fun and develop your skills. Remember: champions are made during the off-season. Prepare during the summer so you can excel in coursework, sports, music, debate, theater, etc. See Appendix B for affordable summer adventures.

- Volunteer for a cause you care about. Colleges want to see that you care about others. Sustained volunteerism for a single cause is huge for private and college-offered scholarships. Get started early.

 ## SOPHOMORE YEAR

Fall:

- Take as rigorous a course load as you can happily manage.

- Take the PSAT in October (the sophomore-year PSAT does not count for the National Merit Scholarship. Still it's good practice.) If you get a 1200 or higher on the PSAT, take SAT/PSAT prep for your junior year October PSAT: a top 1 percent score in your state could mean a national merit scholarship. Or take the ACT in June. A score of 27 or higher indicates that you could finish in the top 1 percent in your state on the October, junior year PSAT (visit www.OnToCollege.com for the best in online or live SAT/PSAT Prep and ACT Prep).

- Get to know your college counselor. She will be writing a recommendation for you senior year, and she has lots of scholarship and college information to share. Be prepared with specific questions—she is busy.

Winter & Spring:

- Typical high school jobs may help you with expenses, but may not help your admission chances much. So only work a job for essential money. Hard work during vacations is great, but avoid working Sunday night through Thursday night during the school year, if feasible.

- Visit colleges when you have vacations.

Summer:

- If you might score extremely well on the upcoming PSAT, take the *OTC* SAT/PSAT Prep course. Top 1 percent PSAT performers in each state typically become National Merit Semifinalists. The PSAT junior year could be the ticket to dozens of excellent schools recruiting you and offering huge merit-based financial aid.

- Any sophomore with a PSAT score of 1200 or higher or an ACT score of 27 or higher is a candidate for a National Merit Scholarship and should prepare vigorously for the October, junior year PSAT.

- Volunteer for a cause you care about. Colleges want to see evidence of compassion, commitment, and leadership; volunteering can demonstrate all three.

- Become great at one extracurricular skill—champions are made during the off-season.

- Remember, colleges want the Big 3: GPA, Test Scores, and one extracurricular skill.

- Job Shadow—this is a great time to test your current preferences regarding a future career. (I thought in high school that I wanted to be an actuary or lawyer—both would've been poor choices for me.)

JUNIOR YEAR

Fall:

- Have the honest 'money talk' so that the student and the parents truly understand the annual college budget.

- Prepare hard for and take the PSAT. Prestigious $2,500 National Merit Scholarships are at stake.

- Take as rigorous a course load as you can happily manage.

- Only work a job for essential money—a higher GPA or an extracurricular school activity can pay more eventually in scholarships than a job pays short term after-tax. For example, doing well in science can help earn a college scholarship that will bring you more money than most high school jobs ever will. And doing well in school will probably require much less time than a job. Work during vacations, but avoid working Sunday night through Thursday night during the school year, if at all feasible. Of course, if you're feeding your family or helping pay the mortgage, lengthy hours at a job may make sense.

- Saving money in the student's name for college is laudable, but may disqualify you for college aid you would have received (see Chapter 9).

- Visit colleges when students are on campus. Refine your list of likes and dislikes.

- If you're looking for financial aid, ask a parent or guardian to handle the search for private scholarships. You write the essays, but let them handle the applications online—filling them out and mailing them in. Have them check the websites and databases in Appendix E.

January:

- Look at your ACT and PSAT scores and decide whether to focus on the ACT or SAT. Occasionally it makes sense to try both tests, though most students soon focus on only one, taking that test twice junior year and twice senior fall (four times total).

February or March:

- Take your first ACT or SAT (if you haven't already). Be sure to take at least two ACTs or two SATs your Junior year.

March or April:

- Visit some colleges that may interest you. Try to visit when the college is in session, and try not to miss any high school time. Visit the leaders of your future extracurricular pursuit (coach, theater department head, editor of the paper, leader of the journalism department, etc.), visit classes, and ask lots of questions (see Chapter 12).

April, May or June:

- Take your second ACT or SAT. Take an ACT Prep or SAT Prep course before your first or second try. Visit www.OnToCollege.com for the best in online and live ACT and SAT Prep courses.

June:

- Take three SAT II Subject Tests if you are thinking of applying to selective colleges (see Chapter 7).

Summer:

- If you're looking for financial aid, ask a parent or guardian to handle the search for private scholarships. You write the essays, but let them handle the applications online—filling them out and mailing them in. Have them check the websites and databases in Appendix E.

- Volunteer for a cause you care about. Colleges and private scholarships want to see evidence of compassion, commitment, and leadership: volunteering can demonstrate all three.

- Make sure this is a summer when you improve yourself and have skill-building experiences. Champions are made during the off-season. You want one developed extracurricular skill by December senior year.

- Market your extracurricular skill to schools through a two-minute YouTube video and resume that you email to coaches, theater department deans, or orchestra leaders. Marketing yourself is nearly free. College web sites offer email addresses of professors and coaches (see Chapter 13).

- Develop the specific criteria you're looking for in a college: student-body size, location, extracurricular opportunities, reputation, foreign study, academic excellence within certain disciplines, climate, etc. (see Chapters 1 & 2).

- Job Shadow—this is a great time to test your current preferences for a future career.

 **SENIOR YEAR**

Fall

September:

- Get an estimate of what the colleges on your list will cost using the Net Price Calculator on each school's website.

- Finalize your list of colleges. Typically, you should apply to seven to sixteen schools (including two financial safety schools) to maximize your chances for admission and scholarships (see Chapters 1 & 2).

- Decide if you'll be applying Early Action or Early Decision somewhere. Your chances are better when applying early. Early Decision is binding—if accepted you must attend. Applying Early Decision can be risky for students seeking financial aid as final aid packages are often not known until the spring, after the application deadline for other colleges. Some colleges do offer the aid package in December for early applicants. For financial aid seekers, Early Action may be a better choice.

- If you're looking for financial aid, ask a parent or guardian to handle the search for private scholarships. You write the essays, but let them handle the applications online, filling them out, and mailing them in. Have them use the websites and databases listed in Appendix E.

- Take as rigorous a course load as you can happily manage.

September or October:

- Retake the ACT and/or SAT. Take the ACT or SAT twice junior year and at least twice senior fall. **Even small score jumps can earn big money.**

- Early admission applications are usually due October 31 or November 15.

- Parents or guardian: submit the FAFSA (fafsa.gov) in early October.

Boosting that ACT or SAT score is the best-paying
job a high school student can have.

Winter

November:

- Retake SAT II Subject Tests, if necessary.

December:

- Retake the ACT or SAT for a final time. The December test, senior year is usually the last one considered by colleges for financial aid and admission. Take the December test senior year!

- Finish all regular admission applications—deadlines are usually January 1 or January 15.

January:

- Complete any still unfinished regular admission applications for schools with January 15 or later deadlines.

February, April, and June:

- Keep taking the ACT if you're trying to get into a rolling admission school, trying to become athletically eligible, or trying to win more aid at a school that gives more financial aid based on a higher score on a spring senior year score.

April:

- Acceptances and rejections arrive.

- Negotiate better aid offers without alienating schools.

- Visit the schools still in the hunt.

- Make your choice. May 1 is typically the deadline. Stay on a school's waitlist if you'd like to keep that option open.

Summer:

- Enjoy yourself, seek productive fun, and have a healthy adventure. Don't let this be an unplanned summer filled with boredom, interrupted only by a mindless job. Sock away money as well—work 60-80 hours a week, if necessary, so you can get by working only ten hours a week at college. Remember—champions are made during the off-season. Be truly great at your extracurricular when you arrive at college.

- You might knock out a course or two at your local community college to save tuition and avoid unwanted but required classes at college.

If you end up attending a two-year college, matriculate in the summer term. Don't wait until the end of summer when poor habits may have developed.

NOTES

CHAPTER 12

THE COLLEGE VISIT: MAKING IT WORTH THE TRIP

Here's your shot to gain a sense of whether a school fits you:

- Ideally, visit the school while it is in session, though not during finals week. Try not to miss meaningful high school class time. Thus, visit primarily during vacations or senior spring, after submitting the applications.

- Before you arrive, call the admissions office to:

  - arrange an interview with an admissions officer, if allowed.

  - reserve a spot in an information session/formal campus tour.

  - reserve an appointment with a financial aid office official, if necessary.

  - ask for a meeting with a professor in your future department or major.

  - if possible, reserve a student host to take you to meals and classes (ideally in your future major) and to host you overnight in the dorms.

  - if you're a jock, schedule a meeting with the coach (for this, call the coach's office directly).

- After you arrive:

  - your parents and you should split up, each going on their own recon mission. You'll have separate experiences and impressions when you reunite. Visiting with a coach or professor together is fine, but students otherwise should be with their student hosts: eating meals, visiting classes, exploring freshmen dorms, testing athletic facilities, and asking questions. Meanwhile, mom and dad can audit their own classes, meet with financial aid representatives, and explore freshman dorms.

- everyone should record impressions, thoughts, feelings, questions for future reference.

- develop a list of likes and dislikes.

- collect all relevant school literature.

- walk or drive around the local community.

- find and keep in touch with the admissions officer who is likely to read your application—a handwritten note soon afterwards is a nice touch.

Questions to have answered (to attend a college for real learning rather than an adult Romper Room):

- What is the academic pulse? Do students actually discuss weighty issues at meals or is this a gathering of social bubbleheads? How many students in freshmen classes?

- Who teaches—grad students or professors?

- Do students actually get to know their professors? Ask them how many professors they plan to call up and visit when they're back in town the year after graduation? Any number less than two suggests that this is a school where professors do not connect with or prioritize undergraduates.

- Am I comfortable with the level of Greek activity?

- Am I comfortable with the ideological and religious leanings of students and faculty?

- Am I comfortable with the level of diversity? Is interaction among races satisfactory?

- Will I be able to participate meaningfully in my foremost extracurricular passion?

NOTES

CHAPTER 13

HOW TO PROMOTE YOURSELF

 JOCKS, PERFORMERS, AND EXTRACURRICULAR STARS:

JOCKS

Use your extracurricular skill as a lever in the application process. Take the initiative to contact college coaches directly; let them know of your interest in their school and their program—same for you actors, musicians, and budding entomologists. Division I and II schools offer athletic scholarships; Division III schools do not (though they often give jocks scholarships for different purposes). It is up to you to cultivate a relationship with the coach or orchestra director and get noticed!

- Craft a list of schools with your current coaches, as well as with your college counselor. This is a large initial list, maybe consisting of twenty to fifty schools.

- Develop an introduction email and an athletic resume (samples on the next pages).

- Gather and edit a game tape (college coaches typically want a tape of a portion of an entire game, not a highlight film). A few video close-ups of your form can be added, as can a quick testimonial given by your varsity coach. Your video should be 1½-2 minutes long—total. Post your video on YouTube or Hudl.com. Check out samples at ACCRecruits.com.

- Attend camps and tournaments that maximize your visibility.

- Send college coaches game and camp schedules.

- Email, call, and write the coaches.

- Keep good notes of all contacts with an excel file.

- Return emails, phone calls, letters, and questionnaires promptly.

- Visit campuses and meet with the coaches and players.

- Become your own best advocate by staying in touch.

Another option is to have a company help you market yourself as an athlete. American College Connection at www.ACCRecruits.com can do the entire job for you. ACC generally leads to excellent results, especially for swimmers. ACC's service starts at around $2,900.

Coaches are not only measuring your athletic ability but also your willingness to commit to their program. By showing your interest through regular and positive communication, a coach may be willing to reserve a valuable spot for you on his list with the admissions office.

Basic School Recruiting Visit Guidelines		
	Division I, II	Division III
Visits per year	5 official	unlimited
Meet with coach?	yes	yes
Attend practice?	yes	yes
Attend classes?	yes	yes
Meet players?	yes	yes
Overnight stays?	usually	sometimes
Expenses paid by:	college	student

When you are invited to campus by a coach, make sure you do the following:

- Attend classes, particularly in a field you might want to study in college.

- Set up an interview with a member of the admissions office (the coach should make the arrangements for you). Ask if your academic credentials are sufficient for admission. If not, what scores and GPA do you need for admission?

- Eat at least one meal in the student dining hall.

- Attend a practice or team workout.

- Spend the night in a regular student dorm, not the jock dorm.

NCAA Clearinghouse

The NCAA has established a clearinghouse for both recruiting and eligibility purposes for student-athletes in Division I and II. You can learn more about the NCAA regulations and rules on the NCAA website at www.ncaa.org/about/student-athlete-eligibility

Sample email introducing you to a college coach (find email address on the athletic department section within the college's website). Attach your resume to the email.

Dear Coach Bell:

I am writing this email to let you know of my interest in playing for you at William & Mary. I am currently a junior at Lincoln Southeast High School in Lincoln, Nebraska. I have started at point guard for the past two years and last year was named First Team All-City. This past summer I attended the Nike All-Star Camp in Las Vegas, Nevada, where I also played in the national AAU tournament for the Nebraska team. I am a 6'0" tall point guard and I averaged 10 points and 5 assists per game last season. My vertical is 27". My GPA is 3.8, and I received a 25 on my first ACT.

On August 10, I will be playing in the State all-star tournament in Kearney, Nebraska. I will be on the North All-Star squad in uniform #23. That game can be seen on NET August 10 at 8pm CDT, which may be available via satellite or cable in your area or online at www.netv.com.

If you feel I could contribute to your program, please send me information on your basketball program. Attached are a copy of my schedule for the remaining 2018 season and my basketball resume. Please click here to watch a short video with highlights and unedited game action.

Thank you very much for your consideration. I hope to hear from you soon regarding whether you think I could be a significant contributor to your program.

Sincerely,

(Your name)

(Phone number)

(Email address)

(Street address)

John Smith
33 Black Top Court, Lincoln, NE 68503
(402) 555-1234 • jsmith@aol.com

6'0" • 185 lbs.	
3.8 GPA • 25 ACT	

Experience:

LSE High School Varsity Basketball: 2016-present

Nebraska AAU select team

First Team: 2016-present

Achievements:

LSE High School

2016-17 Junior Year:

   Starting point guard; leading scorer on the team with a 16.2 pga;

   first in city in assists (4 per game) and steals (2.6 per game);

   First Team All League; team was quarter-finalist in State Tournament.

2015-16 Sophomore Year:

   Starting point guard; second leading scorer with a 12.3 pga;

   led the team in assists and steals;

   All-League Honorable Mention;

   team was Division I semifinalist in State Tournament.

2014-15 Freshman Year:

   Starting point guard; fourth leading scorer with a 8.1 pga;

   led the team in assists and second in steals.

Nebraska All Star Summer Team

2015-2017

   Starting point guard; third leading scorer and assist and steal leader.

   2015 National Tournament

   2016 3rd Team All-Tournament Team.

References:

Mr. Jeff Smith, LSE Basketball Coach

(jsmith@aol.edu, 402-555-4443)

Mr. Matthew DeGreeff, College Counselor

(mdegreeff@aol.edu, 402-555-4442)

Mr. Walter Carty, Nebraska All Star Basketball Coach

(wcarty@aol.edu, 402-555-7737)

Performers

Those of you especially talented in a non-athletic extracurricular pursuit:

Submit a tape of a performance plus a brief resume with references. Get the theater department-head excited, and you have just created an on-campus advocate for your admission.

Sample letter for a special interest leader at a college—attach your resume to the email.

Dear Professor Dramatic,

I am a junior at Crystal Lake South High School and am looking for a college where I can continue my extensive involvement in the technical crew. I have spent most of my extracurricular hours at South assisting in productions of all kinds, from musical theater to one act plays. I simply can't imagine college without tech crew!

I am attaching a resume of my work within South's theater department, as well as photos of the sets I've helped build. Please click here to watch a brief YouTube video of some of my work. I will be visiting your campus on April 8 and would like to meet with you, if possible.

Thank you for replying, especially if you agree that I can meaningfully contribute to your theater department over the next four years.

Sincerely,

(Your name)

(Phone number)

(Email address)

(Street address)

NOTES

CHAPTER 14

THE DREADED ESSAY

 ### YOUR WINDOW REVEALING THE THREE-DIMENSIONAL YOU

Your essays are important. Most out-of-state schools will accept the Common Application (CommonApp.org), which asks for a 650-word long essay. Few in-state colleges require essays. Honors Programs and scholarships, however, often ask for essays.

The 5 Keys to Great Application Essays

1. Be passionate about the topic you choose, one that matters deeply to you. If you're fighting for words, you probably have the wrong topic. Once you decide what important event, moment, or phenomenon in your life to write about, a draft should flow out of you fairly instinctively.

2. Be specific: details, details, details.

    - I was a chubby two-hundred-and-thirty pounds and slower than the corn borer beetles that plague local farmers, but I wanted to be a football player.

3. Show. Don't tell. Show your reaction, don't tell it. Make us feel it with you.

    - On that first hot day, those strangers and I began to run plays they had learned at summer camp. "Ed, get in there at left tackle." I stood, bewildered. "You do know what a left tackle is, don't you?" Red crept into my face as my teammates began to laugh. Tears fell beneath my helmet as I realized that I was unaware of basic football terms and impossibly overweight.

4. Less is More. Choose a narrow subject that you know well and succinctly write about it.

5. Find humor: a little levity goes a long way—if you're by nature a funny person, show it. These admission folks read about 20 to 25 applications daily, 12 to 15 hours a day. Help them smile and like you. Make them laugh out loud, and you've hit a bull's-eye. Just be your self-deprecating, humble, human self, and you should get some smiles. But humor at the expense of someone else can be risky.

   - I stagger out of bed. After donning the latest in farming fashion (ripped jeans, a tattered t-shirt, and rubber boots), I join my dad in the morning chores. We work side-by-side, dumping buckets of feed to silence the earsplitting squeals of the pigs. They devour every morsel, their demanding squeals replaced by satisfied chomping sounds. But for every action there is an equal and opposite reaction. As the stomachs of the pigs are filled, other parts are emptied. So my dad and I continue our work, beginning the odorous task of cleaning pigpen after pigpen. The awful aroma hangs upon us, a pungent pig perfume that can only be removed by countless handfuls of antibacterial soap and bottles of the strongest scented shampoo.

There may be other essays as well if a college requires a supplementary application. Why?

- They want to see that you have researched their college. The essays can show why you and the college would be a good match. Make specific, detailed points about that college.

- They're looking for additional information that will help them draw distinctions among applicants.

So here are some more basics:

- Make sure to answer the essay question and follow all given instructions.

- Start off with a strong opening sentence and paragraph that captures the reader's interest.

- Don't use bad grammar, punctuation, or spelling. Proofread!

- Make a point and stick to it; develop your argument or narrative.

- Check all your facts—if you mention a date, place, or event, make sure it's correct.

- Don't be ambiguous—a confused reader is an unhappy reader.

- Get at least one draft of each essay done before November so you'll have plenty of time to perfect it.

- And most importantly: Be passionate. Show, don't tell. Be specific. Less is more. Add levity. And stay within the word limit.

Possible topics for application essays that allow you to write about what you want:

- Hobbies and non-school pursuits that engage your heart and mind.

- A social cause that you hold dear.

- An event (personal, local, national or international) that has touched you.

- An academic subject that sparks your interest. Has it led to experiences or study outside of school? The best essay material goes beyond the courses you took.

Mistakes to avoid:

- If you're writing about a trip, show how your experiences affected you, and why they were meaningful to you. You are not trying to convince the reader to visit Milan. These are personal essays, not travelogues.

- Make sure the essay is primarily about you. If you are writing a tribute to your grandmother and her influence on you, be personal and specific, not just sentimental. Explain how what she did and said were important to you. Your goal is not to get her admitted, but to get you admitted.

- Don't look for self-pity. If you've overcome obstacles, write about them. But do so with hope and an eye for showing self-growth. If you overcame an athletic injury, your rehab routine alone won't make a compelling essay. Dig deep. Show what it felt like to watch your teammates, instead of playing alongside them. Show how your misfortune is a part of you, but can't define you. Incidentally, the injury topic, along with the divorce topic, are common.

See sample essays in Appendix A.

NOTES

CHAPTER 15

GAP YEAR AS A STRATEGY

 ### CONSIDER A YEAR ABROAD DURING OR JUST AFTER HIGH SCHOOL

A year abroad before college can be a life-changer, whether it's during high school or during the year following high school graduation ("Gap Year"). Just apply to colleges senior year as usual; once accepted, defer for one year and embark on your productive, foreign adventure.

Benefits:

- You could be bilingual and able to avoid your college's foreign language requirements.

- You'll be more mature and self-aware during your freshman year, a notorious year for poor decision making.

- You'll be a more appealing applicant, which means improved college choices.

- If you go during a Gap Year, the year after senior year in high school, you can apply again to a few colleges and even retake the ACT or SAT during that year abroad.

- Gap Year alums get better grades in college than other students, according to admissions pros at Middlebury and Skidmore College. Maturity matters.

Drawbacks:

- If taken during high school, your academic, athletic, extracurricular, and social progress can be interrupted.

Resources for a productive year abroad:

- Rotary Student Exchange is a year abroad with a host family while attending the local high school. Rotary's application is usually due October 1, the fall before you leave.

You pay for the $500 application fee, the open-ended roundtrip plane fare (about $4,000), and health insurance (about $1,200). Rotary will even give you a stipend (about $100/mo). This is a great deal. You apply, name three countries you'd prefer, and hopefully you'll be sent to one of those three. You should not be older than 18-and-a-half when you leave in August, though exceptions are considered. Strong preference is given to those still in high school, though earnest senior-year applicants who convince local Rotarians that this will not be a goof-off year may be accepted. For an application and all the details, contact your local Rotary Club.

- American Field Service (AFS) also offers a year abroad with a host family while attending the local high school.

    AFS will cost you about $16,000 a year. AFS is geared towards a year or semester abroad prior to graduation from high school. However, AFS is developing a few post-high school, pre-college Gap Year programs.

    For an application and all the details, contact AFS at 1-800-AFS-INFO or www.afs.org/usa.

A year abroad before college can be a life-changer.

- The Center for Interim Year Programs helps families craft productive Gap Years.
    www.interimprograms.com   (617) 547-0980

- Dynamy
    www.dynamy.org/internship-year   (508) 755-2571
    Dynamy Internship Year is a potent mix of work, internships, independent living, structure, and coaching for students between high school and college.

- Gap Year
    http://www.gapyear.com/
    The Gap Year is an expansive website with information about time-off options, including students' diaries about their year off.

ONE OTHER POSSIBILITY...

One postgraduate (PG) year at a Boarding School—essentially a second senior-year—can bolster your academic and athletic resume, though it is usually very pricey. Here are a few schools that have particularly well-known PG programs (there are many more):

- Phillips Academy Andover (MA): www.andover.edu

- Hotchkiss School (CT): www.hotchkiss.org

- Putney School (VT): www.putney.com

NOTES

CHAPTER 16

OTC GROUND RULES FOR MAXIMIZING YOUR COLLEGE EXPERIENCE

Learn the latest on getting into your 'best-fit' college at the lowest cost and maximizing your college experience by watching the OnToCollege Show at www.OnToCollege.com, becoming an OnToCollege friend on Facebook, and by following *OTC* on Twitter: @OnToCollege.

1. Meaningfully participate in one extracurricular.

2. Live on campus.

3. Leave your car at home.

4. Get a bike.

5. Small classes only.

6. Good professors/teachers only.

   a. Every college has students with blogs critiquing professors (e.g. ratemyprofessors.com)

7. Continue to apply for privately-offered aid at:

   a. Ffastaid.com and the other sites (see Chapter 9)

   b. Your high school counselor's website

   c. EducationQuest.org (or your state's equivalent)

8. When in college, work a job during vacations or on Friday nights and Saturdays only.

   a. Try not to exceed twelve hours weekly at a job during your time actually in school.

   b. Work 60-plus hours a week during vacations, if necessary.

9. Take at least one semester of these classes.

    a. art history—become more urbane

    b. U.S. social history—become more appreciative

    c. accounting—learn how to run a business

    d. finance—learn how money works

    e. a real college math class—learn to think more quantitatively

    f. a real college science class—learn to think more intelligently

10. Become bilingual by graduation.

    a. At least 1 semester abroad (ideally a full school-year plus summer to ensure you're functionally bilingual for life).

11. Make sure your parents fill out the FAFSA each October (fafsa.gov).

Extra Credit

12. If you're not paying a lot for college and can afford it, take a 5th year.

    a. Go abroad twice (years two and four).

    b. Master a 2nd foreign language.

    c. Complete another major or a masters degree.

    Many students receiving lots of financial aid can graduate from affordable in-state public colleges in five years with two majors and one or two foreign languages. Hello lots of job offers and future job security.

13. Post-college should be years of global and personal exploration, abetted by financial freedom (rather than oppressive monthly loan payments). Hello Peace Corps, teaching or coaching abroad, starting your own business, working for an adventure travel company, living where you've always dreamed, etc.

College should create financial freedom, not indebtedness.

NOTES

NOTES

CHAPTER 17

OTC PRO TIP WRAP UP

Why choose a rigorous college (or a rigorous path in college)?

You'll find vast social opportunities at every college; the question is whether there is an academic/intellectual pulse. You'll never be healthier, be more capable of learning, have fewer responsibilities, or have fewer financial burdens than you will in college. So dive in. Embrace healthy challenges. Surround yourself with bright people. These are years of differentiation. At your high school's fifth reunion, it should be clear who went to a fluff college and who challenged themselves. In ten years and twenty years, it may be even clearer. Small colleges of fewer than 2,000 students typically prioritize undergraduates. You can also get great educations at big universities. Be smart when you shop. Regardless, avoid large, lazy lectures and embrace small, scintillating seminars whenever possible.

Do not waste the summer after senior year in high school.

This has to be the least-planned, most-wasted, three to four months of a young person's life. Sure, have some fun and spend time with your family. Without planning, though, you're in for a summer of boredom interrupted by mindless work. Apply yourself. Don't forget: champions are made during the off-season. Master your extracurricular skill, get a job giving bike tours across Europe (do a Google search and apply), or master Spanish with a six-week immersion program in Argentina or at a camp in Minnesota. Many of you will need to earn at least $4,000 to help mom and dad pay for your freshman year, but there is still time to grow and embrace challenge (and have a sensible amount of fun).

Do not waste your freshman year in college.

Be sure to ask upperclassmen who the best professors are. Check the student blogs critiquing professors. Ask ten upperclassmen: Who are the five professors who have most changed your life? Then take whatever those professors teach. **Life is 30 percent what you do and 70 percent with whom you do it.** Make freshman year count. Take a Gap Year before going to college to maximize your actual freshman year.

What about transferring later?

In life, try to avoid stepping stones. Choose places and endeavors that may be destinations. Perhaps ultimately you'll tire of that choice and move on, but don't go into it knowing that it's a whistle stop. Also, transfer students typically get marginal housing and spend their years trying to catch up academically and socially. Transferring is not glamorous. Do it if you're miserable and/or unchallenged where you are. However, two years at a community college followed by two at a university can make financial sense.

What about a year studying abroad in college?

Great idea, especially if you attend college near your home. By going to a local college, you can get a great education and save dollars, but you may miss a new environmental challenge. Spending at least a summer and semester abroad gives you the best of all worlds (and you'll only pay slightly more than your local college costs for that year in Madrid!). Don't graduate from college still monolingual.

One last pitch for four years of challenge...

It's my experience that few non-job related skills are learned after college graduation. Rent, work, and family soon will fill your time. So you have until college graduation to learn how to play guitar or piano, to act or build theater sets, to debate, to play golf or tennis well, to paint or speak Spanish, etc. What is your passion? Put it off now, and you'll probably never get to it. Gravitate towards ease later in life. Embrace skill-building challenges now.

Get the job done. Don't become an academic casualty (45 percent of college freshmen never graduate). Over a lifetime, four-year college graduates earn about $1 million more than those without college experience; two-year college degree holders earn about $300,000 more than mere high school graduates. Get your degree without over-spending.

NOTES

SAMPLE ESSAYS

First, read again about the keys to great application essays in Chapter 14.

 THE FIVE KEYS:

1. **Be Passionate** (about your topic)

2. **Be Specific**

3. **Show, Don't Tell**

4. **Less is More**

5. **Find Humor**

The College Application (CommonApp.org) is accepted by more than 570 colleges (See Appendix C) and requires a single 650-word essay. There are multiple essay prompts. However, any topic can be massaged to address one of the prompts. So write with passion about what you wish. Below are excellent sample essays.

Interest Essays

∼ Sample Essay #1 ∼

The smell of stale smoke and cheap beer hangs in the air. Wiping perspiration from my palms onto my jeans, I look out at a dimly lit crowd that averages twice my age. Can they hear my heart beat as loud as I can? Stand-up comedians are supposed to be cool.

I like to write jokes. Whether my jokes are shared at a stand-up open mic or on social media, the thrill for me is real. Whenever I get an idea, I grab my notebook, worrying the thought might vanish at any moment. While writing tweets, I scrutinize the grammar, appreciating that the send button grants no second chances. This one has been retweeted to over half a million twitter accounts. I'm amazed too.

Mom makes me take out the garbage

Garbage and I begin to date

I start taking things too fast

Garbage dumps me

A joke that works becomes a game to replicate. What did people like about that? Good jokes involve making connections between two unrelated ideas and presenting them in a creative way. "Hey, see that thing? Well, it's kinda like this thing. Isn't that weird?" It's simple but difficult.

Successful jokes can be so abstract that I feel more like a poet than a comic. I want to make people laugh but also think. My favorite stand up comics—Louis C.K., Bill Burr, and Pete Holmes—all make the audience think differently about the world.

Laughter at my jokes triggers an instant connection. My comedy is an invitation for others to laugh with me. I watched videos of George Carlin getting huge laughs; I knew that I wanted that experience. Knowing that my thoughts and ideas can cause others to have an uncontrollable biological response fuels me. Sometimes a joke falls flat; the crowd doesn't laugh or the tweet isn't retweeted. I learn what doesn't work, refining my skill. If I can share laughter with even one person, the previous challenges have been worth it.

I love performing. My first taste came when I was eleven. I was cast as the lead at a community theater, fittingly named 'The Lofte' due to the building's origins as a pig barn. As Rudy in *Over the Tavern,* I had over three hundred lines, taking the stage thirteen times. Since then, performing is what I've wanted to do most. Being on stage is when I feel I can truly connect with others. I often feel more genuine when I act. Raw, authentic human emotion is so rare in everyday life. Whenever performing on stage, I often get to experience deep emotion, even if it belongs primarily to the character inhabiting me. There's rarely superficial small talk in published scripts: *The Secret Garden* and *The Crucible* are examples of meaningful worlds I got to inhabit. Invented conversation, constructed and written by a playwright, often captures how much deeper real-life interactions should be.

Opportunities to perform stand up are elusive for a high school student; not many open mic bars want an eighteen year-old. Plus, stand up is more of a risk for me than theatre. The emcee calls my name. I take my water and notebook on stage, legs shaking with nervous energy. No one has ever performed what I'm about to say—the reactions remain a mystery.

During a school production, the show consumes me. The day's final bell sends me to the stage, typically rehearsing for three hours, often going over the same scene time and time again, as if a broken Shakespearean record. There is a beautiful monotony to scribbling down blocking, fixing, erasing, and writing it down again.

Growing up in rural Wisconsin, I'm lucky this is my daily work and not cleaning pig pens. Surrounded by corn fields, cattle yards, and farm houses, I find my home on stage.

∼ Sample Essay #2 ∼

I am walking with my grandmother. The lights, the horns, the people introduce me to Times Square. Everyone around me is different: the men with cell phones, the street merchants, the rappers. I am different. We are walking to the New Amsterdam Theater to see my first Broadway show.

My grandmother has promised to take each grandchild to New York for his or her 16th birthday. She lived her entire life in Nebraska, and she often says that if she had seen New York City at the age of 16, she would have lived her life differently. In August 2003, I am 16 and the first grandchild to visit NY. I now understand my grandmother's thinking.

I grew up not in New York, but in York, Nebraska, a small farming town of 8,000. I shared an imaginative childhood with my neighborhood friends. We spent time pretending that we were pioneers: the cornfields were our playgrounds, and our bikes were our horses. We planted corn in our sand boxes and gazed at the crop dusters flying nearby. Thankfully these low buzzing planes never sprayed us.

I enjoyed many of the qualities my grandmother loved about rural life: the safety, the sense of caring, and the essence of community involvement. York was a place where we could play tag downtown on our bikes at night. I wished for more traffic on the days we had lemonade stands but was thankful that we weren't disturbed as we played tennis on roller blades in the streets.

I know that I had an innocent childhood, one in which I was shielded from many of the pressures of a larger place. But York allowed us to become what we wanted to naturally, without pressure from the larger world.

I am who I am today because as a child I was not made into a product of someone else's dreams; instead, I explored for myself whom I wanted to become.

During the summer before eighth grade, we moved to Lincoln, Nebraska, population 250,000. I changed schools, churches, neighborhoods, sports teams, and friends. I'll never forget my first day of school. My mom asked as she dropped me off, "Are you going to be okay?" I barely told her yes before she asked, "Do you know where your locker is?" I said, "No mom, but don't worry, I'll be fine." Though I had been dreading this day, I realized I was ready for something different. I had had a stable, healthy upbringing, but that didn't make me cling to it. I would become grateful for the social and athletic opportunities the bigger city provided me.

My grandmother certainly doesn't regret her life: three children, seven grandchildren, community leadership and social contributions in all corners of the state. But she wishes she had gone to New York City. She took me there not to push me away from Nebraska, but to let me dream and to see my choices.

We often don't know what we have until we sample something else. Now I've seen the billboards of Times Square, and I know it's okay to not know where your locker is. I have learned that throughout my beautiful experiences growing up in Nebraska, and now I am ready to begin an adventure with even greater opportunities.

A

∼ Sample Essay #3 ∼

I escaped the loud monotonous buzz of the enormous machine that encased me. The Hail Mary had worked. A voice came on telling me it was over.

I threw back the stiff white sheets and pulled out the earplugs. After changing, I went back with my mother into the muggy, dimly lit radiology department viewing room. Doctor Matthis was studying the films.

Long white snakes slithered endlessly through a cloud of black. "This here is brain tissue." Doctor Matthis spoke with a southern accent and wore cowboy boots under his white coat.

He pointed to a spot protruding from the right side of my brainstem. I noticed that the white matter had pushed away the right side of my brain. "This protrusion is causing your dizziness."

My mother stayed with Dr. Matthis, while I was asked to step outside, already an hour late for diving practice. Finally the doors swung open and my mother and I escaped from the white walls and buzzing.

We marched past the familiar blue couches. I had walked over the same cream-and-blue-specked tiles too many times in the last three months. I wanted closure. I wanted to know why I was getting dizzy on the diving board, why I couldn't walk straight when I closed my eyes, and what the buzzing sounds were in my ear.

In the car my mother broke. "God, Emma, why?" Confused, I embraced her. Her hands spread black mascara across the sides of her face.

"Mom, it's going to be all right." I tried to rid her of the black streaks. "What did Doctor Matthis say?"

"He doesn't know. He's going to take the films up to Daddy's office. This kind of thing shouldn't happen to a 14 year-old girl, especially when that 14 year-old girl is my daughter."

"Things could be worse. Think of Sam."

"Emma, you have the same symptoms that Sam had two months ago." Sam was a sixth grader in our parish that was slowly dying from a brain tumor that had been detected two months prior. I imagined Sam's white bandages covering his disfigured head. I flinched at the thought of going blind at such an early age. I admired his determination but wasn't sure how much I had. We had been told that Sam had five months left.

Surgery became inevitable. Dr. Fukashima, a neurosurgeon from North Carolina, flew in to Nebraska on July 9th. My father (a vascular surgeon), mother, and several other neurosurgeons from Lincoln consulted together that day about my case. The doctors agreed that the intricate operation would be best left in Dr. Fukashima's hands.

He bowed to the doctors, and then addressed my father. "Ed, I have been in that spot in the brain more than any other doctor in the world. I am the only surgeon that can remove the whole tumor. I would be proud to do this surgery on your daughter." My father was convinced.

At 5:00 a.m. on July 10th, I laid on the surgery bed. The nurse rolled me around a corner; I slowly watched the tears on my mother's face vanish from sight.

We entered the O.R. at Bryan Hospital and trepidation set in. What if something went wrong? The tumor entangled 7 nerves. A simple twitch of Dr. Fukashima's hand and my hearing was gone forever, or the right side of my face might go limp. The drugs took over my body.

I awoke with about two feet of gauze wrapped around my pounding head. My best friend, Megan, and my brother sat in the far corner. Two huge machines lay behind my head. I wanted something to throw up in. Nothing would stay down, yet I was so thirsty that I begged the nurse for some ice chips.

"Oh, Hobbit, how are you feeling?" (Hobbit is Megan's nickname for me because of my size). Slowly putting my finger over my lips I urged her to be quiet and fell asleep again.

Two days later, I was moved from the Intensive Care Unit into the Pediatrics Unit. The gauze was removed and I could feel a small patch of freshly shaved hair on the back of my head. "You can't even tell, Emma, really," my sister tried to assure me.

The familiar sound of cowboy boots clanked outside my door and the muggy smell of the radiology department returned.

Dr. Matthis spoke: "The bad news is that this protrusion we found on Emma's MRIs was in fact a tumor. The good news is that it was benign and there is only a .1 percent chance of recurrence. Emma will dive again."

It would be another five long months before I entered the pool. Every night I thanked God for putting me up to that challenge and for the favorable pathology results. When faced with adversity again, I know that God will be there.

With my first step back inside the pool doors, I could smell the fresh chlorine. The rigid board was an old friend beneath my feet. I approached the end of the blue plank, soared through the air, and fell towards the blue three meters below. It had never felt so good to feel my hands ripping through the water.

A

∼ Sample Essay #4 ∼

It is 12:05 A.M. The NFL (National Forensics League) just announced the debate topic for the next two months—I am deep in the University of Nebraska library stacks. As I grab every book that might be vaguely topical, I congratulate myself on being the first to raid the shelves. At the circulation desk I see a rival team entering. I am not sure what gives me more pleasure: knowing I got there before them or seeing their heads fall because they know they lost the first battle. I saunter past them, grinning like a game show host. What prowess! What cunning! What am I doing? I am losing sleep, losing weight, and losing all sense of decency. I am a debate junkie.

Debaters often describe themselves as having "tunnel vision." The more I am involved in this undertaking the more I realize how true this is. Particularly during the debate season, everything I read, hear, and see is funneled through a debate-shaped cylinder. The term research takes on a whole new meaning—my entire existence is research. You would not believe the kinds of dreams I have.

But that still does not explain what turned me from a good-natured high school student to a somewhat eccentric debater. I guess debate really is like a drug; it can do different things to different people. It forced me to break all the confines of conventional wisdom; it gave me a high I could only get by watching James Carville place a trash bag over his head during the 2002 midterm elections. You know you are an over-the-edge debater when you demand that your friends give supporting evidence for their movie reviews, signpost their argument flow in casual conversation, and wake up at 6:00 A.M. to engage walls in games of locution.

But please, before you evaluate my seemingly deranged mindset, try to understand how I got this way. Try to understand how debate morphed my thinking process. Debaters are often forced to draw connections that most people would cringe at. Do you know what Noam Chomsky, Alexander Hamilton, and Jean Jacques Rousseau have in common? They all would have negated the 2003 January/February resolution. Indeed, debate is its own quirky subculture—immune to the principles of normal socialization. I am merely a derivative.

That momentous October night in the library placed me at an unavoidable junction. Should I continue down my path of analytical ruin—alienating family, friends, colleagues? Or do I take the road more oft' traveled, find moderation and regain some balance. Temperance is for the faint-of-heart—I chose the former. Rather than surrender my passion, I simply became more prudent. No longer do dinnertime conversations focus on the upcoming tournament or my chances of winning state—no more do my friends endure an excruciatingly specific recounting of my final round at Omaha Westside—no more sentences that start with "One time, at debate camp…" No more! I may still be a junkie, but I am a closet junkie, and I do not "peddle" my intellect where it is not wanted. I have since gained sorely needed perspective. You may choose to call me a fanatic; I prefer the term "zealot." You may be kinder and simply refer to me as "moderately fixated." Yeah, I wish.

∽ Sample Essay #5 ∽

The sun rises in the sky over my family farm; a new day peacefully begins. Then, I hear it: a dreaded sound callously disrupts my slumber. No, it is not a rooster. Even small-town Nebraskans have embraced technological advances. The sound belongs to my beeping alarm clock.

I stagger out of bed. After donning the latest in farming fashion (ripped jeans, a tattered t-shirt, and rubber boots), I join my dad in the morning chores. We work side-by-side, dumping buckets of feed to silence the earsplitting squeals of the pigs. They ravenously devour every morsel, their demanding squeals replaced by satisfied chomping sounds. But for every action there is an equal and opposite reaction. As the stomachs of the pigs are filled, other parts are emptied. So my dad and I continue our work, beginning the odorous task of cleaning manure from pigpen after pigpen. The awful aroma hangs upon us, a pungent pig perfume that can only be removed by countless handfuls of antibacterial soap and bottles of the strongest scented shampoo.

As we work, I watch my dad. His clothes are filthy and sweat glistens on his brow. Some dads sit in offices wearing a suit and tie. My dad's office is a hog shed. His suit is a dirty pair of Wrangler jeans. While his profession isn't glamorous, I admire what he does and how he does it. When I see him nurture a newborn pig, gently placing it near its mother to taste its first sip of milk, I see the loving care and attention to detail that make my dad a successful farmer and an even better man.

I see the same attention to detail and work ethic in many of my fellow Nebraskans. They work hard, giving sound effort regardless of the task. And like my dad, Nebraskans are humble and caring. I'm proud of my heritage, but I long for something more. I long for the academic challenges and intellectual rigor more prevalent beyond the gravel roads and cornfields of Nebraska.

To many in this state, football is sacred. The biggest and strongest play the game. On my freshmen football team, I was one of the biggest, a line captain starting every game. But by season's end, I no longer felt passion for football. I gave up my helmet for a yearbook camera. Few of my peers understood. However, pouring myself into the yearbook for hours each afternoon fits me. Coaching my sister's volleyball team for the last five years and going away to summer schools at Yale and Stanford are other passions that my true friends now understand and appreciate.

My dad has always known that I was different from the typical farmer's son. He encourages me to embrace these differences and to enjoy a future beyond our small family farm. And though I appreciate this simpler life, I agree with him. Still, I am no less proud to be the son of a hardworking Nebraska hog farmer.

A

∼ Sample Essay #6 ∼

The standing ovation surprised me. Our self-taught band had just closed my high school's talent show. Teaching myself piano, guitar, and songwriting had always been its own reward, but now it was exhilarating to be appreciated by others as well.

The enthralling feeling of music pouring out of me onto my piano has driven me since I discovered songwriting in 8th grade. Now, despite the typical responsibilities of a 17-year-old, and much to the chagrin of my parents, I find myself spending most late nights pounding out new song creations. It is the process that drives me, not the acclaim.

I have always had the ability to lose myself in things I love. As a nine-year-old, I spent hours setting up elaborate Rube-Goldberg-like booby traps, causing a nerf gun to be fired at an intruder upon invasion. I remember an entire weekend spent rigging my room instead of joining the rest of the neighborhood kids in the backyard football playoffs next door. Although I don't believe a nerf dart ever hit the intended target (my older sister), sabotaging rooms remained a common afternoon activity late into my grade school years. Family members still enter my room with caution.

Fortunately losing myself in what I love has not compromised my performance elsewhere. I still succeed at what I enjoy less. There is a part of me that is proud that I can excel without much passion, but I recognize that skill without passion can be an affliction: many adults seem to choose jobs they can do well rather than careers they love. I want to pursue those activities that ignite my passion. My AP Psychology class research paper, discussions of Hamlet in my AP Lit Comp class, and the real life applications of physics I learned in Physics 211 at UNL have given me the opportunity to lose myself in academics, and I look forward to more such experiences in college.

Meeting society's expectations is not enough for me. Most central to me is a search for an environment that inspires me continuously, allowing me to focus on the academic opportunities that excite me as much as losing myself during the process of writing a song has excited me. I know I'm probably not going to be a rock star, or a home security saboteur for that matter, so I look forward to a college and future that inspires my passionate best at least as often as it demands my ability merely to succeed.

What activity means the most to you?

∼ Sample Essay #1 ∼

It was painfully obvious. Everyone saw it. The third baseman failed to make the tag, but I still called the runner out. The middle-aged, upper-middle class, slightly overweight crowd of respectable suburban professionals was becoming increasingly hysterical. This only further inflamed the coach, who demanded that I consider a second opinion—his opinion. Welcome to the oh-so-competitive sport of baseball—fifth grade baseball— Lincoln YMCA fifth grade baseball.

"I'm sorry sir, baseball is not a democracy." This was my sententious reply to a now astonished coach as I walked away, back to the plate, to await the next pitch.

Baseball is not a democracy? Honestly, when I said it I was not really sure what it meant. Given the circumstances, it seemed like an appropriate response. That was four years ago, soon after I had started umpiring. Before then I had held an unrealistic goal: I wanted to make everyone happy, to be the perfect umpire. This is when I discovered the first parallel between baseball and politics. Umpires, like politicians, can never make everyone happy, but they often succeed in making everyone irritated. Fans that day would have agreed.

Throughout the first year I umpired, my philosophy smacked of Kennedy idealism: I was a visionary, trying to make the baseball diamond a better place for everyone. Since then, idealism has been replaced with realism, creativity with orthodoxy. I now try to bring a sense of totalitarianism to my games—not dissimilar from how Big Brother would umpire. I have come to realize that a good umpire does not always make the right call (to the charge of being human, I plead guilty). But a good umpire acts like he always makes the right call and is not influenced by implacable coaches, impertinent players, or vengeful mobs.

The longer I am involved in baseball the more my umpiring philosophy moves away from benevolence and towards authoritarianism—from Kennedy to King Henry VIII. But umpires, for those hours when we are out on the diamond, justifiably lose all sense of decency and compassion—at least the good ones do. The poet Ernest Thayer, in "Casey at the Bat," explains:

> From the benches, black with people, there went up a muffled roar,
>
> Like the beating of the storm-waves on a stern and distant shore.
>
> "Kill him! Kill the umpire!" shouted some one on the stand;
>
> And it's likely they'd have killed him had not Casey raised his hand.

In a world of such malcontents, Casey does not exist, and democratic baseball becomes an oxymoron.

Of course, some of umpiring's appeal is economic—flipping burgers pays a lot less. But more than that, umpiring is about right and wrong. In a blurred world of grays, I like the clarity of absolutes. I started umpiring when I was 14 years old. Most athletes move to coaching or umpiring after a stellar athletic career. I was never that good at baseball. Most umpires miss playing. Next fall, I will miss umpiring.

A

∼ Sample Essay #2 ∼

It's been a long week. After mornings working on the yearbook, days of classes, and rehearsals in the afternoon, I'm looking forward to a break. So come Friday I'm excited. I'm not going to a movie or hitting Lincoln's scintillating big-city nightlife. I'm going back to school to spend a few hours coaching my sister's volleyball team.

I'm not a star athlete. As a child, I was "that one kid" in P.E. class, lumbering and clumsy, the last to finish every race and the target of every game of dodge ball. But in fifth grade, things began to change. I somehow found some coordination, and my P.E. teacher taught my class the basics of volleyball. As I began to pass, set, and serve, I fell in love with the sport. With time, my passion for the game grew faster than my skills.

In small-town Nebraska, there are countless football and baseball leagues, but the number of boys' volleyball teams barely equals the number of skyscrapers on the Nebraska skyline. So I decided to coach.

I began my "coaching career" in fifth grade playing volleyball with my younger sister— so began a cherished part of our relationship. Separated by four years of age, my sister and I rarely spent much time together before volleyball. Practicing for hours on our backyard patio, passing and setting, not only strengthened our skills, but also our relationship. As we played, we talked. She told me her aspirations of becoming a fashion designer, asking whether she should work in Paris or New York. I opted for Paris, hoping I could visit. I vented my frustrations about my science class. Why does an aspiring news anchor need to know the difference between inertia and momentum? She calmed my anxieties. Our relationship became more than brother and sister, more than player and coach. We became friends.

Where many siblings reenact Gettysburg when they do dishes, my sister and I work together—Rachel washes; I dry. Some brothers never hug their sister in public. Every day after third period, I meet my sister in the hallway and give her a hug. Before Rachel's first junior high dance, she had no idea what to wear. I spent an hour going through her closet, helping her pick out the perfect ensemble for her special night.

In eighth grade, I began helping coach my sister's YMCA and USVBA volleyball teams. At times, this tested our friendship. What I thought was constructive criticism on her passing or serving she sometimes took as a personal attack. Spending four hours in the gym together can strain the relationship of any coach and player. Still, at the end of every match, after the handshakes and "good games," I give her a hug, and say how proud I am of her.

From the first day my sister ever touched a volleyball, I've been there—from the driveway to the state championship in Lincoln last week. I no longer coach because I love the game. I coach because I love my sister.

Why do you want to attend our school?

∼ Sample Essay #1 ∼

"What do you want to be when you grow up?" When my first grade teacher asked me this exact question, she wasn't prepared for the response. I answered without hesitation, "I want to be the President." Later I would change my mind, replacing politics with broadcast journalism, but my desire to make a difference has never subsided.

Actually, superficial reasons initially led to my interest in broadcast journalism. I dreamed of being Peter Jennings or Tom Brokaw, signing multi-million dollar contracts and having national fame. I guess growing up anonymously on a farm where funds were rarely ample affected me. But I have learned that there is more to broadcasting than money and recognition. While attending a summer school at Yale during my junior year, I realized that this desire stemmed from my first grade wish to be the President. I have always had an interest in government. Deep down I still longed to experience the power of politics and to do what I can to help shape the policies of our country.

Yale taught me about the many aspects of our country's government, including the media. In many ways the media is the fourth branch of government. The media tells the American people which issues are important. The media influences policy decisions and holds elected officials accountable for their actions. It has the ability to initiate political change by spotlighting issues that deserve attention. This past summer newspapers and airwaves were filled with countless stories on several child abductions. Because of the barrage of media attention given to the abductions, lawmakers in several states implemented the Amber Alert System, enabling information about an abducted child to be broadcast moments after the child has been reported missing. The media focused on an issue and helped change public policy.

With power comes responsibility. I don't want to be another television bubblehead who reads a teleprompter and smiles for the camera. I long to be a responsible journalist who not only knows what to discuss, but what it means. I have no aspirations of becoming another Carl Bernstein, but I'm convinced I can make a difference. That's why I'm applying to Georgetown. I want to immerse myself in a rigorous education grounded in political science and foreign relations, furthering my education later with law school. Studying at Georgetown will arm me with the prerequisite acumen to truly make a positive difference as a broadcast journalist.

My ambitions have moved from the Oval Office to the newsroom, but one thing has remained—my desire to influence our country's government for the better. An education from Georgetown will put me in the center of our nation's political arena and will give me the tools and experiences needed to accomplish my ultimate goal of responsibly wielding media influence.

A

~ Sample Essay #2 ~

I yearn for a place where my intellectual day does not end when I walk out the classroom door. An essential part of my high school experience has been going to the local coffee house at night to engage in spirited discussions about great ideas. This type of intellectual release sustains me. I have found nothing that enriches my learning more than a group of peers who love what they study, arguing openly about ideas. Thoughtful discussion outside of class is the norm at Swarthmore. Simply, I seek a diverse learning community unified by a central purpose—the pursuit of truth and the enrichment of knowledge. Swarthmore is a cross-fire of ideas, inside and outside the classroom, where hard work comes naturally.

I'm also applying to larger selective schools with vibrant intellectual pulses. But my preference is the intimate classrooms of a smaller college. Small classes ensure accountability. Regardless of the quality of instructor or course content, I don't wish to become a member of the student herd. Further, graduate assistants do not excite me. Swarthmore's size and commitment to professors in every classroom provide the ideal environment for my personal search into philosophical thought—my planned major. Specifically, I most look forward to studying Dr. Eldridge, whose work on Hegelian historical justification I thoroughly enjoyed in my preparation for last spring's national debate, the Tournament of Champions in Lexington, Kentucky.

NOTES

NOTES

AFFORDABLE SUMMER OPPORTUNITIES

Appendix B contains the most current information available at the time of printing. Items are subject to change.

Don't be a summer slug.

Champions are made during the off-season!

Here's the goal: foster your productive passion(s) and become great at ONE extracurricular skill by December of your senior year so you can leverage that skill or interest into the "Best-Fit College for You at the Lowest Cost."

Question: "But what if I don't have TIME for extracurriculars?"

Answer: "That's the beauty of the summer time. Summer vacation is about expanding your horizons."

Objection: "But I want to hang out with my friends during the summer!"

Solution: "Friends are important. But why not get your friends involved in extracurricular activities?

Think about clubs, sports, bands, camps, adventures, volunteer opportunities…"

Conflict: "But I have to work during the summer to make money!"

Resolution: "Then it's time to be creative—think outside of the box and see if there's a way to get PAID to develop your extracurricular skill. And even though making money is a necessity for many high school scholars, don't forget that when you invest in a skill, you are investing in yourself, and that investment could have a financial pay-off when you present your accomplishments to admissions and scholarship committees."

B

DON'T KNOW WHERE TO BEGIN?

Check out these categories below...

Section

*IN THE FOLLOWING PAGES, you will discover a
TREASURE TROVE of life-changing adventures...*

Categorized by type, these activities, camps, organizations, and internships are meant to be examples of the types of summer opportunities that are out there. OnToCollege does not endorse any formally, but we do encourage you to research them thoroughly. This is not an exhaustive list, but serves as a general resource, helping you in the planning stages of your summer adventure!

WHILE ON YOUR ADVENTURE, REMEMBER TO:

1. **KEEP A JOURNAL**, making note of major events and reflections from your summer. You don't have to write your thoughts every day, but the more you write, the easier it will be to write your college application essays later. Record details so you don't have to recreate them in the future.

2. **KEEP IN TOUCH** with new friends and exchange ideas about college plans—maybe they have a friend or sibling at the college of your choice. Harness the college-planning power of social networking applications like Facebook..

3. **KEEP LOOKING** for more future opportunities. Adventure leads to more adventure; connections lead to more connections. If you land one internship, use it as a stepping-stone to NEXT summer's internship!

...and of course: HAVE FUN!

Remember: when you invest in a skill, you are investing in yourself, and that personal investment could have a financial pay-off when you present your accomplishments to scholarship committees. So choose your own adventure!

B

CHECK OUT THE SUMMER OPPORTUNITY COST CHART:

THUMBS UP! "Oh yeah, just tell me where to sign up!"
Between $0 and $100 per week.

BUDGET FRIENDLY: Between $100 and $250 per week.

MID-RANGE: Between $250 and $750 per week.

HIGH END: More than $750 a week.

ART / PHOTOGRAPHY / FILMMAKING:
Not just for the beret-wearing types.

San Francisco Summer Art Experience

San Francisco, California   late June through early August   Grades 10-12

The Pre-College Art Experience program currently offers a mixture of over 40 introductory, intermediate, and advanced level classes spanning all 13 of the undergraduate majors offered at Academy of Art University. The program has been specially designed by our Academic Department Directors to accommodate students from all educational and artistic backgrounds who are interested in exploring the possibilities of an education in art and design.

http://www.academyart.edu/degrees/summer_artexperience.html   Cost: $3,000 plus supplies

Maine Media—Young Artist Workshops

Rockport, Maine   Sessions in June, July, August   Ages 14-17

Maine Media, well known in filmmaking and photography communities for its innovative professional workshops, also offers summer multi-week camps for high school students who like to be behind the camera. Experienced professionals teach subjects like photojournalism, screenwriting, filmmaking, documentary making, acting and fine art. The curriculum includes time in the classroom, computer lab, and darkroom, but it draws more heavily from field work—which can include hiking, kayaking, swimming, and other forms of nature exploration.

http://www.mainemedia.edu/workshops/young-artists   Cost: $1,595-2,995

Camp Shakespeare

Omaha, Nebraska   late June through early July   Ages 8-18

Over the course of two weeks, students work with the professional artists and educators of Nebraska Shakespeare (NS), a nationally-recognized theatre company. The campers are given the tools necessary to understand Shakespeare's 400-year-old version of the English language, and to analyze his broad array of exciting and complex plots and characters. On the final three days of the camp, the students are given the opportunity to share their "Shakesperience" by performing for audiences at NS's Shakespeare on the Green.

http://www.nebraskashakespeare.com/education-programs/camp-shakespeare   Cost: $200

B

Big Red Summer Academic Program—Filmmaking

Lincoln, Nebraska   mid June   Grades 10-12

Put your summer on the big screen! This movie-making adventure will allow you to actually make a film and spend time in the Mary Riempa Ross Media Arts Center. You'll have access to award-winning faculty and see how motion pictures really work. We'll introduce you to one of the few digital film projectors in the world. Participants are welcome to bring their own video cameras.

http://4h.unl.edu/big-red-camps/offerings   **Cost: $600-700**

BUSINESS:
Think bigger than the lemonade stand.

Milwaukee School of Engineering—Focus on Business

| Milwaukee, Wisconsin | Sessions in July | 13-18 years old |

Run your own business for a week! Start the day learning about the functions of a business organization that make companies successful. Also learn how a company gets ideas, develops products, raises money, makes its products, sells them, and accounts for the money earned and spent.

http://www.msoe.edu/admissions/undergraduate/summer-programs-for-business/   Cost: $750

LEAD Summer Business Institute

| Various locations | Sessions in June, July, and August | High School Juniors |

A student must be a high school junior and have at least a 'B' average to apply to the LEAD Summer Business Institute. Recognizing that a lack of role models in corporate America was discouraging students from diverse communities from pursuing careers in business, executives at McNeil Pharmaceutical launched LEAD at The Wharton School in 1980. Their agenda: create an innovative and intensive summer business program that serves as the foundation for lifelong partnerships between students and business schools.

http://www.leadprogram.org/apps/pages/index.jsp?uREC_ID=218898&type=d   Cost: $2,000-3,000

Envision Experience—Business and Innovation

| Various Locations | Sessions in June and July | Grades 9-12 |

Define yourself on an interactive journey that includes hands-on business experience, site visits to leading corporations, and exposure to the knowledge and skills necessary for success in high school, college and beyond!

http://www.envisionexperience.com/explore-our-programs/business-and-innovation

Cost: $2,995-4,190; includes College Credit

CAMP COUNSELING
Get paid to have fun!

Charles Campbell Children's Camp

Billings, Montana   Approx. July 11-17   Ages 15+

Volunteer staff provide nursing, professional food preparation, and supervision of all activities. Lions members and many other caring individuals with your child's interests at heart guide daily activities, provide training for volunteer counselors, and all things that are essential to a successful camp. Counselors must be at least 15 years of age and have an interest in helping children with disabilities.

http://www.billingslions.org/ccc.html

Camp Kindle (for AIDS patients)

Lincoln, Nebraska   Sessions July-August   Ages 16-18

These young people should have past leadership training and possess a desire to be a counselor someday. All potential JC's or CIT's must obtain at least 3 letters of recommendation along with their completed application. Camp Kindle's JC's and CIT's do not have to be directly affected by HIV/AIDS to participate in this program.

http://www.projectkindle.org/forms/

Camp Hertko Hollow (for children with diabetes)

Des Moines, Iowa   Sessions June-early July   Ages 18+

This camp provides an educational and recreational camping program for Iowa's youth between the ages of 6-18 who have diabetes. The Y-Camp's program and staff work with medical personnel and diabetes counselors to provide a meaningful experience for campers.

http://www.camphertkohollow.com/volunteer-staff/apply

Camp Holiday Trails

Charlottesville, Virginia   March-November   Ages 16+

Staff must be at least 16 years old to apply for a paid position at Camp Holiday Trails. Staffing decisions are usually made by early April, so apply early. Camp Holiday Trails is a caring community committed to empowering, encouraging, and educating campers with chronic illnesses. Volunteer positions also available.

http://www.campholidaytrails.org/ways-to-connect/become-a-counselor/

Wonderland Camp

Rocky Mount, Missouri   Summer and Fall   Ages 16+

The mission of Wonderland Camp is to provide a fun, educational camp experience for children, teenagers and adults who have disabilities; to offer a respite from daily caregiving for their family members and healthcare workers; and to provide and nurture a personal development experience for volunteers and staff.

Staff must be at least 16 years old to apply for a paid position at Wonderland Camp. All staff that turn in an application will be required to attend an in person interview with the Program Director. If hired, staff will also be required to attend a weekend Staff Training.

http://www.wonderlandcamp.org/work.asp

Recreational Sports Camps at UC-Berkeley

Berkeley, California   Sessions in June through August   Grades 10-12

Junior Counselors (JCs) gain valuable training and experience by providing support to instructors and group leaders. JCs are supervised by instructors, group leaders, individual Camp Coordinators, and the Strawberry Canyon Youth Programs Director(s). Specific camp activities include gymnastics, martial arts, and skateboarding.

http://camps.berkeley.edu/camps-by-activity/

4-H Nebraska Summer Camps

Gretna, Nebraska & Nebraska National Forest   Sessions in June through August   Ages 15 & up

As summer camp counselors, you will be trained to provide active, hands-on, fun, and cooperative outdoor programming designed to develop respect for self, others, and the environment. You will have the opportunity to affect children's lives in experiential, outdoor settings. You will be challenged to find new ways of teaching, motivating, and playing. You will be a leader and held to high expectations.

http://4h.unl.edu/4hcampemployment

IMPORTANT INSIDER INFO

- Camps for kids with disabilities look for volunteers each year. Most states have many camps with opportunities to serve kids with autism, AIDS, and cerebral palsy, pursuits that impress on a resume or college application—and more importantly, reveal that you used your summer to make a real, positive impact on others' lives.

- When you're googling potential camp opportunities, search for the word "junior counselor." Many camps hire college-aged counselors and high school aged "junior counselors."

- If you're an adventure seeker, look for specialty camps like rock-climbing camps, sailing camps, equestrian camps, and sports camps. Not only will you gain valuable counseling experience, you'll also pick up a variety of other skills, all of which can make you more attractive to colleges.

COLLEGE PREP / HONORS PROGRAMS:
The best paying job...

University of Nebraska-Omaha—Summer Scholars Program

Omaha, Nebraska   early summer Application Deadline: Feb or Mar   Rising 11th

Open to rising juniors in the greater Omaha metropolitan area, this five-week experience operates like a broad pre-college experience. Students live in campus dorms, participate in real college courses for transferable college credit, explore possible future majors and career options, and get a taste of the college life. This program is ideal for students who want an idea of what college feels like before they make major college-related decisions.

http://mca.unomaha.edu/summer.php   **Cost: $0**

UCLA Summer Experience

Los Angeles, California   June, July, August   Ages 15+

Summer time at UCLA is unique in that it is the only time when non-matriculated UCLA students may take advantage of all UCLA has to offer. University students may attend; highly motivated high school students may attend; professionals, members of the community, and alumni may attend.

http://www.summer.ucla.edu/HighSchool/overview.htm   **Cost: $1,800 (for 40 days)**

University of Northern Colorado Summer & Leadership Enrichment Programs

| Greeley, Colorado | mid July | Grades 5-10, 11-12 |

This is a two-week residential program for gifted and creative learners. Students participate in stimulating academic experiences and fun social activities developed by gifted education specialists. These classes are held on the UNC campus and trained counselors provide supervision during all non-class time. 970-351-2683 or sep@unco.edu

http://www.unco.edu/sep   **Cost: $1,775**

IMPORTANT INSIDER INFO

- Pre-college programs may be available in abundance, and many of these programs offer college credit for courses you will take as a student. If your student is academically gifted, you might investigate the honors program at prospective schools and see if they offer summer courses like the one at Indiana University in Pennsylvania.

- If you're signed up for the September ACT, summer gives you lots of time to study! To make sure you stay disciplined, get a study buddy or start an ACT study club. Go out for ice cream after practice tests! You won't have as much time for studying during the school year.

COMPUTERS / TECHNOLOGY
The rise of the machines…

Cybercamps

Various Locations	June, July, August	7-12, 13-18 years old

Whether they are designing games or programming a robot, our campers spend their summer unleashing technology. Courses at our Tech, Digital Media, and Gaming Camps are designed by industry professionals and tested at Giant Campus for fun, relevance, and instructional impact. All of our courses have been updated and are available online to our campers for a whole year after camp. Our campers do hands-on projects and learn new skills in Web design, gaming, digital photography, graphics, video production, programming, robotics, and general computing.

www.idtech.com   **Cost: $1,340-4,199**

Emagination Game Design Camp

Various Locations	June, July, August	8-14, 15-18 years old

Teens experience an intensive two weeks working on a game development team, designing and building a 3D video game. There are no prerequisites. The program runs 14 days and 13 nights. Fun on the weekends with fellow game designers is part of the program and is included. Spend free time challenging other teens to computer gaming tournaments and finalizing components of your team's game.

http://www.computercamps.com/tech-camps/game-design-camp-for-teens/program-overview/
Cost: $2,825-3,295 (2 weeks)

Digital Media Academy

Various Locations	June, July, August	12-17 years old

Learn game development, music-production, filmmaking, programming and more this summer at prestigious universities. Teens can explore career paths, prepare for college, gain real-world skills, and earn Stanford Continuing Studies Credits. Courses are one- or two-weeks long.

http://www.digitalmediaacademy.org/teen-summer-camps/   **Cost: $1,195-2,395**

B

- Teenage fascination with technology has led to the creation of a new breed of tech. Encourage your tech-savvy teen to research new camps and classes that appeal to her individual interests—perhaps smart-phone application design or social networking innovations.

- Think you've mastered the art of Facebook? If you market that skill properly, you might be able to land a paid summer gig as a social networking expert. Companies are paying big to get their name out on Instagram, Facebook, and Twitter. Do some research, brainstorm with your parents, and see if you can Twitter up some summer income.

- While some of these opportunities are expensive, check your local community college or schools to see if they offer more affordable options. Also, note that most of the camps offer need-based scholarships.

DEBATE
All right, you win this argument.

Jayhawk Debate Institute at the University of Kansas

Lawrence, Kansas — Sessions in June/July — Rising 9-12

The Jayhawk Debate Institute at the University of Kansas is a premier high school debate camp providing first class instruction at an good value. The JDI offers students of all levels of debate experience the opportunity to further their development through a low student-to-staff ratio and interaction with strong faculty.

https://debate.ku.edu/debate-camp-info   **Cost: $1,800 (two weeks) $2,400 (three weeks)**

Debate Camp, Cameron University

Lawton, Oklahoma — mid-late July — Rising 9-12

This is an inexpensive summer debate camp hosted by Cameron University on the NFL topic. This camp has five different tracks: Beginning Team CX Debate, Intermediate Team CX Debate, Advanced Team CX Debate, Beginning Lincoln-Douglas Debate, Intermediate Lincoln-Douglas Debate, and Advanced Lincoln-Douglas Debate.

http://www.cameron.edu/academic/liberal_arts/communications/spchcamp/

Cost: $415-455

B

ENGINEERING
Build your summer.

Engineering Summer Programs, North Carolina State University

Raleigh, North Carolina   June and July   Rising 3-5, 6-8, 9-10, 11-12

Each summer, the College of Engineering at NC State University offers high school students the opportunity to experience engineering, science, and technology. A multidisciplinary week-long day camp is offered for rising 9th & 10th graders and discipline-specific residential camps are offered for rising 11th & 12th graders. The residential program allows students to explore a particular field of engineering in more depth.

http://www.engr.ncsu.edu/theengineeringplace/summerprograms/   **Cost: $225-800**

Engineering Summer Program (ESP), University of Wisconsin—Madison

Madison, Wisconsin   June 16-July 27   Rising 11-12

ESP is designed to focus on academic enrichment related to math, science. Participants will interact with UW faculty/staff, students, program alumni, and other talented peers who share the same interest in mathematics, science and engineering.

http://studentservices.engr.wisc.edu/diversity/esp/   **Cost: $0, plus a $500 stipend**

Introduction to Engineering, Notre Dame University

Notre Dame, Indiana   June and July   Rising 12

Over two weeks of the summer between your junior and senior years in high school will give you an introduction to engineering that includes a chance to meet the faculty of the College of Engineering, an update on career opportunities in engineering, a look at the many facets of engineering, and an overview of the elements of engineering design and computer programming.

http://www.nd.edu/~iep/   **Cost: $1,850 (partial scholarships available)**

Nuclear Engineering Camp, University of Missouri-Rolla

Rolla, Missouri   late June   Rising 11, 12, and undecided college freshmen

This one-week summer program will introduce you to the fascinating world of nuclear power and the outstanding opportunities in nuclear engineering.

http://futurestudents.mst.edu/summercamps/nuce/   **Cost: $650**

Women in Engineering Summer Camp

Dayton, Ohio   mid July   Rising 9-12

Explore engineering on your own terms with other girls your age from across the country. Live in a dorm with others who share your interests. Guided by UD professors, you'll conduct experiments, innovate, make cool stuff, take things apart—then put them back together again—in engineering classrooms and laboratories. You'll visit a job site and meet women engineers.

https://www.udayton.edu/engineering/k-12-programs/women_in_engineering_summer_camp/index.php
Cost: $665

Michigan Technological University—Explorations in Engineering Workshop

Houghton, Michigan   Sessions June-August   Completed grades 6-8, 9-11

Which field would you like to explore—mechanical, chemical, electrical, civil? Get a taste of these as you test the memory of metal, design bridges, purify water, and assemble a computer.

http://www.syp.mtu.edu/apply.php   **Cost: $945**

University of Vermont Summer Engineering Institute for High School Students

Burlington, Vermont   Session in mid July   15-16 years old

The UVM/GIV Engineering Institute enrolls approximately 100 high school freshmen, sophomores, and juniors. The Institute focuses on implementing sustainable engineering practices. Students will be empowered with knowledge about how technology affects the world. Through hands-on engineering projects, laboratory experiences, faculty presentations, and tours, students will work on real projects in project groups using systems approach solutions.

http://www.uvm.edu/~cems/giv/   **Cost: $1,708 (some financial assistance available)**

B

ENVIRONMENT
Think green.

Student Conservation Association Internships

United States   Varies   15-19 years

Each year, the Student Conservation Association helps thousands of people 18 and over find a way to make a difference. SCA offers 3-to-12 month, expense-paid internship opportunities in all 50 states and in more than 50 professional fields with the National Park Service, the U.S. Forest Service, the Bureau of Indian Affairs, the U.S. Fish and Wildlife Service, the U.S. Geological Survey, and state and local agencies.

http://www.thesca.org/serve/youth-programs   **Cost: $0 (Paid internship)**

SeaWorld Resident Camps

Tampa Bay, Orlando, San Antonio, and San Diego   1 week in June-August   Grades 7-9, 10-12

Each SeaWorld/Busch Gardens resident camp session provides up-close, behind-the-scenes, hands-on experiences with amazing animals, including many threatened or endangered species. Alongside veterinarians, trainers, and other animal care experts, you'll have the opportunity to feed and care for animals ranging from belugas and manatees to giraffes and great apes. Swim with dolphins, snorkel, kayak, or surf and more.

http://seaworldparks.com/en/seaworld-orlando/Educational-Programs/Resident-Camps
Cost: $1,200

IMPORTANT INSIDER INFO

- For those looking for an adventure between high school and college, consider WWOOFing for a couple of months out of the summer. World Wide opportunities on Organic Farms connects organic farmers from across the globe with volunteers over the age of 18. This is a great chance to learn more about organic farms, food production, and to see different parts of the country/world. For more information, go to wwoof.org.

JOURNALISM
Get the scoop.

 Nebraska High School Press Association Journalism Camp, UNL

Lincoln, Nebraska | late July | Rising 9-12

Choose from workshops on editorial leadership, yearbook, journalistic writing, video production, newspaper productions, and digital photography.

http://nhspaonline.org/wordpress/?page_id=51 **Cost: $300**

 High School Journalism Institute, Indiana University

Bloomington, Indiana | All sessions in July | Rising 9-12

While learning about the proper role of media, students improve their journalism and publication skills both through skill-building and through comparative criticism of a variety of high school publications. Similar programs (on different dates) are available for yearbook, television news, business and advertising, and photojournalism.

http://journalism.indiana.edu/programs/hsji/ **Cost: $399**

 Summer Journalism Workshops, University of Iowa

Iowa City, Iowa | late July | 14-18 years old

Students and instructors have access to the latest in computer technology and software in workshops for advanced news writers, editors-in-chief, social media domination, adventure journalism, yearbook, photojournalism, broadcast, and advanced graphic design.

http://www.iowajournalism.com/ **Cost: $450**

B

IMPORTANT INSIDER INFO

- Journalism workshops abound, so look for options at your in-state colleges. Some camps, such as the one offered by Indiana University, offer different tracks, so investigate the details before applying.

- Take the initiative! Contact your local newspaper and find out if it offers any internship opportunities for high school students. Often, newspapers are looking for a "young voice."

- If you are seriously interested in a future career in journalism, involve yourself in related activities at your school—sign up for Yearbook Staff and contribute to the school newspaper!

LEADERSHIP
Stand up. Stand out.

Leadership Studies Program at The Frances A. Karnes Center for Gifted Studies, University of Southern Mississippi

Hattiesburg, Mississippi   mid June   Grades 6-11

Training will include fundamentals of leadership, written and oral communication, group dynamics, problem solving, planning, personal skills, and decision-making. Avenues for becoming leaders in school, community, and religious affiliation will heighten leadership potential. Two advanced programs with a psychological focus are offered for returning students. Need-based aid is available.

http://www.usm.edu/karnes-gifted/leadership-studies-program   **Cost: $600**

General Shelton Challenge—Leadership Initiative

various locations in North Carolina   Sessions in June/July   Rising 9-12

The Shelton Challenge is a six-day residential experience to help students expand their knowledge of what it takes to be a leader. Students will participate in activities leading to greater understanding for personal leadership assessment and interpersonal dynamics, role of values and ethics in leadership, leadership traits and approaches, teambuilding and empowering others, civic and social responsibility, and goal setting.

https://sheltonleadership.ncsu.edu/shelton-challenge-applications-open/   **Cost: $700**

National Teen Leadership Program

various locations in California   July and August   Grades 8-12

Three days and two nights, the National Teen Leadership Program encourages students to understand that it is within their power to help those in need and to show peers how they can contribute. Our mission is to empower, motivate, and inspire teens to creatively and positively influence their community.

http://www.ntlp.org   **Cost: $449**

YMCA Leadership Training Programs

Estes Park, Colorado   June-Aug   15-18 years old

Over two weeks in beautiful Estes Park, grow in confidence and communication skills by participating in adventurous activities like hiking, rafting, backpacking, horseback riding, and mountain biking.

http://campchiefouray.org/camps/leadership-training-program/   **Cost: $785-1,040**

IMPORTANT INSIDER INFO

- Many leadership camps are known more for their flashy, gold-embossed invitations than for their academic rigor. When googling for good leadership camps, find out exactly what activities will be conducted. Make sure your student will be more than just a consumer of a politician's canned lectures.

- You don't have to go to leadership camp to learn how to be a leader. Start by volunteering! Lead tours at an art gallery; help lead a 4H or scout club; volunteer as an assistant coach to Little Leaguers…

LIBERAL ARTS
It's classic.

Great Books Summer Program, Sir Thomas More College

Merrimack, New Hampshire   Sessions in June/July   Rising 11-12

During this two-week program, you will surround yourself with a community of learners all dedicated to renewing that spirit of learning and living developed in the schools of Greece and Rome, and in the universities of the Middle Ages. Here you will build friendship meant to last as you study, play sports, hike, and pray together.

http://www.thomasmorecollege.edu/summerprogram/collegiate   **Cost: $975**

Summer Great Books Program, Thomas Aquinas College

Santa Paula, California   July-August   Rising 12

Students of exceptional ability from around the country gather on the campus of Thomas Aquinas College with members of the faculty as a community of teachers and learners for two weeks to read and discuss works selected from Plato, Euclid, Sophocles, Pascal, Boethius, St. Thomas Aquinas, and others. These two weeks are an opportunity for forging new friendships, for enjoying the give and take of rational argument, and for engaging first-hand in the ideas that civilize, ennoble, and liberate.

http://www.thomasaquinas.edu/admission/high-school-summer-program   **Cost: $975**

Liberal Arts Experience, Carleton College

Northfield, Minnesota   early July   Rising 11

The Carleton Liberal Arts Experience (CLAE) will select 50 high school students who are current sophomores and bring them to Carleton, all expenses paid, for a one-week summer program that introduces the strengths of a liberal arts education through an array of courses in science, art, social sciences, and technology.

http://apps.carleton.edu/summer/clae/   **Cost: $0**

MATHEMATICS
Calling all mathletes.

Mathematics Summer Camp for High School Girls (All Girls, All Math) at UNL

Lincoln, Nebraska   2 Sessions in July   Rising 10-12

Students take week-long courses on encryption, bioinformatics, aerodynamics, and number theory, while working with women professors and graduate students.

http://www.math.unl.edu/programs/agam/

$175 for Nebraska residents. Financial aid is available.

Program in Mathematics for Young Scientists, Boston University

Boston, Massachusetts   late June-early August   Rising 10-12

PROMYS is a six-week summer program at Boston University designed to encourage motivated high school students to explore the creative world of mathematics in a supportive community of peers, counselors, research mathematicians, and visiting scientists.

www.promys.org   Cost: $3,800 Financial aid is available.

The Ross Program, Ohio State University

Columbus, Ohio   mid June 18-late July   Ages 14-18

The central goal of the six-week Ross Program has always been to instruct bright young students in the art of mathematical thinking and to inspire them to discover for themselves that abstract ideas are valuable and important. First year participants take the basic course in number theory. For most students, this is the first time they are asked to consider entirely new questions, to develop methods that they have not seen before, and to justify every answer.

https://people.math.osu.edu/ross/   Cost: $4,000. Some financial aid available.

Girls Adventures in Mathematics, Engineering, and Science

Urbana-Champaign, Illinois   mid July   Rising 9-12

G.A.M.E.S. is an annual week-long camp designed to give talented middle school aged girls an opportunity to explore exciting engineering and scientific fields through demonstrations, classroom presentations, hands-on activities, and contacts with women in these fields.

http://publish.illinois.edu/womeninengineering/camps/g-a-m-e-s- camp/

Cost: $1,000 (financial aid available)

Michigan Math and Science Scholars Program—University of Michigan

Ann Arbor, Michigan   two-week sessions in June & July   Rising 10-12

Michigan Math and Science Scholars (MMSS) is a program designed to expose high school students to developments and research in the sciences and to encourage the next generation to develop and retain a love of mathematics and science. Students are given the opportunity to participate in the exciting research that is ongoing at the University of Michigan, attending courses with titles such as Fibonacci Numbers, Roller Coaster Physics, Human Anatomy, and Physiology.

http://www.math.lsa.umich.edu/mmss/   **Cost: $2,000**

B

IMPORTANT INSIDER INFO

- While math camps are not quite as common as science camps, many options exist for the math student who wants to hang with his and her intellectual peers. Check out this list compiled by the American Mathematical Society: http://www.ams.org/employment/mathcamps.html.

- Keep your math skills sharp over the summer. Hire a reasonably-priced math tutor and meet weekly or bi-weekly. Or offer your tutoring services to friends, neighbors, and family. You might get paid, and you will certainly learn a lot!

- GIRLS: go to a science or math camp each summer and watch colleges recruit you!

MEDICAL
Try it out before you declare that pre-med major.

Milwaukee School of Engineering—Focus on Nursing

Milwaukee, Wisconsin　　　　Two sessions in July　　　　Rising 10-12

Teens interested in the medical field can spend a week at the Milwaukee School of Engineering learning about medical computer systems, the history of nursing, and the assessment of patients and working in MSOE's state-of-the-art critical care laboratory.

http://www.msoe.edu/admissions/undergraduate/summer-programs-for-nursing/　　　Cost: $750

National Institutes of Health—Summer Internship Program (SIP)

Many laboratory locations, including: Baltimore, MD; Park, NC; Phoenix, AZ; Detroit, MI; Hamilton, MT.

Eight weeks minimum   16 years+

If you land a spot in this highly competitive program, you'll get the chance to work alongside pioneering scientists in various fields of biomedical research—this experience will be priceless for any pre-med student and extremely impressive on college applications.

http://www.training.nih.gov/programs/sip   Cost: $0 (monthly stipend awarded)

Summer at Georgetown Medical Institute

Washington D.C.   8 days—June-August   Rising 10-12

You will be introduced to the traditional disciplines that medical students encounter through a hands-on laboratory setting in the Georgetown Medical Center. During your eight-day institute, you will get a snapshot of the Georgetown medical school curriculum and address such topics as human anatomy and physiology, microbiology and infectious disease, surgery, cancer, and biomedical ethics. Students will have the opportunity to work with a patient simulator and focus on some of today's basic medical issues, such as preventive medicine, heart disease, and HIV. The Georgetown Medical Center includes the School of Medicine and School of Nursing & Health Studies, in addition to the renowned Lombardi Cancer Center.

http://scs.georgetown.edu/courses/1252/medical-institute   Cost: $2,795

B

MUSIC
Be a REAL guitar hero.

Omaha Jazz Workshop, University of Nebraska—Omaha

Omaha, Nebraska   mid June   Grades 7-12

Budding musicians can enhance their skills through instrument and voice master classes, improvisation, and the performance of combo big band, and/or vocal jazz music. This week-long camp concludes with students performing as the opening act for an internationally renowned jazz artist. This workshop runs daily from 9 a.m. to 3 p.m.

http://unojazzcamp.com/   Cost: $330

Senior High Band and Orchestra Institute at the University of Kansas

Lawrence, Kansas   Sessions in June & July   Rising 9-12

A schedule geared to the musical needs of high school players features full orchestras and bands, jazz ensembles, chamber ensembles, private lessons, and electives in each session. Fees include supervision, recreation, social activities, and recitals. Costs for private lessons, audio and video recordings, pictures, camp shirts, snacks, and souvenirs are in addition to the camp fee.

http://www.musiccamp.ku.edu/   Cost: $625 (talent-based scholarships available)

Iowa Summer Music Camps at the University of Iowa

Iowa City, Iowa   sessions in June   Rising 8-12, Adults

The Iowa Summer Music Camps offer students musical training and experience, including group instruction, master classes, and classroom instruction in most phases of instrumental music. The entire program is an invaluable experience for young people, not only in music but also in human relations.

http://www.uiowa.edu/ismc/   Cost: $820 (Scholarships available.)

Solo Singer High School Workshop, Nebraska Wesleyan University

Lincoln, Nebraska   June   15+ years

Nebraska Wesleyan University presents this three-day intensive Workshop for the High School Solo Singer that allows high school students to explore aspects involved in the healthy development of the voice. Technical work will include the development of posture, breathing, resonance, and articulation. Daily master classes in performance will deal with performance practices, style, phrasing, how to practice, and textural communication. College credit available.

https://www.nebrwesleyan.edu/academics/academic-departments-and-programs/music-department/
high-school-singers-workshop   **Cost: $310**

Marching Band Camp, University of Nebraska—Lincoln

Lincoln, Nebraska   July   Grades 9-12

The University of Nebraska-Lincoln (UNL) Cornhusker Summer Marching Band Camp fosters leadership, fundamental marching, and performance skills in all areas of the high school marching band. Participants receive intensive instruction from clinicians on an individual and group basis. The camp finale is an exhibition performance in Memorial Stadium on the final day of the camp. All camp participants perform at this exhibition. Cost: [typically paid by student's school]

http://www.unl.edu/band/hsbandcamp.shtml   **Cost: $285-345**

Ithaca College Summer Piano Institute

Ithaca, New York   10 days in June-July   12-18 years old

The Summer Piano Institute at Ithaca College is a comprehensive program of varied musical experiences held on the beautiful Ithaca College campus. Participants use the superb facilities of the James J. Whalen Center for Music, where a nationally- and internationally-known piano faculty provides a lively array of daily lessons, workshops, classes, and supervised practice.

http://www.ithaca.edu/gps/piano/   **Cost: $1,880 (Scholarships available.)**

Summer Music Camps—Florida State University

| Tallahassee, Florida | Sessions in June & July | Grades 7-8, 9-12 |

Florida State University offers one- to two-week camps in 14 areas of musical interest from Honors Piano to Choral ensemble under the direction of FSU faculty members.

http://music.fsu.edu/Quicklinks/Summer-Music-Camps   **Cost: $462-870**

IMPORTANT INSIDER INFO

- Get great at music over the summer—for college admissions, for college, and for life.

POLITICAL SCIENCE / ECONOMICS
Run for office!

Discover Unicameral Youth Conference, University of Nebraska—Lincoln

| Lincoln, Nebraska | Approx. June 10-15 | Rising 9-12 |

The Unicameral Youth Conference is a four-day legislative simulation for current high school students who take on the role of a lawmaker. Student senators sponsor bills, conduct committee hearings, debate legislation, and discover the unique process of the nation's only unicameral.

http://4h.unl.edu/4hcamps/bigredcamps/campofferings   **Cost $350-450**

World Affairs Seminar

| Waukesha, Wisconsin | late June | 15-18 years |

Hundreds of students from around the world meet at the World Affairs Seminar to discuss the pressing global issues while learning about each other's culture. Students spend their days listening to experts speak on a wide variety of topics related to globalization, international relations, human rights, arms control, and the environment. Local service organizations (Rotary Club, Lions, Kiwanis, Optimists, Key Club) often provide scholarships.

http://www.worldaffairsseminar.org/   **Cost: $680 (scholarships available)**

Economics for Leaders

| Various Locations | Sessions June-August | Rising 12 |

Through interactive and engaging lesson plans, participants attain an understanding of economic reasoning principles and how to employ these concepts for successful and effective leadership. Participants achieve a heightened awareness of the impact their decisions have on others and the responsibility that awareness imposes.

http://www.fte.org/student-programs/economics-for-leaders-program/   Cost: $850-1,200

JSA Institute

| Various Locations | Early August | 14-18 years old |

The problems and opportunities facing greater Los Angeles are the focus of this five-day exploration of Southern California politics. From analyzing questions of law and justice with the Chief of Police and District Attorney to interacting with the award-winning staff of the *Los Angeles Times*, the Symposium is a chance to debate and discuss politics with leaders and students from across the region. Look for JSA camps in your region.

http://www.jsa.org/summer-programs/jsa-institutes-2   Cost: $2,750-5,750

American Legion Boys State

Various locations   Various dates   Rising 12

American Legion Boys State is among the most respected and selective educational programs of government instruction for high school students. It is a participatory program where each participant becomes a part of the operation of his local, county, and state government. At American Legion Boys State, participants are exposed to the rights, privileges, duties, and responsibilities of a franchised citizen. The training is objective and practical with city, county, and state governments operated by the students elected to the various offices.

http://www.boysandgirlsstate.org/boys.html   **Cost: Varies**

American Legion Auxiliary Girls State

Various locations   Various dates   Rising 12

The American Legion Auxiliary Girls State Program has provided high school Juniors all across the country the opportunity to participate in a hands-on citizenship training program for over 60 years. These young ladies learn government by actually creating a mythical state through the election of public officials on local, county, and state levels and then by carrying out the duties of these respective offices.

www.boysandgirlsstate.org/girls.html   **Cost: Varies**

SCIENCE
Put on those safety goggles—this is no home-made volcano.

 Chincoteague Bay Marine Science Pre-College Summer Camp

Wallops Island, Virginia · Weeklong sessions June-July · Ages 8-18

Students benefit from experienced instructors and the geography and biology of Virginia's barrier islands. Classes offered include CSI (Costal Sea Investigation), Aquaculture, Dolphin and Marine Mammal Behavior, Shark Biology, Advanced Marine Science, Dangerous Creatures, Life Along the Atlantic Coast, and Introduction to Sea Kayaking.

http://www.cbfieldstation.org/#/youth-camps/4579051262 · **Cost: $850**

 Research Science Institute at the Center for Excellence in Education at MIT

Cambridge, Massachusetts · late June 24-early August · Rising 12, PG

RSI scholars first participate in a week of intensive STEM classes with accomplished professors. The heart of RSI is the five-week research internship where students conduct individual projects under the tutelage of mentors who are experienced scientists and researchers. During the final week of RSI, students prepare written and oral presentations on their research projects.

http://www.cee.org/research-science-institute

Cost: $25 application fee. January application deadline.

 Minority Introduction to Engineering and Science (MITES) Program at MIT

Cambridge, Massachusetts · June-August · Rising 12

MITES is an intense six-week program meant to introduce rising seniors to careers in science, engineering, and entrepreneurship. Students study mathematics, physics, chemistry and biochemistry, engineering design, writing, and high technology. MIT's engineering and science faculty members are highly involved. Underrepresented minorities are encouraged to apply, although all applications are accepted.

http://web.mit.edu/mites/www · **Cost: $0. February 1 application deadline.**

Summer Science Camps, Hillsdale College

Hillsdale, Michigan   Approx. June 24-29   Rising 10-12

The science camps seek to promote scientific literacy among high school students. These camps are designed to instill a deeper appreciation of what science is about and the idea that science is both exciting and practical.

http://www.hillsdale.edu/outreach/camps   Cost: $75 deposit

Operation Catapult at Rose-Hulman Institute of Technology

Terre Haute, Indiana   two-week sessions in June and July   Rising 12

One of the important features of Operation Catapult is the exposure to engineering and applied science through project work. Each Catapulter will work on a project, to be selected either from a list of suggestions or self-initiated because it presents a challenge to tackle.

http://www.rose-hulman.edu/admissions-financial-aid/early-planning/operation-catapult.aspx
                    Cost: $2,500

Young Nebraska Science Camp

various locations in Nebraska   Sessions in June and July   Rising 10-11

You will be a part of creating a new community of students of science, learn what science is about, and see what exciting career options are available in the sciences. Your three-day or week-long experience culminates in a team-oriented poster presentation allowing you to demonstrate what you have accomplished to your peers, parents, and university faculty, staff, and students.

http://yns.nebraska.edu/Research.aspx   Cost: $100-250

Big Red Summer Academic Camps—Discover Weather & Climate Science

Lincoln, Nebraska   June   Grades 10-12

Find out how scientists observe and forecast the weather as well as monitor the changing climate. During the week, participants will use instruments to make their own weather observations: learn how to forecast the weather, visit with National Weather Services forecasters, and learn about the local weather and climate of Nebrask—from tornadoes to blizzards.

http://4h.unl.edu/4hcamps/bigredcamps/campofferings   Cost: $500-600

Big Red Summer Academic Camps—Culinary Arts & Food Science

Lincoln, Nebraska   June   Grades 10-12

Learn new culinary arts skills and understand the science of food. Impress friends and family with your new culinary skills and knowledge. Explore local foods, food product development, and learn food preparation skills.

http://4h.unl.edu/4hcamps/bigredcamps/campofferings   Cost: $600-700

Big Red Summer Academic Camps—Veterinary Science

Lincoln, Nebraska   June   Grades 10-12

Explore various aspects of veterinary medicine and discover what veterinarians need to know to help sick animals. Learn about anatomy, bacteriology, parasitology, surgery, and toxicology. Learn how to give an animal a physical examination. Learn from scientists and veterinarians studying how animal diseases progress and are diagnosed, treated and prevented. Learn about an exciting career as a veterinarian.

http://4h.unl.edu/4hcamps/bigredcamps/campofferings   Cost: $600-700

IMPORTANT INSIDER INFO

- Science camps are in abundant supply, everywhere from Hawaii to Virginia. The trick is finding low-cost alternatives to the larger, pricey camps. Most big research universities offer something in the sciences for teens, especially girls. Some camps for minority students offer free tuition or large discounts.

- If you have a love for zoology or botany, consider volunteering at your local zoo or arboretum. Many wildlife sanctuaries and public gardens hire scientifically-minded high school students for all kinds of positions.

B

Cosmosphere Camps

Hutchinson, Kansas   June/July, weeklong sessions   Rising 9-12

Six-day overnight camps for students. Several different camps available.

http://cosmo.org/explore/camps   **Cost: varies**

Astronaut Academy at the Strategic Air and Space Museum

Ashland, Nebraska   June and July   Ages 13-16

Let this amazing camp launch your dreams into orbit as you begin to train like the best at NASA. Campers fulfill their dreams of space exploration, aviation, and engineering. Campers sharpen analytical skills and problem solving techniques in an entertaining, hands-on environment. Five days and four nights.

http://www.sasmuseum.com/education/summer-camps/   **Cost: $500**

Illinois Aerospace Institute Summer Camp, University of Illinois at Urbana-Champaign

Urbana-Champaign, Illinois   July   Rising 9-12

Many students have some experience with aerospace, through model rockets, remote control airplanes, or a family member who is a pilot. But no experience is necessary—just an interest in learning about aerospace engineering. Students will learn about a topics regarding aerospace engineering through classroom sessions, laboratories, demonstrations, and hands-on activities.

http://iai.aerospace.illinois.edu/   **Cost: $650 plus $100 deposit**

John D. Odegard School of Aerospace Sciences Summer Camp, University of North Dakota

| Grand Forks, North Dakota | week-long sessions in June and July | Rising 11-12 |

What makes this seminar unique is the amount of flight training each student receives. We are very interested in students who truly want to experience collegiate aviation. Your counselors, flight instructors, and professors are leaders in aerospace education. You'll start with the basics of flying, experience new and exciting technology, and explore career opportunities in aerospace.

http://www.aviation.und.edu/currentStudents/AEROCAMP/Default.aspx   **Cost: $1,375**

SPORTS / OUTDOORS
Because who wants to spend summer inside?

Nike Advanced Soccer Camps

| Varies | Sessions June, July, August | HS Students |

Nike Advanced Soccer Camps have attracted some of the most respected and accomplished soccer instructors and coaches in the country. They stress what is needed of a camper to play at the next level in college!

http://www.ussportscamps.com/soccer/nike/advanced/#camp-locations   **Cost: varies by activity**

Darlington Summer Programs

| Rome, Georgia | Sessions June-August | 8-18 years old |

For over 100 years, Darlington has been preparing young men and women for college and life according to the motto, "Wisdom more than Knowledge, Service beyond Self, Honor above Everything." Their overnight camps include lacrosse, tennis, wrestling, and soccer, as well as several other options.

http://www.darlingtonschool.org/summer/overview-schedule.aspx

Cost: $475-2,600 (varies by activity)

B

Camp Berachah Ministries

Auburn, Washington   Sessions June, July, August   5-17 years old

For over 35 years, they have been providing events and camps for thousands of youth, adults, families, and churches throughout the Pacific Northwest. Aside from their popular summer camps, their wide variety of programs and facilities are available for Christian churches, non-profit organizations, and families.

http://blackdiamond.org/summer/sports-camp.php   **Cost: $126-345 (varies by activity)**

IMPORTANT INSIDER INFO

- Sports camps are everywhere. They can be a cost-effective way to gain visibility and a college scholarship, and/or they can be overcrowded and short on personal instruction. Be strategic: seek visibility in front of college coaches as well as opportunities to truly improve, thanks to personal attention. When researching a sports camp, read through its schedule closely and ask the directors/coaches lots of questions about their philosophy.

- If you're just looking for some exercise and time outside, explore low cost options in your area, perhaps at a YMCA or local high schools.

SPY/LAW ENFORCEMENT
Mission: Impossible.

"Days of Intrigue" Summer Program—University of Mississippi

Oxford, Mississippi   June   Rising 11-12

For rising juniors and seniors interested in pursuing careers in the intelligence community. The Days of Intrigue is an Intelligence Case Study program that offers an opportunity to learn about the intelligence community and to work on an intelligence case, not unlike something the Intelligence Community would face.

http://ciss.olemiss.edu/summer-program/   **Cost: $425**

American Legion Junior Law Cadet

Grand Island, Nebraska   June   Rising 12th

Each year, high school juniors from each of the American Legion's 15 Districts are chosen to participate in the Junior Law Cadet Program. Participants will stay at the Nebraska Law Enforcement Training Center in Grand Island, where they will experience aspects of law enforcement and receive training from representatives of city, county, state and federal law enforcement officers. Cadets participate in daily calisthenics, firearms training, and self-defense tactics, as well as learn the latest in law enforcement technology, including fingerprinting, K-9 handling, and accident and criminal investigation.

http://www.nebraskalegion.net/Programs/JRLaw.html   **Cost: $0**

B

WEB DESIGN
Do more than surf.

Camps that educate students in the graphic arts can run the gamut: elite, pricey camps to lower-cost day workshops. To find similar camps, look up key terms like "graphic design," "animation," or "industrial design."

Web Design, Information Science and Technology Summer Workshops

Omaha, Nebraska   June 4-8   Ages 14-17

Students will develop their very own internet websites. They will start by learning how websites work and the basics of HTML and PHP programming language. Students will learn about databases and how to use database-driven content on their website as well as how to plan a website, what makes for good navigation, how to make design decisions, and how to use cross browser or special considerations for making web pages. By the end of the week, the students will have enough knowledge to make a website. Previous HTML experience is a plus.

https://techademy.unomaha.edu/index.php?p=index   **Cost: $150**

NOTES

NOTES

THE MORE THAN 500 COLLEGES THAT ACCEPT THE COMMON APPLICATION

C

Alabama

Birmingham-Southern College
Samford University
Spring Hill College
University of Alabama at Birmingham
University of Alabama at Birmingham

Alaska

Alaska Pacific University

Arizona

Benedictine University (AZ)
Prescott College

Arkansas

Hendrix College
Lyon College

California

American Jewish University
California College of the Arts
California Institute of Technology (Caltech)
California Lutheran University
Chapman University
Charles R. Drew University of Medicine and Science
Charles R. Drew University of Medicine and Science

Claremont McKenna College
Columbia College Hollywood
Concordia University Irvine
Dominican University of California
Harvey Mudd College
Holy Names University
Hult International Business School– San Francisco
Hunt International Business School
Loyola Marymount University
Marymount California University
Menlo College
Mills College
Minerva Schools at KGI
Minerva Schools at KGI
Mount Saint Mary's University, Los Angeles
Notre Dame de Namur University
Occidental College
Pepperdine University
Pitzer College
Point Loma Nazarene University
Pomona College
Saint Mary's College of California
Santa Clara University
Scripps College
Soka University of America
Stanford University
The Culinary Institute of America
University of La Verne

C

University of Redlands
University of San Diego
University of San Francisco
University of Southern California
University of the Pacific
Westmont College
Whittier College
Woodbury University
Zaytuna College

Colorado

Colorado College
Colorado State University
Johnson & Wales University-Denver
Naropa University
Regis University
University of Colorado Boulder*
University of Denver
Western State Colorado University

Connecticut

Albertus Magnus College
Central Connecticut State University
Connecticut College
Eastern Connecticut State University
Fairfield University
Mitchell College
Quinnipiac University
Sacred Heart University
Southern Connecticut State University
Trinity College
University of Bridgeport
University of Connecticut
University of Hartford
University of New Haven
University of Saint Joseph

Wesleyan University
Western Connecticut State University
Yale University

Delaware

University of Delaware

Florida

Ave Maria University
Barry University
Eckerd College
Flagler College
Florida Institute of Technology
Florida Southern College
Jacksonville University
Johnson & Wales University-North Miami
Keiser University Flagship Campus–West Palm
    Beach Florida
Lynn University
New College of Florida
Nova Southeastern University
Ringling College of Art and Design
Rollins College
Saint Leo University
St. Thomas University
Stetson University
University of Central Florida
University of Miami
University of Tampa

Georgia

Agnes Scott College
Berry College
Brenau University
Clark Atlanta University

Emory University

Georgia College

Georgia Institute of Technology

Georgia State University

Mercer University

Morehouse College

Oglethorpe University

Piedmont College

Savannah College of Art and Design

Spelman College

Hawaii

Hawai'i Pacific University

Idaho

Northwest Nazarene University

The College of Idaho

University of Idaho

Illinois

Augustana College (Illinois)

Benedictine University

Benedictine University

Bradley University

Chicago State University

Columbia College Chicago

Concordia University Chicago

DePaul University

Illinois College

Illinois Institute of Technology

Illinois Wesleyan University

Knox College

Lake Forest College

MacMurray College

McKendree University

Millikin University

Monmouth College (IL)

North Park University

Northwestern University

Principia College

School of the Art Institute of Chicago

Trinity Christian College

University of Chicago

University of Illinois at Chicago

Western Illinois University

Western Illinois University

Indiana

Butler University

DePauw University

Earlham College

Franklin College

Goshen College

Hanover College

Indiana University–Bloomington

Indiana University–Purdue University Fort Wayne (IPFW)

Manchester University

Purdue University

Saint Joseph's College (IN)

Saint Mary-of-the-Woods College

Saint Mary's College, Notre Dame

University of Evansville

University of Indianapolis

University of Notre Dame

Valparaiso University

Wabash College

Iowa

Coe College

Cornell College

C

Drake University
Grinnell College
Luther College
Saint Ambrose University
Simpson College
St. Ambrose University
University of Dubuque
University of Northern Iowa
Upper Iowa University
Wartburg College

Kansas

Benedictine College

Kentucky

Centre College
Eastern Kentucky University
Transylvania University
University of Kentucky

Louisiana

Centenary College of Louisiana
Dillard University
Loyola University New Orleans
Tulane University
Xavier University of Louisiana

Maine

Bates College
Bowdoin College
Colby College
College of the Atlantic
Husson University
Maine Maritime Academy
Saint Joseph's College of Maine

The University of Maine
Thomas College
Unity College
University of Maine at Farmington
University of Maine at Fort Kent
University of Maine at Machias
University of Maine at Presque Isle
University of New England
University of Southern Maine

Maryland

Capitol Technology University
Coppin State University
Goucher College
Hood College
Johns Hopkins University
Loyola University Maryland
Maryland Institute College of Art
McDaniel College
Notre Dame of Maryland University
Salisbury University
St. John's College (MD)
St. Mary's College of Maryland
Stevenson University
University of Maryland, Baltimore County
Washington College

Massachusetts

Amherst College
Anna Maria College
Assumption College
Babson College
Bard College at Simon's Rock–The Early College
Bay Path University
Becker College
Bentley University

Boston College

Boston University

Brandeis University

Clark University

College of the Holy Cross

Curry College

Dean College

Elms College

Emerson College

Emmanuel College

Framingham State University

Franklin W. Olin College of Engineering

Hampshire College

Harvard University

Lasell College

Lesley University

Massachusetts College of Art and Design

Massachusetts College of Liberal Arts

Massachusetts College Of Pharmacy & Health Sciences

Merrimack College

Mount Holyoke College

Mount Ida College

Newbury College

Nichols College

Northeastern University

Pine Manor College

Regis College

Simmons College

Smith College

Springfield College

Stonehill College

Suffolk University

Tufts University

University of Massachusetts Amherst

University of Massachusetts Boston

University of Massachusetts Dartmouth

University of Massachusetts Lowell

Wellesley College

Wentworth Institute of Technology

Western New England University

Wheaton College

Wheelock College

Williams College

Worcester Polytechnic Institute

Michigan

Albion College

Alma College

Calvin College

Hillsdale College

Hope College

Kalamazoo College

Kettering University

Lawrence Technological University

Spring Arbor University

University of Detroit Mercy

University of Michigan

University of Michigan-Flint

University of Michigan–Flint

Wayne State University

Minnesota

Augsburg College

Carleton College

College of Saint Benedict

Concordia College at Moorhead

Gustavus Adolphus College

Hamline University (MN)

Macalester College

Saint John's University

Saint Mary's University of Minnesota

C

St. Catherine University
St. Olaf College
University of St. Thomas (MN)

Mississippi

Millsaps College
University of Southern Mississippi

Missouri

Columbia College
Cottey College
Drury University
Maryville University of St. Louis
Saint Louis University
St. Louis College of Pharmacy
Stephens College
Stephens College
Truman State University
Washington University in St. Louis
Webster University
Westminster College (Missouri)
William Jewell College

Montana

Carroll College (Montana)
University of Great Falls

Nebraska

Creighton University
Hastings College
Nebraska Wesleyan University

Nevada

Cottey College
Sierra Nevada College

New Hampshire

Colby-Sawyer College
Dartmouth College
Franklin Pierce University
Keene State College
New England College
Plymouth State University
Rivier University
Saint Anselm College
Southern New Hampshire University
University of New Hampshire

New Jersey

Bloomfield College
Caldwell University
Centenary College (NJ)
College of Saint Elizabeth
Drew University
Felician University
Georgian Court University
Kean University
Monmouth University
New Jersey City University
New Jersey Institute of Technology
Princeton University
Ramapo College of New Jersey
Rider University
Rowan University
Saint Peter's University
Seton Hall University
Stevens Institute of Technology
Stockton University
The College of New Jersey
William Paterson University of NJ

New Mexico

St. John's College (NM)

New York

College & University System NY New York
   University
Adelphi University
Albany College of Pharmacy and Health Sciences
Alfred University
Bard College
Barnard College
Canisius College
Cazenovia College
Clarkson University
Colgate University
College of Mount Saint Vincent
Columbia University
Concordia College
Cornell University
Daemen College
D'Youville College
Elmira College
Fordham University
Hartwick College
Hilbert College
Hobart and William Smith Colleges
Hofstra University
Houghton College
Iona College
Ithaca College
Keuka College
Le Moyne College
List College The Jewish Theological Seminary
LIU Brooklyn
LIU Post

Manhattan College
Manhattanville College
Marist College
Marymount Manhattan College
Mercy College
Molloy College
Mount Saint Mary College
Nazareth College
New York Institute of Technology (NYIT)
New York School of Career & Applied Studies of
   Touro College & University System
Niagara University
Pace University
Paul Smith's College
Rensselaer Polytechnic Institute
Roberts Wesleyan College
Rochester Institute of Technology
Russell Sage College
Sage College of Albany
Sarah Lawrence College
Siena College
Skidmore College
St. Bonaventure University
St. John Fisher College
St. John's University (NY)
St. Joseph's College – Brooklyn Campus
St. Joseph's College - Long Island Campus
St. Lawrence University
St. Thomas Aquinas College
SUNY College at Brockport
SUNY Alfred State College
SUNY Binghamton University
SUNY Buffalo State College
SUNY Cobleskill
SUNY College at Geneseo
SUNY College at Old Westbury

C

SUNY College at Oneonta
SUNY College of Environmental
    Science & Forestry
SUNY College of Technology at Canton
SUNY Cortland
SUNY Delhi
SUNY Farmingdale State College
SUNY Fredonia
SUNY Maritime College
SUNY Morrisville State College
SUNY New Paltz
SUNY Oswego
SUNY Plattsburgh
SUNY Polytechnic Institute (formerly SUNYIT)
SUNY Potsdam
SUNY Purchase College
SUNY Stony Brook University
SUNY University at Albany
SUNY University at Buffalo
Syracuse University
The College of New Rochelle
The College of Saint Rose
The Cooper Union for the Advancement of
    Science and Art
The Culinary Institute of America
The New School
Union College
University of Rochester
Utica College
Vassar College
Wagner College
Wells College

North Carolina

Brevard College
Davidson College

Duke University
Guilford College
High Point University
Johnson & Wales University-Charlotte
Meredith College
North Carolina State University
Queens University of Charlotte
Salem College
St. Andrews University
University of North Carolina Asheville
University of North Carolina at Chapel Hill
University of North Carolina Wilmington
Wake Forest University
Warren Wilson College

Ohio

Antioch College
Baldwin Wallace University
Bowling Green State University – Main Campus
Bowling Green State University-Main Campus
Capital University
Case Western Reserve University
College of Wooster
Denison University
Hiram College
John Carroll University
Kenyon College
Lake Erie College
Lourdes University
Malone University
Marietta College
Miami University (Ohio)
Oberlin College
Oberlin Conservatory of Music
Ohio Northern University
Ohio University

Ohio Wesleyan University
Otterbein University
The Ohio State University
The University of Findlay
University of Akron Main Campus
University of Cincinnati
University of Dayton
University of Toledo
Ursuline College
Wilberforce University
Wittenberg University
Xavier University

Oklahoma

Oklahoma City University
The University of Oklahoma
The University of Tulsa

Oregon

Concordia University - Portland, OR
George Fox University
Lewis & Clark College
Linfield College
Pacific University
Reed College
University of Portland
Willamette University

Pennsylvania

Albright College
Allegheny College
Alvernia University
Arcadia University
Bryn Mawr College
Bucknell University

Cabrini College
Carnegie Mellon University
Cedar Crest College
Chatham University
Delaware Valley University
DeSales University
Dickinson College
Drexel University
Elizabethtown College
Franklin & Marshall College
Gannon University
Gettysburg College
Haverford College
Immaculata University
Juniata College
Keystone College
King's College
La Roche College
La Salle University
Lafayette College
Lebanon Valley College
Lehigh University
Lycoming College
Marywood University
Mercyhurst University
Millersville University
Moravian College
Muhlenberg College
Neumann University
Pennsylvania Academy of the Fine Arts
Philadelphia University
Robert Morris University (PA)
Rosemont College
Saint Francis University
Saint Joseph's University
Saint Vincent College

C

Seton Hill University
Susquehanna University
Swarthmore College
Temple University
The University of Scranton
Thiel College
University of Pennsylvania
University of the Sciences
Ursinus College
Villanova University
Washington & Jefferson College
Westminster College (Pennsylvania)
Wilkes University
Wilson College

Rhode Island

Brown University
Bryant University
Johnson & Wales University-Providence
Providence College
Rhode Island College
Rhode Island School of Design
Roger Williams University
Salve Regina University
University of Rhode Island

South Carolina

Columbia College
Converse College
Furman University
Newberry College
Presbyterian College
Wofford College

South Dakota

Augustana University

Tennessee

Belmont University
Christian Brothers University
Fisk University
Middle Tennessee State University
Middle Tennessee State University
Rhodes College
Sewanee: The University of the South
The University of Tennessee Knoxville
Vanderbilt University
Watkins College of Art, Design & Film

Texas

Austin College
Baylor University
Rice University
Southern Methodist University
Southwestern University
St. Edward's University
Texas Christian University
The Culinary Institute of America (TX)
Trinity University
University of Dallas
University of North Texas

Utah

Westminster College

Vermont

Bennington College
Castleton University
Champlain College
College of St. Joseph
Goddard College
Green Mountain College

Johnson State College
Lyndon State College
Marlboro College
Middlebury College
Norwich University
Saint Michael's College
Sterling College
University of Vermont

Virginia

Christopher Newport University
Emory & Henry College
George Mason University
Hampden-Sydney College
Hollins University
Lynchburg College
Marymount University
Old Dominion University
Randolph College
Randolph-Macon College
Roanoke College
Sweet Briar College
The College of William & Mary
University of Mary Washington
University of Richmond
University of Virginia
Virginia Commonwealth University
Washington and Lee University

Washington

Gonzaga University
Pacific Lutheran University
Saint Martin's University
Seattle Pacific University
Seattle University
University of Puget Sound

Whitman College
Whitworth University

West Virginia

Bethany College
West Virginia University
West Virginia Wesleyan College
Wheeling Jesuit University

Wisconsin

Beloit College
Carroll University
Carthage College
Concordia University Wisconsin
Edgewood College
Lawrence University
Marquette University
Northland College
Ripon College
St. Norbert College
University of Wisconsin-Madison

Washington DC

American University
Howard University
The Catholic University of America
The George Washington University

NOTES

Don't forget to subtract the student's annual contribution of $11K (or at least $8,500) from your family's Net Cost. See pages 3 and 4.

Yes, college can be affordable. **$11K Paves The Way.** Your eventual annual Net Cost equals the college's Retail Sticker Price minus your student's Scholarships. But the family's actual annual cost is Net Cost minus $11,000—the student's yearly contribution. **$11K Paves The Way!**

So, subtract $11,000 from your expected annual Net Cost—the student can borrow up to $5,000 a year, earn at least $3,500 during breaks each year, and possibly qualify for $2,500 each year thanks to the American Opportunity Tax Credit. **$11K Paves The Way!** As for the student's pizza and laundry costs, they can earn that working at most ten hours per week on campus while at school.

THE *OTC* SCHOOL-PROVIDED SCHOLARSHIP DATABASE

Appendix D contains the most current information available at the time of printing. Items are subject to change.

The following pages provide a listing of the various merit-based scholarships offered by out-of-state colleges and universities all across the country, from liberal arts colleges and private schools to large public universities and schools of regional interest.

1. Each scholarship should bring the Net cost of attending each school to less than $30,000 per year.

2. The list includes scholarships offered mainly by universities and liberal arts colleges ranked by *U.S. News and World Report.**

   **U.S. News and World Report* rankings are based on a range of factors including admissions criteria and selectivity, retention, faculty/financial resources, graduation rate, and peer assessment.

   http://colleges.usnews.rankingsandreviews.com/usnews/edu/college/rankings/rankindex_brief.php

OTC does not encourage students to use any ranking system.

Thoughts:

- Scholarships that require an extra application will require more work but consequently have less competition. Your chances improve if there is a separate application.

- Be realistic. Duke offers a full-ride scholarship, but only about 30 of them (with no separate application). You'll need to be one of a few chosen from the entire applicant pool. It's tough enough just getting admitted to Duke. Meanwhile, Emory, also a highly selective school, offers about 150 two-thirds tuition scholarships with a separate application.

Use Appendix D in conjunction with OTC's America's Most Affordable Colleges, our book filled with dozens of colleges that each cost less than $24,000 a year.

D

Agnes Scott College

Decatur, Georgia   800-868-8602   www.agnesscott.edu

Basic Profile:
enrollment: 927 (women only)
average ACT: 23-27
average SAT: 1048-1270
U.S. News ranking: 61 (liberal arts)
Student/Faculty Ratio: 10/1

Financial Information:
$40,920 = tuition
$12,330 = room/board
$240 = fees
$53,490 = total billed cost per year
Students Receiving Aid: 64%

Application:
early decision: 11/15 binding
scholarship: 1/15 non-binding
regular decision: 3/15
common app: yes (supplement)

Presidential Scholarships
award   full tuition, room & board; renewable for 4 years; awarded to fewer than 10 freshmen.
eligibility   outstanding academic merit, service, etc.
application   all applicants who apply by early decision or scholarship decision are considered; no separate application.
deadline   1/15 (scholarship decision); interviews with Scholarship Committee in March.

Goizueta Foundation Scholarhsips
award   full tuition, room & board; renewable for 4 years
eligibility   in recognition of an excellent overall record.
application   all applicants who apply by early decision or scholarship decision are considered; no separate application.
deadline   1/15 (scholarship decision); committee interviews with finalists in March.

Elizabeth Kiss Trailblazer Scholarship
award $25,000 renewable for four years
eligibility   3.75 GPA and 26 ACT or 1250 SAT
application   all applicants who apply by early decision or scholarship decision are considered; no separate application.
deadline   1/15 (scholarship decision); committee interviews with finalists in March.

Total billed cost per year does NOT include travel, books, or pizza money.

D

Baker University

Baldwin City, Kansas   785-594-6451   www.bakerU.edu

Basic Profile:

enrollment: 2,689 (private)
average ACT: 20—25
average SAT: 885—1110
U.S. News ranking: 46 (regional midwest)
Student/Faculty Ratio: 13/1

Financial Information:

$29,300 = tuition
$8,310 = room/board
$630 = fees
$38,240 = total billed cost per year
Students Receiving Aid: 79%

Application:

early decision: n/a
regular decision: 3/15

common app: no

Harter Scholarship

award	full tuition; renewable for 4 years; one semester at Haraxton College in England, 2-5 freshmen.
eligibility	combination of GPA and ACT or SAT score
application	all applicants accepted are considered; no separate application.
deadline	admitted by January 15.

Calculated Awards

Scholarship/Award	Institutional Rating*	Amount
Honors Scholarship	combination of GPA and ACT or SAT score	$13,000
Academic Merit Scholarship	combination of GPA and ACT or SAT score	$10,000
Wildcat Scholarship	combination of GPA and ACT or SAT score	$8,000
University Award	combination of GPA and ACT or SAT score	$6,000

Presidential Scholarship

award	$1,000 to $6,000
eligibility	Honors and Academic Merit Scholarship recipients.
application	Competition for this award will be during Scholarship Recognition Day.

STEM

award	$1,000-$4,000
eligibility	students interested in science, technology, engineering, or mathematics and academic merit
application	Competition for this award will be during Scholarship Recognition Day.

Ball State University

Muncie, Indiana   765-289-1241   www.bsu.edu

Basic Profile:

enrollment: 21,196 (public)
average ACT: 20—24
average SAT: 1010—1190
U.S. News ranking: 187

Financial Information:

$24,462 = tuition (non-resident)
$10,112 = room/board
$2,126 = fees
$35,976 = total billed cost per year

Application:

early decision: none
priority decision: 3/1
* rolling admission
common app: no

Whitinger Scholars

award	full tuition, room & board; renewable for 4 years; awarded to 10 freshmen.
eligibility	academic superiority, character, creativity, leadership, etc.; 3.7+ GPA, 29+ ACT (26+ on Math and English subscores)/1950+ SAT (600+ on Critical Reading, Math, and Writing subscores).
application	upon acceptance to Honors College, qualifying students will receive Whitinger application; interview; essay.
deadline	1/18 (Honors College), 3/1 (complete interview), all materials must be received 5 days before interview.

Presidential Scholars Program

award	out-of-state: $12,000/year; in-state: $4,500/year; renewable for four years.
eligibility	academic excellence, leadership, test scores, activities.

Total billed cost per year does NOT include travel, books, or pizza money.

Baylor University

Waco, Texas   800-229-5678   www.baylor.edu

Basic Profile:
enrollment: 16,263 (private)
average ACT: 23-29
average SAT: 1234
U.S. News ranking: 75
Student/Faculty Ratio: 15/1

Financial Information:
$41,194 = tuition
$13,038 = room/board
$4,598 = fees
$58,830 = total billed cost per year
Students Receiving Aid: 90%

Application: 6/15

common app: no

Regents' Gold Scholarship

award	SAT score (Reading + Math)	ACT score	Award/year
	1520-1600	36	$45,360
	1450-1510	34-36	$44,194
	1390-1440	32-33	$43,194
eligibility	limited number available, first come first serve basis; class rank also considered, renewable up to 4 years.		
application	considered upon acceptance, must maintain a 3.5 college GPA.		

Other Scholarships—Scholarship Estimator available at www.baylor.edu/estimator/
President's Gold Scholarship $19,000-$22,000/year
Provost's Gold Scholarship $16,000-$18,000/year
Deans' Gold Scholarship $7,000-$12,000/year

eligibility	based on a combination of a student's rank in class and SAT (Critical Reading and Math) or ACT score.
application	considered upon acceptance.

Berea College

Berea, Kentucky   859-985-3500   www.berea.edu

Basic Profile:
enrollment: 1,643
average ACT: 24-25
average SAT: 1160
U.S. News ranking: 68 (liberal arts)
Student/Faculty Ratio: 11/1

Financial Information:
Free = tuition
$6,534 = room/board
$570 = fees
$7,104 = total billed cost per year
To be eligible to attend, students must come from low income families.
See Berea's web site for income eligibility information.

Application:
priority: 10/31
final deadline: 3/31

Berea is a highly competitive college committed to offering students a quality education at a fraction of the cost. Four years of tuition is covered when a student is admitted to Berea. For a small school, Berea offers several outstanding majors: Engineering and Environmental Design, Computer and Physical Science, Biological Sciences, Communications and the Arts, Agriculture, Health Professions (nursing), and Social Sciences.

Total billed cost per year does NOT include travel, books, or pizza money.

D

Boston College

Chestnut Hill, Mass.   617-552-8000   www.bc.edu

Basic Profile:

enrollment: 13,851 (private)
average ACT: 29-32
average SAT: 2032-2400
U.S. News ranking: 32
Student/Faculty Ratio: 12/1
One time Freshman Fee: $474

Financial Information:

$54,600 = tuition
$14,142 = room/board
$1,401 = fees
$70,143 = total billed cost per year
Students Receiving Aid: 55%

Application:

early action: 11/1 binding
regular decision: 1/1
common app: yes (supplement)

Presidential Scholars

award	full tuition for 4 years; awarded to 20 freshmen; enter Honors Program; 3 summer programs.
eligibility	academic excellence, leadership, community service, potential.
application	no separate application is required, but must apply for admission through the early action program.
deadline	application for admission must be submitted by 11/1.

Boston University

Boston, Mass.   617-353-2000   www.bu.edu

Basic Profile:

enrollment: 32,694 (private)
average ACT: 27-31
average SAT: 1200-1410
U.S. News ranking: 37
Student/Faculty Ratio: 10/1

Financial Information:

$52,816 = tuition
$15,720 = room/board
$1,132 = fees
$69,668 = total billed cost per year
Students Receiving Aid: 57%

Application:

early decision: 11/1 binding
regular decision: 1/2
common app: yes (supplement)

Trustee Scholarship

award	full tuition and fees; renewable for 4 years; awarded to about 20 freshmen.
eligibility	academic merit, leadership, etc.; GPA: 4.0, rank: top 5-10%.
application	must receive nomination from principal and complete separate application/essays (available online).
deadline	all materials must be received no later than 12/1.

Presidential Scholarship

award	$20,000; renewable for 4 years; 5% of incoming freshman class.
eligibility	academic merit; involvement beyond classroom.
application	no separate application; all applicants are considered via their admission application.
deadline	11/1 (early decision), 12/1 (regular decision).

Brandeis University

Waltham, MA   781-736-3500   www.brandeis.edu

Basic Profile:

enrollment: 5,729
average ACT: 29-32
average SAT: 1250-1470
U.S. News ranking: 34
Student/Faculty Ratio: 10/1

Financial Information:

$53,260 = tuition
$15,260 = room/board
$1,780 = fees
$70,300 = total billed cost per year
Students Receiving Aid: 63%

Application:

early decision I: 11/1
early decision II: 1/1
regular decision: 1/1

Brandeis University requires all students to submit the CSS/PROFILE for scholarship eligibility. Brandeis offers several specialty scholarships available at www.brandeis.edu/admissions/financial/scholarships.html. Six specialty scholarships are offered to incoming freshman and can be accessed at the website.

Total billed cost per year does NOT include travel, books, or pizza money.

Carnegie Mellon University

Pittsburg, PA   412-268-2028   www.cmu.edu

Basic Profile:

enrollment: 13,961
average ACT: 31-34
average SAT: 1360-1540
U.S. News ranking: 25
Student/Faculty Ratio: 13/1

Financial Information:

$54,244 = tuition
$14,418 = room/board
$1,221 = fees
$69,883 = total billed cost per year
Students Receiving Aid: 82%

Application:

early decision: 11/1
early admission: 1/1
regular decision: 1/1

Presidential Scholarship

award   amounts vary, renewable for eight semesters.
eligibility   All qualified U.S. citizens and permanent residents are eligible.
application   Must submit all required CMU financial aid documents by deadlines to be considered. Renewable with 2.0 GPA.
Several major-specific full-tuition scholarships also available. See http://admission.enrollment.cmu.edu/pages/grants-scholarships for details.

Case Western Reserve University

Cleveland, Ohio   216-368-4450   www.case.edu

Basic Profile:

enrollment: 11,340 (private)
average ACT: 30-33
average SAT: 1300-1490
U.S. News ranking: 37
Student/Faculty Ratio: 11/1

Financial Information:

$48,604 = tuition
$15,190 = room/board
$438 = fees
$64,232 = total billed cost per year
Students Receiving Aid: 82%

Application:

early action: 11/1 non-binding
regular decision: 1/15
common app: yes (supplement)

Milton A. And Roslyn Z. Wolf Scholarship

award   full tuition, room & board, fees, books, elective summer experiences; renewable for 4 years.
eligibility   academic achievement, leadership potential, essay.
application   all qualified applicants for admission are considered; no separate application is required.
deadline   admission application must be received by 2/1.

Several major-specific full-tuition scholarships also available. See http://admission.case.edu/affording-cwru/scholarships/ for details.

Total billed cost per year does NOT include travel, books, or pizza money.

D

Central Michigan University

Mount Pleasant, Michigan   989-774-4000   www.cmich.edu

Basic Profile:
enrollment: 23,000
average ACT: 23
average SAT: 1140
U.S. News ranking: 207
Student/Faculty Ratio: 22/1

Financial Information:
$12,510 = tuition (non-resident)
$9,736 = room/board
$1,000 = fees
$23,476 = total billed cost per year
Students Receiving Aid: 94%

Application:
regular decision: 2/1

CMU President's Award
award   The President's Award is granted to non-Michigan resident high school seniors with at least a 2.75 (on a 4.0 scale) GPA and to non-Michigan resident transfer students who have earned 30 or more credit hours with a cumulative GPA of at least 2.75(on a 4.0 scale) and who enroll directly at Central Michigan University as full-time, on-campus students. The value of the award is equal to the difference between in-state and out-of-state tuition for the academic year. In state tuition is $11,850.

Centralis Scholar Award
award   full tuition, room & board, books; renewable for 4 years; 20 available.
eligibility   open to high school seniors with a GPA of 3.7 or higher and an ACT 27 or above.
application   selected from an on-campus essay competition.
deadline   10/15

Centralis Gold Award
award   full tuition; renewable for 4 years; 130 available.
eligibility   open to high school seniors with a GPA of 3.7 or higher and an ACT 27 or above.
application   selected from an on-campus essay competition.
deadline   10/15

Academic Prestige Award
award $6,000 per academic year; renewable for 4 years.
eligibility   open to high school seniors with a GPA of 3.25 or higher and an ACT 27 or above.
application   no additional application.
deadline   priority given to applications received by 11/1.

Academic Excellence Award
award $4,500 per academic year; renewable for 4 years.
eligibility   open to high school seniors with a GPA of 3.0 or higher and an ACT 23 or above.
application   no additional application.
deadline   priority given to applications received by 11/1.

Academic Success Award
award $3,000 per academic year; renewable for 4 years.
eligibility   open to high school seniors with a GPA of 3.0 or higher and an ACT 21 or 22.
application   no additional application.
deadline   priority given to applications received by 11/1.

*2018 scholarship policy: students may receive two renewable merit scholarships. Students selected for more than two renewable scholarships may select the two scholarships that are the most generous.

Total billed cost per year does NOT include travel, books, or pizza money.

Centre College

Danville, Kentucky   800-423-6236   www.centre.edu

Basic Profile:
enrollment: 1,367 (private)
average ACT: 26-31
average SAT: 1110-1400
U.S. News ranking: 46 (liberal arts)

Financial Information:
n/a = tuition
n/a = room/board
n/a = fees
$52,180 = comprehensive fee per year
Students Receiving Aid: 97%

Application:
early decision: 11/15 binding
early action: 12/1 non-binding
regular decision: 1/15
common app: yes (supplement)

Brown Fellows Scholarship and Grissom Scholars
award	full tuition, room and board, 4 summer enrichment programs, awarded to 10 incoming freshmen for each award.
eligibility	academic merit, leadership, 3.95 GPA, 32+ACT, 1360+ SAT, at or very near top of class.
application	apply to college, finalists submit a written project proposal; interview.
deadline	application submitted by Jan. 15.

Merit Scholarships
award	$5,000-$25,000/year; renewable for 4 years; about 50% of incoming students.
eligibility	academic merit, extracurricular accomplishment, character.
application	all applicants for admission are considered; no separate application is required.
deadline	application for admission must be received by 2/1.

Claremont McKenna College

Claremont, California   909-621-8088   www.claremontmckenna.edu

Basic Profile:
enrollment: 1,349 (private)
average ACT: 29-33
average SAT: 1340-1530
U.S. News ranking: 8 (liberal arts)
Student/Faculty Ratio: 9/1

Financial Information:
$54,160 = tuition
$15,538 = room/board
$500 = fees
$69,698 = total billed cost per year
Students Receiving Aid: 50%

Application:
early decision I: 11/1 binding
early decision II: 1/1 binding
regular decision: 1/1

Seaver Leadership Award
award	full tuition, renewable for 4 years; two $4,000 stipends for summers. Awarded to approx. 3 students.
eligibility	academic achievement and demonstrated leadership.
application	Mark box in common application that student is interested in merit based scholarships, CMC writing supplement.
deadline	12/1

Interdisciplinary Science Scholarship
award	full tuition, renewable for 4 years. Awarded to 20 students.
eligibility	science and non-science double or dual major, science leadership, some financial need.
application	Mark box in common application that student is interested in merit based scholarships, CMC writing supplement.
deadline	12/1

McKenna Scholars Award
award	$15,000/year, renewable for 4 years; Awarded to 15 students.
eligibility	entering freshmen
application	Mark box in common application that student is interested in merit based scholarships, CMC writing supplement.
deadline	12/1

Total billed cost per year does NOT include travel, books, or pizza money.

D

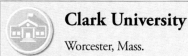

Clark University

Worcester, Mass.   508-793-7711   www.clarku.edu

Basic Profile:

enrollment: 3,485 (private)
average ACT: 24-28
average SAT: 1217
U.S. News ranking: 81
Student/Faculty Ratio: 9/1

Financial Information:

$45,380 = tuition
$9,170 = room/board
$3,057 = fees
$57,607 = total billed cost per year
Students Receiving Aid: 83%

Application:

early decision: 11/15 binding
scholarship deadline: 2/1
regular decision: 1/15
common app: yes (supplement)

Presidential Scholarship

award   full tuition; renewable for 4 years; number awarded varies each year.
eligibility   academic merit
application   all applicants who apply for admission are considered; no separate application is required.
deadline   admission application must be received by the scholarship deadline of 1/15.

Traina Scholarship

award $20,000 per year; renewable for 4 years; $3,000 stipend, awarded to a few select Presidential Scholars.
eligibility   all Presidential qualifications apply; studying the sciences.
application   all applicants who apply for admission are considered; no separate application is required.
deadline   admission application must be received by the scholarship deadline of 1/15; interviews on Feb. 24.

Achievement Scholarship

award $15,000 per year; renewable for 4 years; number awarded varies each year.
eligibility   academic merit.
application   all applicants who apply for admission are considered; no separate application is required.
deadline   admission application must be received by the scholarship deadline of 1/15.

Jonas Clark Scholarship

award $10,000 per year; renewable for 4 years; number awarded varies each year.
eligibility   academic merit.
application   all applicants who apply for admission are considered; no separate application is required.
deadline   admission application must be received by the scholarship deadline of 1/15.

Coastal Carolina

Conway, South Carolina   843-347-3161

public state school

www.coastal.edu

Basic Profile:

enrollment: 10,479
average ACT: 20-24
average SAT: 910-1080
U.S. News ranking: 52 (regional south)
Student/Faculty Ratio: 17/1

Financial Information:

$26,648 = tuition & fees (non-resident)
$9,190 = room/board
$35,838 = total billed cost per year

Application:

priority: 12/1
post 12/1: rolling admission

CCU Scholarship money is first come-first served. Awards given to those who apply, are accepted, and qualify—until money runs out.
Rolling Admissions, but if apply by December 1, you get it. Each scholarship increases with increases in tuition.

Presidential Scholarship (60% of tuition)

award $15,990 per year; renewable for 4 years with 30 credits per year and 3.0 GPA.
eligibility   SAT of 1400 or ACT of 32 and high school GPA of 3.75+.
application   online scholarship application.
deadline   12/1
                Money is first come-first served. Awards given to those qualifying until money runs out.

President's Scholar Award (45% of tuition)

award $11,992 per year; renewable for 4 years with 30 credits per year and 3.0 GPA.
eligibility   SAT of 1250 or ACT of 27 and high school GPA of 3.5+.

Total billed cost per year does NOT include travel, books, or pizza money.

application   online scholarship application.
deadline   12/1

Provost's Scholar Award (35% of tuition)
award $9,328 per year; renewable for 4 years with 30 credits per year and 3.0 GPA.
eligibility   SAT of 1200 or ACT of 26 and high school GPA of 3.5+.
application   online scholarship application.
deadline   12/1

Coastal Scholar Award (25% of tuition)
award $6,662 per year; renewable for 4 years with 30 credits per year and 3.0 GPA.
eligibility   SAT of 1100 or ACT of 24 and high school GPA of 3.5+.
application   online scholarship application.
deadline   12/1

College of the Holy Cross
Worcester, Mass.   800-442-2421   www.holycross.edu

Basic Profile:

enrollment: 3,020 (private)
average ACT: 26-30
average SAT: 1220-1380
U.S. News ranking: 33 (liberal arts)
Student/Faculty Ratio: 10/1

Financial Information:

$52,100 = tuition
$15,520 = room/board
$670 = fees
$67,290 = total billed cost per year
Students Receiving Aid: 53%

Application:

early decision: 12/15 binding
regular decision: 1/15
common app: yes

Merit-Based Scholarships

include   Brooks Scholarship (music major) and Bean Scholarship (classics major).
award   Full tuition; renewable for 4 years; awarded to one freshman for each scholarship.
eligibility   based on excellence in area and interest in specific major.
application   all applicants for admission are considered; no separate application is necessary.

Colorado College

Colorado Springs, Colorado 800-542-7214 www.coloradocollege.edu

Basic Profile:

enrollment: 2,131(private)
average ACT: 28-31
average SAT: 1240-1420
U.S. News ranking: 23 (liberal arts)
Student/Faculty Ratio: 10/1

Financial Information:

$54,996 = tuition
$12,512 = room/board
$474 = fees
$67,982 = total billed cost per year
Students Receiving Aid: 49%

Application:

early decision I: 11/10 binding
early action: 11/10 non-binding
early decision II: 1/15 binding
regular decision: 1/15
common app: yes (supplement)

Otis A. Barnes Scholarship

award	full tuition; renewable for 4 years; awarded to approx. 2 freshmen per year.
eligibility	academic merit; for outstanding students planning on majoring in math and science-related fields.
application	separate application is required, essay, three letters of recommendation.
deadline	all application materials, including application for admission, must be sent by 1/15.

Margaret T. Barnes Scholarship

award	full tuition; renewable for 4 years; awarded to approx. 2 freshmen per year.
eligibility	academic merit; for outstanding students planning on majoring in any of the natural sciences other than chemistry: biology, environmental sciences, geology, mathematics, neuroscience, physics, psychology.
application	separate application is required, essay, three letters of recommendation.
deadline	all application materials, including application for admission, must be sent by 1/15.

Leadership Scholarship

award	$5,000 per semester
eligibility	with admission application; outstanding academic, leadership and extracurricular achievement

Trustee Scholarship

award	$3,500 per semester
eligibility	with admission application; outstanding academic, leadership and extracurricular achievement

Presidential Scholarship

award	$2,500 per semester
eligibility	with admission application; outstanding academic, leadership and extracurricular achievement

Cooper Union for the Advancement of Science & Art

New York City, NY 212-353-4120 www.cooper.edu

Basic Profile:

enrollment: 972
average ACT: 29—33
average SAT: 1190—1480
U.S. News ranking: 1 (regional north)
Student/Faculty Ratio: 10/1
Cooper Union is exclusively dedicated to art, architecture, and engineering. Public programs work towards civic, cultural, and practicable enrichment of New York City.

Financial Information:

$43,250 = tuition
$16,270 = room/board
$250 = fees
$59,775 = total billed cost per year
Students Receiving Aid: 96%

Application:

early decision: 12/1 binding
regular decision: varies
common app: no

Cooper Union Tuition Scholarship

award	half tuition (approx. $20,400/year); renewable for 4 years.
eligibility	academic ability, achievements; all accepted applicants to Cooper Union are awarded this scholarship.
application	all applicants to Cooper Union are considered; no separate application is required.
deadline	admission application must be received by 12/1 (early decision), regular decision varies.

Other merit-based scholarships may be offered to exceedingly exceptional students.

Total billed cost per year does NOT include travel, books, or pizza money.

Dakota Wesleyan

Mitchell, South Dakota   800-333-8506   www.dwu.edu

Basic Profile:

enrollment: 991 (private)
average ACT: 18-24
average SAT: 770-1030
U.S. News ranking: 30 (regional midwest)
Student/Faculty Ratio: 12/1

Financial Information:

$26,700 = tuition
$6,950 = room/board
$330 = fees
$33,980 = total billed cost per year
Students Receiving Aid: 99%

Application:

rolling deadlines

John Wesley Scholarship
Award: $13,000-14,750 renewable up to ten semesters
Eligibility: 3.7 GPA and 27 ACT or 1210 SAT
Application: no separate application required

Trustee Scholarship
Award: $12,000-13,750 renewable up to ten semesters
Eligibility: 3.5 GPA and 24 ACT or 1090 SAT
Application: no separate application required

Presidential Scholarship
Award: $8,750-13,000 renewable up to ten semesters
Eligibility: 3.0 GPA and 18 ACT or 860 SAT
Application: no separate application required

Tiger Award
Award: $3,500-10,000 renewable up to ten semesters
Eligibility: 2.5 GPA and below 18 ACT or 860 SAT
Application: no separate application required

DWU Grant
Award: $3,500 renewable up to ten semesters
Eligibility: 2.49 or below GPA
Application: no separate application required

Davidson College

Davidson, North Carolina   704-894-2000   www.davidson.edu

Basic Profile:

enrollment: 1,784 (private)
average ACT: 29-32
average SAT: 1260-1440
U.S. News ranking: 10 (liberal arts)
Student/Faculty Ratio: 10/1

Financial Information:

$51,447 = tuition and fees

$14,372 = room/board
$65,819 = total billed cost per year
Students Receiving Aid: 70%

Application:

early decision I: 11/15 binding
early decision II: 1/2 binding
regular decision: 1/2
common app: yes (supplement)

John Montgomery Belk Scholarship
award   full tuition, room & board, fees, two $3,000 summer stipends for "leadership activities," international leadership conferences; renewable for 4 years; awarded to 8 freshmen per year.
eligibility   academic excellence, character, service, athletics, nomination from high school is recommended.
application   separate application required for nomination and application found here: https://admission.davidson.edu/belknomination/, one nomination per school.
deadline   nomination due 11/8; application must be received by 12/1.

Total billed cost per year does NOT include travel, books, or pizza money.

D

Lowell L. Bryan Scholarship
award: $30,000 renewable for 4 years, awarded to 2 freshman per year
eligibility: Students who contribute in a superlative manner to their sports as well as their academic life
application: nomination and application form foundon school website

Missy and John Kuykendall Scholarship
award $25,000/year, renewable for 4 years; awarded to 2 freshmen per year.
eligibility   You can provide the kind of servant leadership that characterized the presidency of John W. Kuykendall.
application   no separate application is required; all Davidson applicants are considered.
deadline   application for admission must be received by ½.

William Holt Terry Scholarship
award   Full tuition, renewable for 4 years, and one $1,500 summer stipend; awarded to 2 freshmen per year.
eligibility   You have demonstrated exemplary leadership skills and personal qualities through student government, athletics, service, or other activities.
application   no separate application is required; all Davidson applicants are considered.
deadline   application for admission must be received by 1/2.

Other merit-based and major-specific scholarships available. See website for details.

Deep Springs College
Big Pine, California   760-872-2000   www.deepsprings.edu/

Basic Profile:

enrollment: 30

average SAT: 1400

Financial Information:

$50,000 = tuition and fees
$ — = room/board
$ — = other charges
$50,000 = total billed cost per year **

Application:

early decision I: 11/15 binding
early decision II: 1/2 binding
regular decision: 1/2
common app: yes (supplement)

**Every single student accepted at Deep Springs receives a comprehensive scholarship that covers tuition and room and board in full, an estimated value of over $50,000. Students are only expected to pay for books, incidentals, and travel, which the school estimates run less than $2,800 per year.

Deep Springs is an unusual college. The student body is all-male with a maximum of 30 students on campus. This is a two year college (not a community college). Students work on a ranch performing both manual labor as well as administrative duties. Deep Springs describes the experience: "students stay dedicated to on-campus living to preserve the intensity and integrity of the program. Classes are seminar based liberal arts in nature with extensive student self-government. The mission at Deep Springs is to prepare students by stressing character, intellect of skill and purpose to prepare students for a life of service through endowing them with significant responsibility.

Deep Springs is highly selective, with only 6-15% of applicants accepted. Students graduating from Deep Springs are often accepted at the most selective colleges and universities in America.

Denison University

Granville, Ohio   1-800-DENISON (800-336-4766)   www.denison.edu

Basic Profile:

enrollment: 2,254 (private)
average ACT: 28
average SAT: 1270
U.S. News ranking: 46 (liberal arts)
Student/Faculty Ratio: 9/1

Financial Information:

$50,790 = tuition
$12,710 = room/board
$1,170 = fees
$64,670 = total billed cost per year
Students Receiving Aid: 99%

Application:

early decision I: 11/15 binding
early decision II: 1/15 binding
regular decision: 1/15
common app: yes (supplement)

Wells Scholarship in the Sciences

award	$46,000; renewable for 4 years.
eligibility	Based on superior academic achievement, outstanding leadership and personal merit. These awards require the student to be nominated by the admissions committee.
application	no separate application required, all Denison applicants considered.
deadline	admission application and scholarship application must be received by 1/15.

Dunbar Scholarship in the Humanities

award	$46,000; renewable for 4 years.
eligibility	Based on superior academic achievement, outstanding leadership and personal merit. These awards require the student to be nominated by the admissions committee.
application	no separate application required, all Denison applicants considered.
deadline	admission application and scholarship application must be received by 1/15.

Dr. Betty Lovelace Scholarship

award	$46,000; renewable for 4 years.
eligibility	Based on superior academic achievement, outstanding leadership and personal merit, and to recognize Denison's ongoing commitment to diversify the community. These awards require the student to be nominated by the admissions committee.
application	no separate application required, all Denison applicants considered.
deadline	admission application and scholarship application must be received by 1/15.

Dr. Desmond Hamlet Scholarship

award	$46,000; renewable for 4 years.
eligibility	Based on superior academic achievement, outstanding leadership and personal merit, and to recognize Denison's ongoing commitment to diversify the community. These awards require the student to be nominated by the admissions committee.
application	no separate application required, all Denison applicants considered.
deadline	admission application and scholarship application must be received by 1/15.

Bob and Nancy Good Scholarship

award	$24,000; renewable for 4 years.
eligibility	Based on academic achievement, leadership and personal merit, and to recognize Denison's ongoing commitment to diversify the community.
application	no separate application required, all Denison applicants considered.
deadline	admission application and scholarship application must be received by 1/15.

Hia/Fisher Scholarship

award	$20,000; renewable for 4 years.
eligibility	Based on academic achievement, leadership and personal merit, and to recognize Denison's ongoing commitment to diversify the community.
application	no separate application required, all Denison applicants considered.
deadline	admission application and scholarship application must be received by 1/15.

Total billed cost per year does NOT include travel, books, or pizza money.

D

DePauw University

Greencastle, Indiana   765-658-4800   www.depauw.edu

Basic Profile:
enrollment: 2,265 (private)
average ACT: 25-29
average SAT: 1060-1290
U.S. News ranking: 53 (liberal arts)
Student/Faculty Ratio: 9/1

Financial Information:
$47,026 = tuition
$12,529 = room/board
$812 = fees
$60,367 = total billed cost per year

Application:
early decision: 11/1 binding
early action: 12/1
regular decision: 2/1
common app: yes (supplement)

Rector Scholarships
award	three-quarter or full tuition; renewable for 4 years; number awarded varies each year.
eligibility	academic achievement; top DePauw applicants; SAT/ACT scores.
application	applicants must be nominated by high school guidance counselor or teacher, finalists for full tuition scholarships invited to campus for interview.
deadline	admission application must be received by 11/1 (early decision), 12/1 (early notification), or 2/1.

Holton Scholarships
award	up to full tuition per year; renewable for 4 years; number awarded varies each year.
eligibility	academic achievement, demonstrated leadership, commitment to community service.
application	all Early Decision and Early Action applicants who apply for admission to DePauw are considered; no separate application is required.
deadline	application for admission and scholarship application must be received by 2/1.

Drew University

Madison, New Jersey   973-408-3000   www.drew.edu

Basic Profile:
enrollment: 2,082 (private)
average ACT: 21-28
average SAT: 970-1220
U.S. News ranking: 112 (liberal arts)
Student/Faculty Ratio: 10/1

Financial Information:
$38,668 = tuition
$14,108 = room/board
$832 = fees
$53,608 = total billed cost per year
Students Receiving Aid: 98%

Application:
early decision I: 11/15 binding
early decision II: 1/15 binding
regular decision: 2/1
common app: yes (supplement)

Francis Asbury Scholarship
award:	annual amount of $20,000
eligibility:	earned A average in high school, with a minimum SAT score of 1260 or 26 ACT. Students must maintain 3.6 GPA for renewal.
application	separate application is required (http://www.drew.edu/undergraduate/admissions/scholarships/civic).
deadline	3/1

Baldwin Honors Scholarship
award:	annual amount of $2,500
eligibility:	recipients of the Asbury Scholarship who indicate their interest in the Baldwin Honors Program will be considered for this additional amount.
application	separate application is required (http://www.drew.edu/undergraduate/admissions/scholarships/civic).
deadline	3/1

Presidential Scholarship
award:	annual amount of $15,000
eligibility:	earned A- average in high school, with a minimum SAT score of 1150 or 24 ACT. Students must maintain 3.6 GPA for renewal.
application	separate application is required (http://www.drew.edu/undergraduate/admissions/scholarships/civic).
deadline	3/1

Dean's Scholarship
Award:	Annual amount of $12,000
Eligibility:	Earned B+ average in high school. Test scores are not required for this award.
application	separate application is required (http://www.drew.edu/undergraduate/admissions/scholarships/civic).
deadline	3/1

Total billed cost per year does NOT include travel, books, or pizza money.

Civic Engagement Scholarship

award	$2,500/year; renewable for 4 years; number awarded varies each year.
eligibility	outstanding leadership in community service and civic engagement, essay, recommendations, resume.
application	separate application is required (http://www.drew.edu/undergraduate/admissions/scholarships/civic).
deadline	3/1

Drew Scholarship

award	$7,000/year; renewable for 4 years; number awarded varies each year.
eligibility	awarded to applicants with a minimum high school GPA in the B range in an honors curriculum
application	separate application is required (http://www.drew.edu/undergraduate/admissions/scholarships/civic).
deadline	3/1

Duke University

Durham, North Carolina   919-684-3214   www.duke.edu

Basic Profile:

enrollment: 15,984 (private)
average ACT: 31-34
average SAT: 1360-1550
U.S. News ranking: 9
Student/Faculty Ratio: 6/1

Financial Information:

$55,960 = tuition and fees
$15,944 = room/board
$71,904 = total cost per year

Students Receiving Aid: 62%

Application:

early decision I: 11/1 binding
regular decision: 1/3
common app: yes (supplement)

Angier B. Duke Memorial Scholarship

award	full tuition, fees, room & board, paid study abroad at Oxford; renewable for 4 years, $5,000 for research; awarded to approximately 15 freshmen per year.
eligibility	academic excellence, extreme intellectual curiosity and ambition, unique personal qualities.
application	no separate application is necessary; all applicants who apply for admission to Duke are considered; top applicants in the applicant pool will be invited for an on-campus scholarship interview.
deadline	all application materials must be received by 11/1 (early decision) or 1/3 (regular decision).

Robertson Scholars Leadership Program (see: http://www.robertsonscholars.org)

award	full tuition, room & board; renewable for 4 years, funding for three summer experiences; awarded to approximately 20 freshmen per year.
eligibility	academic achievement, leadership, dedication to community service.
application	no separate application is necessary; all applicants who apply for admission to Duke are considered; top applicants will be invited for an on-campus scholarship interview.
deadline	all application materials must be received by 11/1 (early decision) or 1/3 (regular decision).

University Scholars Program

award	full tuition, fees, room & board, renewable for 4 years, $7,000 for research.
eligibility	ability to explore new academic horizons.
application	no separate application is necessary; all applicants who apply for admission to Duke are considered; top applicants will be invited for an on-campus scholarship interview.
deadline	all application materials must be received by 11/1 (early decision) or 1/3 (regular decision).

Total billed cost per year does NOT include travel, books, or pizza money.

D

Eckerd College

St Petersburg, Florida   800-456-9009   www.eckerd.edu

Basic Profile:
enrollment: 2,023 (private)
average ACT: 23-28
average SAT: 1000-1210
U.S. News ranking: 128 (liberal arts)
Student/Faculty Ratio: 12/1

Financial Information:
$43,914 = tuition
$12,588 = room/board
$626 = fees
$57,128 = total billed cost per year
Students Receiving Aid: 96%

Application:
early decision: 11/15
regular decision: 12/1
*rolling admission

common app: yes (supplement)

Academic Achievement Scholarships

award   award if standardized score and GPA are met; renewable for 4 years.
application   all applicants who apply are considered; no separate application is necessary.

Scholarship	Amount	GPA	ACT Score	SAT Score
Founders	$21,000	3.8	29	1310
Trustee	$19,000	3.6	27	1280
Presidential	$17,000	3.4	25	1230
Dean	$16,000	3.2	23	1180
Academic Achievement	$11,000	2.99	22	1130

Emory University

Atlanta, Georgia   404-727-6123   www.emory.edu

Basic Profile:
enrollment: 13,788 (private)
average ACT: 29-33
average SAT: 1270-1490
U.S. News ranking: 21
Student/Faculty Ratio: 9/1

Financial Information:
$50,590 = tuition
$14,506 = room/board
$716 = fees
$65,812 = total billed cost per year
Students Receiving Aid: 51%

Application:
early decision I: 11/1 binding
early decision II: 1/1 binding
regular decision: 1/1

common app: yes (supplement)

Emory Scholars Program

award   up to full tuition, room & board, fees; renewable for 4 years.
eligibility.   academic excellence, extracurricular achievements, varied cultural interests, leadership.
application   students nominate themselves via their Common Application, two teacher letters of recommendation, one counselor letter of
               recommendation, written application under Emory University section of Common Application.
deadline   all application and nomination materials must be received by Nov. 15.

Evergreen State College

Olympia, Washington   360-867-6170   www.evergreen.edu

Basic Profile:
enrollment: 4,190 (public)
average ACT: 20-26
average SAT: 940-1190
U.S. News ranking: 33 (regional west)
Student/Faculty Ratio: 22/1

Financial Information:
$25,326 = tuition (non-resident)
$11,346 = room/board
$870 = fees
$37,542 = total billed cost per year
Students Receiving Aid: 86%

Application:
early decision: none
regular decision: 3/15

common app: no

Merit Awards

award   several major-specific awards available—up to full tuition.
eligibility   all may apply.
application   varies—see http://www.evergreen.edu/scholarships/home.htm
deadline   Feb. 1.

Franciscan University of Steubenville

Steubenville, Ohio   740-283-3771   www.franciscan.edu

Basic Profile:

enrollment: 2,759 (private)
average ACT: 23-28
average SAT: 1060-1270
U.S. News ranking: 19 (Midwest)

Student/Faculty Ratio: 14/1

Financial Information:

$27,170 = tuition
$8,500 = room/board
$630 = fees
$36,300 = total billed cost per year

Application:

early decision: none
regular decision: 11/30
common app: no

Students Receiving Aid: 99%

Father Michael Scanlan Scholarship Competition

award	full tuition, renewable; two awarded.
eligibility	exceptional academic achievement and distinctive personal accomplishment; extracurricular involvement; Invitation only—open to Presidential and Chancellor Scholarship recipients.
application	those invited participate in a two day event, including a written essay, oral interview, and a group project.
deadline	must submit by regular deadline to be considered.

Chancellor Scholarship

award	$10,000/year, renewable
eligibility	31+ ACT or 1420+ SAT and certain GPA.
application	no separate application
deadline	must submit by regular deadline to be considered.

Dean's Scholarship

award	$8,000/year, renewable
eligibility	27+ ACT or 1280+ SAT and certain GPA.
application	no separate application
deadline	must submit by regular deadline to be considered.

Provost Scholarship

award	$7,000/year, renewable.
eligibility	23+ ACT or 1130+ SAT, and 3.0+ GPA.
application	no separate application
deadline	must submit by regular deadline to be considered.

St. Elizabeth Scholarship

award	$4,000/year, renewable.
eligibility	21+ ACT or 1080+ SAT, and 2.4+ GPA.
application	no separate application
deadline	must submit by regular deadline to be considered.

Total billed cost per year does NOT include travel, books, or pizza money.

Furman University

Greenville, South Carolina   864-294-2034   www.furman.edu

Basic Profile:
enrollment: 3,003 (private)
average ACT: 25-30
average SAT: 1180-1370
U.S. News ranking: 53 (liberal arts)
Student/Faculty Ratio: 11/1

Financial Information:
$49,152 = tuition
$13,438 = room/board
$380 = fees
$62,970 = total billed cost per year
Students Receiving Aid: 97%

Application:
early decision: 11/1 binding
regular decision: 1/5
common app: yes (supplement)

James B. Duke Scholarship
award	full tuition; study away stipend of up to $2,000; renewable for 4 years.
eligibility	exceptional academic achievement and distinctive personal accomplishment; extracurricular involvement; 32+ ACT/1400+ SAT.
application	Furman admission application and Merit-based Scholarships Applications; interviews in late March.
deadline	both applications must be received by 11/15 (early decision) or 1/15 (regular decision).

John D. Hollingsworth/Charles H. Townes Scholarships
award	$35,000; renewable for 4 years; study away stipend of up to $2,000; two of each awarded.
eligibility	awarded to students from/outside of South Carolina respectively; exceptional leadership skills and distinctive personal accomplishment; community impact.
application	Furman admission application and Merit-based Scholarships Applications; interviews in late March.
deadline	both applications must be received by 11/15 (early decision) or 1/15 (regular decision).

Grand Valley State University

Allendale, Michigan   616-331-5000   www.gvsu.edu

Basic Profile:
enrollment: 25,460
average ACT: 24
average SAT: n/a
U.S. News ranking: 29 (regional midwest)
Student/Faculty Ratio: 17/1

Financial Information:
$17,064 = tuition (non-resident)
$9,000 = room/board
$26,064 = total billed cost per year
Students Receiving Aid: 87%

Application:
rolling admission

total billed cost per year

Presidential Scholarship
award	$4,000 to $7,000; renewable for 4 years.
eligibility	Minimum ACT of 32 or SAT of 1470 and high school GPA of 3.8; maintain college GPA of 3.5.
application	must participate in scholarship competition to be eligible
deadline	31-Dec

Faculty Scholarship
award	$1,000 to $3,000; renewable for 4 years.
eligibility	Minimum ACT of 30 or SAT of 1400 and high school GPA of 3.6; maintain college GPA of 3.5.
application	must participate in scholarship competition to be eligible
deadline	31-Dec

Award for Excellence Scholarship
award	$5,000; renewable for 4 years.
eligibility	Minimum ACT of 26 and high school GPA of 3.5; maintain college GPA of 3.25.
application	no additional application
deadline	31-Dec

Laker Scholarship
award	$2,000; renewable for 4 years.
eligibility	Minimum SAT score of 1070 and high school GPA of 3.5; maintain college GPA of 2.85.
application	no additional application
deadline	31-Dec

Total billed cost per year does NOT include travel, books, or pizza money.

Grinnell College

Grinnell, Iowa   641-269-4000   www.grinnell.edu

Basic Profile:
enrollment: 1,705 (private)
average ACT: 30-33
average SAT: 1300-1510
U.S. News ranking: 18 (liberal arts)
Student/Faculty Ratio: 9/1

Financial Information:
$51,924 = tuition
$12,810 = room/board
$468 = fees
$65,202 = total billed cost per year
Students Receiving Aid: 92%

Application:
early decision I: 11/15 binding
early decision II: 1/1 binding
regular decision: 1/15
common app: yes

President's Scholarship

award:	$50,000 per year, for a total of $200,000
eligibility:	awarded on a holistic basis during the admission process, taking into account each student's academic achievement, extracurricular involvement, demonstrated leadership, and/or special talents. Renewable each year for four years with cumulative GPA of at 2.75.
application	all applicants for admission to Grinnell are considered; no separate application is necessary.
deadline	application for admission must be received by 11/20, 1/1 (early decisions), or 1/20 (regular decision).

Dean's Scholarship

award:	$25,000 per year, for a total of $100,000
eligibility:	awarded on a holistic basis during the admission process, taking into account each student's academic achievement, extracurricular involvement, demonstrated leadership, and/or special talents. Renewable each year for four years with cumulative GPA of at 2.75.
application	all applicants for admission to Grinnell are considered; no separate application is necessary.
deadline	application for admission must be received by 11/20, 1/1 (early decisions), or 1/20 (regular decision).

Founder's Scholarship

award:	$12,000 per year, for a total of $48,000
eligibility:	awarded on a holistic basis during the admission process, taking into account each student's academic achievement, extracurricular involvement, demonstrated leadership, and/or special talents. Renewable each year for four years with cumulative GPA of at 2.75.
application	all applicants for admission to Grinnell are considered; no separate application is necessary.
deadline	application for admission must be received by 11/20, 1/1 (early decisions), or 1/20 (regular decision).

Gustavus Adolphus College

St. Peter, Minnesota   507-933-8000   www.gustavus.edu

Basic Profile:
enrollment: 2,379 (private)
average ACT: 25-30
average SAT: 1225
U.S. News ranking: 85 (liberal arts)
Student/Faculty Ratio: 11/1

Financial Information
$44,900 = tuition
$9,910 = room/board
$700 = fees
$55,510 = total billed cost per year
Students Receiving Aid: 90%

Application:
early action: 11/1
regular decision: 5/1
*rolling admission
common app: yes (supplement)

Presidential Scholarship

award	up to $27,000 per year; renewable for 4 years.
eligibility	academic excellence; 30+ ACT/1400+ SAT; essay; interview.
application	separate application is required and can be found at https://apply.gustavus.edu/register/PresidentsScholarship.
deadline	both the application for admission and scholarship application must be received by 1/1.

Dean's Scholarship

award	$13,000-$24,000 per year; renewable for 4 years.
eligibility	academic excellence.
application	no separate application required.
deadline	both the application for admission and scholarship application must be received by 1/1.

Hendrix College

Conway, Arkansas   501-329-6811   www.hendrix.edu

Basic Profile:

enrollment: 1,338 (private)
average ACT: 25-32
average SAT: 1120-1340
U.S. News ranking: 76 (liberal arts)
Student/Faculty Ratio: 11/1

Financial Information:

$45,440 = tuition
$12,284 = room/board
$350 = fees
$58,074 = total billed cost per year
Students Receiving Aid: 100%

Application:

early action I: 11/15 binding
early action II: 2/1
regular decision: after 2/1
common app: yes (supplement)

Hendrix College Scholarship

award	$18,000 up to full tuition
eligibility	based on GPA, standardized test scores, leadership and extracurricular activities, recommendations
application	no separate application

Hays Memorial Scholarship

award	full tuition, fees, room and board; renewable for 4 years.
eligibility	3.6+ GPA; 32+ ACT/1410+ SAT.
application	separate application due 2/1; apply by Early Action I date; finalists will be invited to an on-campus. interview in March.

Hillsdale College

Hillsdale, Michigan   517-437-7341   www.hillsdale.edu

Basic Profile:

enrollment: 1,526 (private)
average ACT: 27-31
average SAT: 1210-1400
U.S. News ranking: 71 (liberal arts)
Student/Faculty Ratio: 10/1

Financial Information:

$26,300 = tuition
$11,000 = room/board
$1,278 = fees
$38,578 = total billed cost per year

Application:

early action I: 11/15 binding
early action II: 2/1
regular decision: after 2/1
common app: yes (supplement)

Academic Merit Awards

award	$1,000 to half tuition with a few three-quarter to full-tuition awards given each year, renewable for four years
eligibility	Superior academic achievement and leadership, an interview with an Admissions representative is strongly recommended.
application	all applicants considered upon admission, no separate application necessary
deadline	application for admission must be submitted by priority decision date 1/2

Total billed cost per year does NOT include travel, books, or pizza money.

Hobart & William Smith Colleges

Geneva, New York   315-781-3000   www.hws.edu

Basic Profile:

enrollment: 2,351 (private)
average ACT: 24-27
average SAT: 1080-1270
U.S. News ranking: 65 (liberal arts)
Student/Faculty Ratio: 10/1

Financial Information:

$54,060 = tuition
$14,035 = room/board
$1,195 = fees
$69,290 = total billed cost per year
Students Receiving Aid: 87%

Application:

early decision I: 11/15 binding
early decision II: 1/15 binding
regular decision: 2/1
common app: yes (supplement)

Blackwell Scholars Program

award: $30,000 annual award
eligibility: top 10% of their high school class, 90 GPA or equivalent, 28 ACT or 1300 SAT, and completed advanced science coursework, relevant research or participated in science related experiences. Must maintain a minimum 3.0 cumulative GPA for renewal
application: all applicants considered upon admission, no separate application necessary
deadline: application for admission must be submitted by early decision date of January 15

Seneca Scholarship

award: Full tuition annual award
eligibility: awarded by the admissions staff to the 3 top scholars in attendance at Scholar Recognition Day.
application: all applicants considered upon admission, no separate application necessary
deadline: application for admission must be submitted by early decision date of January 15

Illinois College

Jacksonville, Illinois   217-245-3030   www.ic.edu

Basic Profile:

enrollment: 960 (private)
average ACT: 21-27
average SAT: n/a
U.S. News ranking: 138 (liberal arts)
Student/Faculty Ratio: 12/1

Financial Information:

$32,540 = tuition
$9,280 = room/board
$550 = fees
$42,342 = total billed cost per year
Students Receiving Aid: 100%

Application:

early decision: n/a
regular decision: 3/1
common app: yes (supplement)

Trustee Scholarship

award: full tuition; renewable for 4 years; 5 freshmen.
eligibility: top 10% of that year's pool, as based on ACT scores, GPA, essays, and extracurricular involvements.
application: all applicants accepted are considered; no separate application.
deadline: 12/1 of student's senior year.

Edward Beecher Scholarship

award: $13,000-$21,000/year; renewable for 4 years.
eligibility: academic achievement
application: all applicants accepted are considered; no separate application.
deadline: 12/1 of student's senior year

Illinois College Opportunity Scholarship

award: $12,000/year; renewable for 4 years.
eligibility: academic achievement
application: all applicants accepted are considered; no separate application.
deadline: 12/1 of student's senior year

Total billed cost per year does NOT include travel, books, or pizza money.

D

Johns Hopkins University

Baltimore, Maryland   410-516-8171   www.jhu.edu

Basic Profile:

enrollment: 5,366 (private)
average ACT: 32-34
average SAT: 1360-1530
U.S. News ranking: 11
Student/Faculty Ratio: 7/1

Financial Information:

$53,740 = tuition and fees
$16,338 = room/board

$70,078 = total billed cost per year
Students Receiving Aid: 63%

Application:

early decision: 11/1 binding
regular decision: 2/15
common app: yes (supplement)

Hodson Trust Scholarship

award	Up to $30,500 per year; automatically renewed for 4 years; awarded to <20 freshmen per year.
eligibility	academic excellence, intellectual curiosity, leadership, community service.
application	all applicants for admission to Johns Hopkins are considered; no separate application is required.
deadline	application for admission must be sent by 11/15 (early decision) or 1/1 (regular decision).

Charles R. Westgate Scholarship in Engineering

award	full tuition and stipend; renewable for 4 years; awarded to 2 freshmen per year.
eligibility	outstanding academic record & achievements, leadership, success in science fairs, independent research.
application	all applicants for admission to Johns Hopkins who indicate an interest in majoring in engineering are considered; no separate application is required.
deadline	application for admission must be sent by 11/15 (early decision) or 1/1 (regular decision).

Kansas State University

Manhattan, Kansas   785-532-6250   www.k-state.edu

Basic Profile:

enrollment: 24,146 (public)
average ACT: 20-27
U.S. News ranking: 145
Student/Faculty Ratio: 18/1

Financial Information:

$24,606 = tuition (non-resident)
$9,430 = room/board
$862 = fees
$34,898 = total billed cost per year
Students Receiving Aid: 85%

Application:

early decision: 12/15
regular decision: 3/1
common app: no

Presidential Scholarship

award	$20,000, renewable for 4 years; two awarded each year.
eligibility	32+ ACT/1450+ SAT, 3.85+ GPA, top 10% of class, interview.
application	K-State application and scholarship application.
deadline	12/9

Midwest Student Exchange Program

award	students pay 150% of in state tuition (approx.$12,000/year); automatically renewed for 4 years.
eligibility	must be a resident of Indiana, Michigan, Minnesota, Missouri, Nebraska, North Dakota, Wisconsin, or Illinois. 3.5+ GPA, 24+ ACT/1090+ SAT; Must be enrolled in one of the curriculum covered by the MWSEP (list found here: http://www.k-state.edu/admit/mwsep.htm.)
application	contact the Campus Administrator, as well as mark on the normal application that you seek admission as a MWSEP student.
deadline	application for admission must be sent by 11/1 (early decision) or 3/1 (regular decision).

Purple and White Scholarship

award	$12,000 per year; renewed for 4 years with 3.5 GPA.
eligibility	3.5+ GPA, 24+ ACT/1160+ SAT; out-of-state graduating seniors.
application	K-State application and scholarship application.
deadline	application for admission must be sent by 11/1 (early decision) or 3/1 (regular decision).

Denison Award

award	$8,000 per year; renewed for 4 years with 3.5 GPA.
eligibility	3.5+ GPA, 21-23 ACT/1060 - 1150 SAT; out-of-state graduating seniors.
application	K-State application and scholarship application
deadline	application for admission must be sent by 11/1 (early decision) or 3/1 (regular decision).

Total billed cost per year does NOT include travel, books, or pizza money.

Lehigh University

Bethlehem, Penn   610-758-3100   www.lehigh.edu

Basic Profile:

enrollment: 7,059 (private)
average ACT: 29-32
average SAT: 1230-1420
U.S. News ranking: 46
Student/Faculty Ratio: 9/1

Financial Information:

$52,480 = tuition
$13,600 = room/board
$650 = fees
$66,730 = total billed cost per year
Students Receiving Aid: 67%

Application:

early decision I: 11/1
early decision II: 1/1
regular decision: 2/1
common app: yes (supplement)

Founders and Trustees Scholarship Awards

award   full or half tuition and fees; renewable for 4 years with 3.0 GPA.
eligibility   awarded to students in top tier of applicant pool
application   all applicants for admission to Lehigh are considered; no separate application is required.

Dean's Scholars

award $12,000 per year; renewable for 4 years with 3.0 GPA.
eligibility   awarded to students in top tier of applicant pool
application   all applicants for admission to Lehigh are considered; no separate application is required.

Lewis & Clark College

Portland, Oregon   503-768-7000   www.lclark.edu

Basic Profile:

enrollment: 3,526 (private)
average ACT: 26-31
average SAT: 1200-1340
U.S. News ranking: 76 (liberal arts)
Student/Faculty Ratio: 11/1

Financial Information:

$50,574 = tuition
$12,594 = room/board
$3,061 = fees
$66,229 = total billed cost per year
Students Receiving Aid: 94%

Application:

early action: 11/1 non-binding
regular decision: 1/15
common app: yes (supplement)

Barbara Hirschi Neely Scholarship

award   full tuition and fees; renewable for 4 years; up to 5 awarded per year.
eligibility   academic excellence, character, leadership; preference given to students interested in math/science or international education/
                 issues; min. GPA: 3.98, min. rank: top 10%, min. SAT: 1410, min. ACT: 31.
application   all applicants for admission to Lewis & Clark are considered; no separate application is required.
deadline   1/15

Lewis & Clark Merit Scholarship

award $15,000-$24,000 per year; renewable for 4 years; must maintain satisfactory academic progress.
eligibility   academic excellence, character, leadership.
application   all applicants for admission to Lewis & Clark are considered; no separate application is required.
deadline   1/15

Loras College

Dubuque, Iowa   800-245-6727   www.loras.edu

Basic Profile:
enrollment: 1,528 (private)
average ACT: 21-26
average SAT: 920-1110
U.S. News ranking: 13 (regional Midwest)
Student/Faculty Ratio: 12/1

Financial Information:
$32,524 = tuition
$8,275 = room/board
$1,660 = fees
$42,459 = total billed cost per year
Students Receiving Aid: 100%

Application:
early decision: none
*rolling admission
common app: no

Loras Merit Awards
award	$12,000-$22,000/year; renewable for 4 years.
eligibility	academic achievement
application	all applicants who apply for admission to Loras are considered; no separate application is required.
deadline	accepted to college prior to Jan. 31.

Louisiana State University

Baton Rouge, Louisiana   225-578-1175   www.lsu.edu

Basic Profile:
enrollment: 31,524
average ACT: 23-28
average SAT: 1010-1260
U.S. News ranking: 133
Student/Faculty Ratio: 22/1

Financial Information:
$28,051 = tuition & fees (non-resident)
$8,752 = room/board
$36,803 = total billed cost per year

Application:
scholarship priority: 11/15
*rolling admission

Penelope W. and E. Roe Stamps IV Leadership Scholars Award
award	full cost of attendance and up to $14,000 in enrichment experiences.
eligibility	top five entering freshmen to Honors College with competitive SAT or ACT writing score, essay, resume, and interview with a panel.
deadline	11/15

Chancellor's Alumni Scholars Awards
award	tuition, room and board; $1,500 per year, $2,000 study abroad, possible research funding.
eligibility	33 ACT or 1490 SAT and 3.5 GPA top ten entering freshmen to Honors College with competitive SAT or ACT writing score, essay, resume, and interview with a panel.
deadline	11/15

Flagship Scholars Award
award	receive $20,500 per year; renewable for 4 years.
eligibility	students with an ACT score of 33 to 36 or an SAT score of 1330 to 1490, as well as a 3.0 high school GPA.
deadline	11/15

LSU Academic Scholars Award
award	receive $15,500 per year; renewable for 4 years.
eligibility	students with an ACT score of 30 to 32 or an SAT score of 1330 to 1390, as well as a 3.0 high school GPA.
deadline	11/15

Tiger Excellence Award
award	receive $7,600 per year; renewable for 4 years.
eligibility	students with an ACT score of 28 to 29 or an SAT score of 1250 to 1310, as well as a 3.0 high school GPA.
deadline	11/15

Loyola University of Chicago

Chicago, Illinois   773-274-3000   www.luc.edu

Basic Profile:

enrollment: 16,437 (private)
average ACT: 24-29
average SAT: 1040-1260
U.S. News ranking: 103
Student/Faculty Ratio: 14/1

Financial Information:

$41,720 = tuition
$14,200 = room/board
$7,258 = fees
$63,178 = total billed cost per year
Students Receiving Aid: 95%

Application:

early decision: none
priority decision: 3/1
*rolling admission
common app: no

Academic Scholarships

Requirements vary yearly; awards range from $16,000-$21,000/year

Rambler Award

award	$7,500/year; renewable for 4 years.
eligibility	academic excellence, commitment to service and leadership
application	no separate application is required, all applicants to Loyola are considered.
deadline	admitted by Feb. 1.

Luther College

Decorah, Iowa   800-458-8437   www.luther.edu

Basic Profile:

enrollment: 2,337 (private)
average ACT: 23-29
average SAT: 970-1265
U.S. News ranking: 987 (liberal arts)
Student/Faculty Ratio: 11/1

Financial Information:

$41,950 = tuition
$9,460 = room/board
$340 = fees
$51,750 = total billed cost per year
Students Receiving Aid: 98%

Application:

early decision: 3/1
*rolling admission
common app: yes (supplement)

Founders Scholarship

award	$24,000/year; renewable for 4 years
eligibility	28+ ACT, 4.0 GPA, rank in top 5% of class
application	no separate application is required, all applicants to Luther are considered.

President's Scholarship

award	$22,000/year; renewable for 4 years
eligibility	27+ ACT, 3.85+ GPA
application	no separate application is required, all applicants to Luther are considered.

Dean's Scholarship

award	$20,000/year; renewable for 4 years
eligibility	24+ ACT, 3.6+ GPA
application	no separate application is required, all applicants to Luther are considered

Martin Luther Award

award	$18,000/year; renewable for 4 years
eligibility	23+ACT, 3.3 GPA
application	no separate application is required, all applicants to Luther are considered

Achievement Award

award	$10,000/year; renewable for 4 years
eligibility	20+ACT, 3.0 GPA
application	no separate application is required, all applicants to Luther are considered

Total billed cost per year does NOT include travel, books, or pizza money.

D

Marquette University

Milwaukee, Wisconsin   800-222-6544   www.marquette.edu

Basic Profile:

enrollment: 11,491 (private)
average ACT: 24-30
average SAT: 1070-1300
U.S. News ranking: 90
Student/Faculty Ratio: 14/1

Financial Information:

$41,290 = tuition
$12,720 = room/board
$580 = fees
$54,570 = total billed cost per year
Students Receiving Aid: 100%

Application:

early decision: none
closing date: 12/1
*rolling admission
common app: yes

Père Marquette Awards

award	up to $14,000; renewable for 4 years
eligibility	academic achievement, leadership, community service.
application	no separate application required
deadline	12/1

Several other major-specific scholarships available at http://marquette.edu/explore/scholarships.php.

Mississippi State University

Starkville, Mississippi   662-325-2323   www.msstate.edu

Basic Profile:

enrollment: 21,622
average ACT: 21-29
average SAT: 960-1260
U.S. News ranking: 171
Student/Faculty Ratio: 20/1

Financial Information:

$22,358 = tuition & fees (non-resident)
$9,614 = room/board
$31,972 = total billed cost per year
Students Receiving Aid: 95%

Application:

rolling admission

Annual Merit Awards

ACT	SAT	GPA	Award/year
33-36	1490-1600	3.0	$20,000
30-32	1390-1480	3.0	$14,000
26-29	1240-1380	3.0	$12,500
24-25	1160-1230	3.0	$7,000
24-25	1160-1230	3.5	$9,000
22-23	1100-1150	3.5	$8,000

Total billed cost per year does NOT include travel, books, or pizza money.

Montana State University

Bozeman, Montana   406-994-2452   www.montana.edu

Basic Profile:

enrollment: 16,703
average ACT: 25
average SAT: 1213
U.S. News ranking: 207
Student/Faculty Ratio: 19/1

Financial Information:

$24,992 = tuition & fees (non-resident)
$10,100 = room/board
$35,092 = total billed cost per year

Students Receiving Aid: 86%

Application:

rolling admission

Freshman Achievement Awards
award	awards range from $1,000 to $15,000 per year; renewable for 4 years
eligibility	range from min ACT of 23 and min SAT of 1560
deadline	12/1

Presidential Scholarship
award	full tuition renewable for 4 years; up to 20 awards and stipend applied to room and board.
eligibility	minimum 3.75 GPA and 30 ACT or 1390 SAT, intellectual or creative distinctions, extracurricular activities, letters of reference and essay.
deadline	12/1

Mount Holyoke College

South Hadley, Mass.   413-538-2023   www.mtholyoke.edu

Basic Profile:

enrollment: 2,327 (women)
average ACT: 27-31
average SAT: 1220-1430
U.S. News ranking: 36 (liberal arts)
Student/Faculty Ratio: 10/1

Financial Information:

$49,780 = tuition
$14,660 = room/board
$218 = fees
$64,658 = total cost per year
Students Receiving Aid: 82%

Application:

early decision I: 11/15 binding
early decision II: 1/1 binding
regular decision: 1/15

Trustee Scholarship
award	Full tuition; renewable for 4 years; approx. 5 awarded each year.
eligibility	outstanding record of scholarship, cocurricular achievement, and considerable leadership potential.
application	all applicants who apply for admission to Mt. Holyoke are considered; no separate application is required.
deadline	application for admission must be received by 11/15, 1/1 (early decisions), or 1/1 (regular decision).

Mount Holyoke Twenty First Century Scholarship
award	$25,000 per year; renewable for 4 years; approx. 35 awarded each year.
eligibility	academic excellence, outstanding extracurricular achievement; average 33 ACT/1446 SAT, 4.0 GPA.
application	all applicants who apply for admission to Mt. Holyoke are considered; no separate application is required.
deadline	application for admission must be received by 11/15, 1/1 (early decisions), or 1/1 (regular decision).

Chin Scholars
award	$25,000 scholarship annually, renewable for four years. 25 awarded each year.
eligibility	he average recipient of this award demonstrates a 4.0 GPA, 33 ACT and ranks in the top 5% of their class rank
application	First-year applicants are considered automatically for these awards, no additional application is required.
deadline	application for admission must be received by 11/15, 1/1 (early decisions), or 1/1 (regular decision).

Northeastern University

Boston, Mass.   617-373-2200   www.northeastern.edu

Basic Profile:

enrollment: 20,381 (private)
average ACT: 31-34
average SAT: 1340-1510
U.S. News ranking: 40
Student/Faculty Ratio: 14/1

Financial Information:

$48,560 = tuition
$15,660 = room/board
$937 = fees
$65,157 = total billed cost per year
Students Receiving Aid: 75%

Application:

regular decision: 1/1
early action: 11/1
early decision: 11/1
common app: yes

Merit Scholarships

award	$10,000-$25,000 first year; renewable for 4 years at $5,000-$10,000/semester.
eligibility	top 15% of admitted freshman considered.
application	no additional application
deadline	1/15

Northeastern University Scholars Program

award	full tuition; renewable for 4 years; awarded to 75 incoming freshman.
eligibility	academic distinction, demonstrated curiosity and creativity.
application	no additional application
deadline	1/15

Torch Scholars

award	full tuition, room and board; renewable for 4 years
eligibility	awarded to students who have overcome exceptional odds and demonstrate potential to excel.
application	no additional application, must be nominated by an education professional.
deadline	1/15

Ohio University

Athens, Ohio   740-593-1000   www.ohio.edu

Basic Profile:

enrollment: 29,712 (public)
average ACT: 22-26
average SAT: 990-1210
U.S. News ranking: 151
Student/Faculty Ratio: 18/1

Financial Information:

$21,360 = tuition & fees (non-resident)
$12,612 = room/board
$33,972 = total billed cost per year

Students Receiving Aid: 92%

OHIO Success Scholarship

award	$1,000-$7,000
eligibility	minimum 24 ACT, based on sliding scale based on test scores and GPA
application	no separate application
deadline	1/15

OHIO Focus Award

award	up to $1,000
eligibility	minimum 22 ACT, based on sliding scale based on test scores and GPA
application	no separate application
deadline	1/15

Total billed cost per year does NOT include travel, books, or pizza money.

Ohio Wesleyan University

Delaware, Ohio   800-922-8953   www.owu.edu

Basic Profile:

enrollment: 1,671 (private)
average ACT: 25
U.S. News ranking: 101 (liberal arts)
Student/Faculty Ratio: 10/1
Test-optional (3.5+ GPA = no ACT/SAT required)

Financial Information:

$45,500 = tuition and fees
$12,430 = room/board
$260 = fees
$58,190 = total billed cost per year
Students Receiving Aid: 97%

Application:

regular decision: 3/1 binding
early decision: 11/15
early action: 12/1, 1/15
common app: yes

Branch Rickey Scholarship

award	$30,000, renewable for up to four years
eligibility	3.4 cumulative high school GPA and 1150 SAT or 23 ACT
application	first-year applicants are considered automatically for these awards, no additional application is required.
deadline	admissions application submitted by January 15.

Olin College of Engineering

Needham, Mass.   781-292-2300   www.olin.edu

Basic Profile:

enrollment: 378
average ACT: 32-35
average SAT: 1440-1600
U.S. News ranking: 3
Student/Faculty Ratio: 7/1
Scholarship Policy—every admitted student receives a four-year, half-tuition scholarship.

Financial Information:

$50,400 = tuition
$16,300 = room/board
$3,336 = fees
$70,036 = total billed cost per year
Students Receiving Aid: 100%

Application:

regular decision: 1/1 binding
early action: n/a
common app: yes

Pacific Lutheran University

Tacoma, Washington   253-535-7411   www.plu.edu

Basic Profile:

enrollment: 3,170 (private)
average ACT: 22-28
average SAT: 980-1230
U.S. News ranking: 16 (regional west)
Student/Faculty Ratio: 11/1

Financial Information:

$40,352 = tuition and fees
$10,520 = room/board
$370 = fees
$51,242 = total billed cost per year
Students Receiving Aid: 98%

Application:

regular decision: 10/15, 11/15, 12/15, 1/15
early action: n/a
common app: yes, essay, recomm.

Academic Merit Scholarship

award	$15,000-$25,000/year; renewable for 4 years; number awarded varies.
Eligibility	academic merit
application	no separation application required
deadline	10/15, 11/15, 12/15, 1/15

President's Scholarship

award	$26,000; renewable for 4 years; 125 awarded per year, invited to compete for Harstad Founder's and Regents' Scholarships in February.
Eligibility	3.8+ GPA or 1310+ SAT or 28+ ACT
application	President's supplemental application, found at https://forms.plu.edu/475,
deadline	12/1

Harstad Founder's Scholarship

award	$31,000; renewable for 4 years; 10 awarded per year from 125 President's Scholars
eligibility	President's Scholars
application	President's supplemental application, found at https://forms.plu.edu/475,
deadline	12/1

Regents' Scholarship

award	full tuition; renewable for 4 years; 5 awarded per year from 125 President's Scholars
eligibility	President's Scholars
application	President's supplemental application, found at https://forms.plu.edu/475,
deadline	12/1

Purdue University—West Lafayette

West Lafayette, Indiana   765-494-4600   www.purdue.edu

Basic Profile:

enrollment: 40,472
average ACT: 25-31
average SAT: 1080-1330
U.S. News ranking: 56
Student/Faculty Ratio: 12/1

Financial Information:

$28,804 = tuition and fees (non-resident)
$10,030 = room and board
$38,834 = total billed cost

Students Receiving Aid: 63%

Application:

early action: 11/1
regular decision: 1/1
common app: yes

Trustees Scholarship

award	$12,000-$16,000; renewable for 4 years, 100+ awarded per year.
Eligibility	based on academic achievement and demonstrated leadership.
Application	considered upon admission.
Deadline	11/1

Presidential Scholarship

award	$5,000-$10,000; renewable for 4 years, 900+ awarded per year.
Eligibility	based on academic achievement and demonstrated leadership.
Application	considered upon admission.
Deadline	11/1

Total billed cost per year does NOT include travel, books, or pizza money.

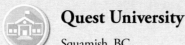

Quest University

Squamish, BC   888-783-7808   www.questu.ca

Basic Profile:

enrollment: 540

Financial Information (Canadian dollars):

$35,000 = tuition
$13,450 = room/board
$1,000 = fees
$49,450 = total billed cost per year (est. $36,000 US)

Application:

vary: spring/fall

David W. Strangway Scholarship

award   four year tuition
eligibility   3.75 GPA and above are considered
application   300 word essay

Presidential Scholarships

award   varies from $2,000 to $18,000 a year
eligibility   academic record and extracurricular activities are considered for award as well as difficulty of classes taken
                  in high school.

Quest University does not use test scores or GPA for admission decisions. Quest is, however, deeply committed to recruiting students who have taken challenging classes or have pursued a passionate endeavor or interest.

Rice University

Houston, Texas   713-348-7423   www.rice.edu

Basic Profile:

enrollment: 6,855 (private)
average ACT: 32-35
average SAT: 1390-1560
U.S. News ranking: 14
Student/Faculty Ratio: 6/1

Financial Information:

$46,600 = tuition
$14,000 = room/board
$750 = fees
$61,350 = total billed cost per year
Students Receiving Aid: 65%

Application:

early decision: 11/1 binding
regular decision: 1/1
common app: yes (supplement)

Trustee Distinguished Scholarship

award $24,000-$26,500; renewable for 4 years
eligibility   students whose personal talents distinguish them from the pool of applicants.
application   all admitted students automatically considered

Trustee Diversity Scholarship

award $24,000-$26,500; renewable for 4 years
eligibility   students whose diverse life experiences and contributions distinguish them from the pool of applicants.
application   all admitted students automatically considered

Barbara Jordan Scholarship

award $24,000, renewable for 4 years
eligibility   Students who have distinguished themselves through initiatives that build bridges between cultural, racial, and ethnic groups.
application   all admitted students automatically considered

Other major-specific scholarships available. Details found at http://financialaid.rice.edu/scholarships.aspx.

Total billed cost per year does NOT include travel, books, or pizza money.

Rhodes College

Memphis, Tenn.   901-843-3000   www.rhodes.edu

Basic Profile:
enrollment: 2,063 (private)
average ACT: 27-32
average SAT: 1180-1380
U.S. News ranking: 51 (liberal arts)
Student/Faculty Ratio: 10/1

Financial Information:
$47,580 = tuition
$11,403 = room/board
$310 = fees
$59,290 = total billed cost per year
Students Receiving Aid: 94%

Application:
early decision I: 11/1 binding
early decision II: 1/1 binding
regular decision: 1/15
common app: yes (supplement)

Bellingrath Scholarship

award	full tuition; renewable for 4 years; awarded to 1 freshman per year
eligibility	outstanding academic achievement, leadership, and dedication to service;
application	no separate application is required,
deadline	nomination form must be received by 11/1; application for admission must be received by 1/1.

Merit Scholarships

award	$22,000 to $35,000
eligibility	outstanding academic achievement, leadership, and dedication to service;
application	no separate application is required,
deadline	nomination form must be received by 11/1; application for admission must be received by 1/1.

Rollins College

Winter Park, Florida   407-646-2000   www.rollins.edu

Basic Profile:
enrollment: 3,260 (private)
average ACT: 19-24
average SAT: 940-1140
U.S. News ranking: 2 (regional south)
Student/Faculty Ratio: 10/1

Financial Information:
$48,335 = tuition and fees
$14,730 = room/board
$63,065 = total billed cost per year

Students Receiving Aid: 85%

Application:
early decision: 11/15
early decision II: 1/15
priority decision: 2/15

common app: yes (supplement)

Alfond Scholars Program

award	full tuition, fees, room & board; renewable for 4 years; awarded to 10 freshmen.
eligibility	academic superiority, leadership; 1510+ SAT/ 32+ ACT and 3.6+ GPA
application	considered upon admission
deadline	admission application due 9/1

Dean's Scholarships

award	$30,000 annually, renewable for 4 years
eligibility	academic superiority, leadership; 1400+ SAT/ 30+ ACT and 3.6+ GPA
application	considered upon admission
deadline	admission application due 9/1

Presidential Scholarships

award	$24,000 annually, renewable for 4 years
eligibility	academic superiority, leadership; 1290+ SAT/ 27+ ACT and 3.3+ GPA
application	considered upon admission

Centennial Scholarships

award	$5,000-$17,000 annually, renewable for 4 years
eligibility	academic superiority, leadership; 1270+ SAT/ 26+ ACT and 3.1+ GPA
application	considered upon admission

Total billed cost per year does NOT include travel, books, or pizza money.

Santa Clara University

Santa Clara, California   408-554-4000   www.scu.edu

Basic Profile:

enrollment: 8,680 (private)
average ACT: 27-32
average SAT: 1210-1400
U.S. News ranking: 2 (regional west)
Student/Faculty Ratio: 11/1

Financial Information:

$51,081 = tuition and fees
$15,837 = room/board
$66,918 = total cost per year

Students Receiving Aid: 72%

Application:

early action: 11/1
regular decision: 1/7

common app: yes

Johnson Scholars Award

award	full tuition, room & board, summer stipend; renewable up to four years; 10 awarded yearly.
eligibility	3.8+ GPA, 30+ ACT/ 1400+ SAT, leadership and service.
application	no separate application is necessary; all applicants who apply for admission are considered.
deadline	all application materials must be received by 1/7

Presidential at Entry Scholarship

award	full tuition; renewable up to four years
eligibility	academic merit and leadership
application	no separate application is necessary; all applicants who apply for admission are considered.
deadline	all application materials must be received by 1/7

Seton Hall University

South Orange, New Jersey   973-761-9000   www.shu.edu

Basic Profile:

enrollment: 9,836 (private)
average ACT: 23-27
average SAT: 1060-1230
U.S. News ranking: 124
Student/Faculty Ratio: 13/1

Financial Information:

$39,900 = tuition
$14,498 = room/board
$1,170 = fees
$55,568 = total cost per year
Students Receiving Aid: 98%

Application:

early action: 11/15
early action II: 12/15
regular decision: 2/1, 3/1
common app: yes

Dan Barney Memorial Scholarship

award	one-time, up to $1,000
eligibility	have permanent residence in Indiana, Illinois, Michigan, Minnesota, Kansas, Nebraska, Wisconsin, Missouri, Iowa, Oklahoma, North Dakota, or South Dakota. 3.0+ GPA, 1170+ SAT/ 23+ ACT
application	separate application: https://setonhall.formstack.com/forms/admissions_dan_barney_scholarship
deadline	application and admission application must be received by Jan 15.

Public Tuition Rate Scholarship

award	up to $22,500; renewable up to four years.
eligibility	28+ ACT, 1310+ SAT (CR&M) and in the top 10% of graduating class.
application	no special application required.
deadline	admission application must be received by Dec 15.

University Scholarship

award	$4,000-$20,000, renewable up to four years. Increases incrementally with increasing academic profile.
eligibility	based on academic achievement
application	no special application required.
deadline	admission application must be received by Dec 15.

Total billed cost per year does NOT include travel, books, or pizza money.

D

Southern Methodist University

Dallas, Texas   214-768-2000   www.smu.edu

Basic Profile:

enrollment: 11,739 (private)
average ACT: 28-32
average SAT: 1220-1410
U.S. News ranking: 61
Student/Faculty Ratio: 11/1

Financial Information:

$54,364 = tuition & fees
$16,950 = room/board
$71,314 = total cost per year

Students Receiving Aid: 75%

Application:

early action: 11/1 non-binding
early decision: 1/1, 1/15 binding
regular decision: 1/15
common app: yes

President's Scholar Award

award   full tuition and fees; renewable up to four years; tuition and transportation for semester/year study.
eligibility   academic achievement and leadership
application   no separate application is necessary; all applicants who apply for admission to SMU are considered; finalists will be invited for an on-campus scholarship interview in March.
deadline   all application materials must be received by 1/15

Nancy Ann & Ray L. Hunt Leadership Scholars Program

award $42,000 annually, renewable for four years; tuition and transportation for semester/year study abroad. program; awarded to 20-25 freshmen per year
eligibility   academic merit, extraordinary leadership; top 25% of class, 1270+ SAT (CR&M)/ 28+ ACT
application   letter of recommendation and a separate 2-3 page application essay is required - topic available from Admissions Office; finalists will be invited for an on-campus scholarship interview in March.
deadline   all application materials must be received by 1/15

Other major-specific scholarships available at http://www.smu.edu/Admission/Academics/Honors/MeritScholarships.

St. Louis University

St. Louis, Missouri   800-758-3678   www.slu.edu

Basic Profile:

enrollment: 17,047 (private)
average ACT: 25-31
average SAT: 1090-1340
U.S. News ranking: 94
Student/Faculty Ratio: 9/1

Financial Information:

$43,160 = tuition
$11,146 = room/board
$724 = fees
$55,030 = total billed cost per year
Students Receiving Aid: 98%

Application:

priority decision: 12/1
closing: 8/1
*rolling admission
common app: yes

Presidential Scholarship

award   full tuition; renewable for 4 years; $1,200 towards an "Investigative Learning Experience;" 35 awarded.
eligibility   superior academic achievement, leadership, 3.85+ GPA, 30+ ACT/ 1390+ SAT, on-campus interview.
application   separate application - contact admission counselor, essay, resume, two letters of recommendation.
deadline   application for admission must be received by 12/1 (priority decision)

Martin Luther King, Jr. Scholarship

award $13,000-$24,000/year, number awarded varies each year , contact admission counselor for information.
eligibility   superior academic achievement, leadership, 3.25+ GPA, 23+ ACT/ 1130+ SAT
application   separate application - contact admission counselor, essay, resume, two letters of recommendation.
deadline   application materials must be received by 2/1

Total billed cost per year does NOT include travel, books, or pizza money.

St. Olaf College

Northfield, Minnesota　　　　507-786-2222　　　　www.stolaf.edu

Basic Profile:

enrollment: 3,046 (private)
average ACT: 26-31
average SAT: 1140-1410
U.S. News ranking: 57 (liberal arts)
Student/Faculty Ratio: 12/1

Financial Information:

$47,840 = tuition and fees
$10,850 = room/board
$58,690 = total billed cost per year

Students Receiving Aid: 77%

Application:

early decision I: 11/15
early decision II: 1/8
regular decision: 1/15
common app: yes

St. Olaf College Scholarship Program

award	$10,000-$25,000 per year; renewable for 4 years; up to 100 awarded.
eligibility	exceptional academic performance
application	no additional application, interview during Scholars' Days in March
deadline	early decision deadline, 11/15

Texas Christian University

Fort Worth, Texas　　　　817-257-7000　　　　www.tcu.edu

Basic Profile:

enrollment: 10,304 (private)
average ACT: 25-30
average SAT: 1080-1280
U.S. News ranking: 78
Student/Faculty Ratio: 13/1

Financial Information:

$46,860 = tuition
$13,290 = room/board
$90 = fees
$60,240 = total billed cost per year
Students Receiving Aid: 92%

Application:

early action I: 11/1 non-binding
early action II: 1/1
regular decision: 2/15
common app: yes

Chancellor's Scholarship

award	full tuition for four years
eligibility	4.0 unweighted GPA, 34 ACT score or 1500 SAT score
application	scholarships are not guaranteed regardless of academic marks, application for admission must be received by priority decision date of December 15.
deadline	application for admission must be received by 12/15 (priority decision)

Dean's Scholarship

award	$21,000 renewable for four years
eligibilit	3.87 unweighted GPA, 33 ACT score or 1460 SAT score
application	scholarships are not guaranteed regardless of academic marks, application for admission must be received by priority decision date of December 15.
deadline	application for admission must be received by 12/15 (priority decision)

Faculty Scholarship

award	$18,000 renewable for four years
eligibility	3.75 unweighted GPA, 30 ACT score or 1380 SAT score
application	scholarships are not guaranteed regardless of academic marks, application for admission must be received by priority decision date of December 15.
deadline	application for admission must be received by 12/15 (priority decision)

TCU Scholarship

award	$14,000 renewable for four years
eligibility	3.7 unweighted GPA, 29 ACT score or 1340 SAT score
application	scholarships are not guaranteed regardless of academic marks, application for admission must be received by priority decision date of December 15.
deadline	application for admission must be received by 12/15 (priority decision)

Founder's Scholarship

Award	$10,000 renewable for four years
Eligibility	3.65 unweighted GPA, 28 ACT score or 1320 SAT score
Application	scholarships are not guaranteed regardless of academic marks, application for admission must be received by priority decision date of December 15.

Total billed cost per year does NOT include travel, books, or pizza money.

D

Thomas More College

Crestview Hills, Kentucky   859-344-3332   www.thomasmore.edu

Basic Profile:

enrollment:1,959 (private)
average ACT: 20-24
average SAT: 820-1000
U.S. News ranking: 80 (regional south)
Student/Faculty Ratio: 16/1

Financial Information:

$29,700 = tuition
$8,650 = room/board
$1,500 = fees
$39,850 = total billed cost per year
Students Receiving Aid: 100%

Application:

priority deadline: 3/15
common app: no

James Graham Brown Honors Scholarship

award	full tuition; renewable for 4 years;
eligibility	exceptional academic performance; 3.6+ GPA; 28+ ACT/ 1340+ SAT
application	admissions and scholarship applications must be completed - http://www.thomasmore.edu/PDFs/jgb_app.pdf

Presidential Scholarship

award	$10,000-$15,000; renewable for 4 years;
eligibility	exceptional academic performance; 3.5+ GPA; 26+ ACT/ 1240+ SAT
application	no separate application required

Dean's Scholarship

award	$9,000-$14,000; renewable for 4 years;
eligibility	exceptional academic performance; 3.0+ GPA; 20+ ACT/ 1020+ SAT
application	no separate application required

Trinity University

San Antonio, Texas   800-TRINITY (800-874-6489)   www.trinity.edu

Basic Profile:

enrollment: 2,438 (private)
average ACT: 27-32
average SAT: 1160-1370
U.S. News ranking: 44 (national liberal arts)
Student/Faculty Ratio: 9/1

Financial Information:

$42,976 = tuition and fees
$13,464 = room/board
$56,440 = total billed cost per year

Students Receiving Aid: 98%

Application:

early decision I, II: 11/1 binding, 1/1
early action I, II: 11/1, 1/1
regular decision: 2/1
common app: yes (supplement)

Academic Merit Scholarships

award and eligibility

Scholarship	ACT	SAT	GPA	Award/year
Murchison	32+	1410+	3.5+	$25,000-full tuition
Trustee's	30+	1300-1410	3.5+	$22,000
President's	27+	1220-1290	3.5+	$17,000
Dean's	25-26	1150-1220	3.25+	$12,500
	*each scholarship has a sliding scale			

application	no separate application is required
deadline	admission application must be received no later than 2/1

Total billed cost per year does NOT include travel, books, or pizza money.

Truman State University

Kirksville, Missouri   660-785-4000   www.truman.edu

Basic Profile:
enrollment: 5,898 (public)
average ACT: 27
average SAT: 1280
U.S. News ranking: 8 (regional Midwest)
Student/Faculty Ratio: 16/1

Financial Information:
$14,136 = tuition (non-resident) $7,352 for MO residents
$8,638 = room/board
$654 = fees
$23,428 = total billed cost per year
Students Receiving Aid: 99%

Application:
priority decision: 12/15
regular decision: 4/1
common app: no

Midwest Student Exchange Program
award	reduces tuition to 150% of in-state tuition rate
eligibility	automatically awarded to admitted students from Illinois, Indiana, Kansas, Minnesota, Michigan, Nebraska, North Dakota, or Wisconsin who do not qualify for the Non-Resident Tuition Scholarship.
application	all applicants for admission to Truman State are considered; no separate application is necessary.
deadline	application for admission must be received by 12/1 (must be accepted by 1/10)

General John J. Pershing Scholarship
award	full tuition, room & board, $4,000 for semester abroad; renewable for 4 years; 12 awarded/year.
eligibility	outstanding academic achievement, exceptional leadership, community service; usually top 3% of high school class and top 3% of national ACT / SAT scores.
application	all applicants for admission to Truman State are considered; no separate application is necessary; finalists will be invited for an on-campus scholarship interview
deadline	application for admission must be received by 12/1 (must be accepted by 1/15)

TruMerit Automatic Scholarship
award	$3,000 per year for four years
eligibility	must be a nonresident incoming freshman who meets the minimum requirements, if they do not meet reciprocity requirements; 27 ACT or 1280 SAT and cumulative 3.50 GPA
application	all applicants for admission to Truman State are considered; no separate application is necessary.
deadline	application for admission must be received by 12/1 (must be accepted by 1/15)

TruMerit Automatic Scholarship
award	$2,500 per year for four years
eligibility	must be a nonresident incoming freshman who meets the minimum requirements, if they do not meet reciprocity requirements; 25 ACT or 1200 SAT and cumulative 3.50 GPA
application	all applicants for admission to Truman State are considered; no separate application is necessary.
deadline	application for admission must be received by 12/1 (must be accepted by 1/15)

TruMerit Automatic Scholarship
award	$2,000 per year for four years
eligibility	must be a nonresident incoming freshman who meets the minimum requirements, if they do not meet reciprocity requirements; 23 ACT or 1130 SAT and cumulative 3.50 GPA
application	all applicants for admission to Truman State are considered; no separate application is necessary.
deadline	application for admission must be received by 12/1 (must be accepted by 1/15)

Total billed cost per year does NOT include travel, books, or pizza money.

D

Tulane University

New Orleans, Louisiana   504-865-5000   www.tulane.edu

Basic Profile:

enrollment: 12,485 (private)
average ACT: 29-32
average SAT: 1240-1410
U.S. News ranking: 40
Student/Faculty Ratio: 8/1

Financial Information:

$52,960 = tuition & fees
$14,536 = room/board
$67,496 = total billed cost per year

Students Receiving Aid: 76%

Application:

early action: 11/15 non-binding
early decision: 11/1 binding
regular decision: 1/15

common app: yes

Dean's Honor Scholarships

award	full tuition; renewable for 4 years; awarded to 100 freshmen per year.
eligibility	academic excellence; leadership, extracurricular involvement; top 5% of class.
application	separate application is required http://www.admission.tulane.edu/aid/merit.php#dhs
deadline	both the application for admission and scholarship application must be received by 12/5.

Paul Tulane Award

award	full tuition; renewable for 4 years; awarded to 50 freshmen per year.
eligibility	academic excellence; leadership, extracurricular involvement; top 5% of class.
application	separate application is required http://www.admission.tulane.edu/aid/merit.php#dhs
deadline	both the application for admission and scholarship application must be received by 12/15.

United States Air Force Academy

Colorado Springs, Colorado   www.usafa.af.mil

Basic Profile:

enrollment: 4,237
average ACT: 30
average SAT: 1296
U.S. News ranking: 26 (liberal arts)
Student/Faculty Ratio: 9/1

Financial Information:

$ — = tuition
$ — = room/board
$ — = fees
$ — = total billed cost per year
Students Receiving Aid: 76%

Application:

application checklist on website

The Air Force Academy provides a full ride to each successful applicant worth $415,000. A five year post graduate commitment is required to attend the academy. A monthly stipend is awarded each cadet while enrolled at the academy. Cadets also receive free medical care
Tuition assistance is provided for MA degrees while serving out the five-year commitment
*The application process is rigorous. All steps for successful admission are listed and explained on the Air Force Admissions web page and must be followed to be considered for admission.
Graduates begin military service as an officer in the Air Force and are obligated to serve five years. Tuition assistance is provided by the Air Force for MA programs while serving the five-year commitment

Total billed cost per year does NOT include travel, books, or pizza money.

University of Alabama
Tuscaloosa, Alabama   205-348-6010   www.ua.edu

Basic Profile:
enrollment: 37,908 (public)
average ACT: 27
average SAT: 1080
U.S. News ranking: 110
Student/Faculty Ratio: 23/1

Financial Information:
$30,030 = tuition & fees (non-resident)
$13,402 = room/board
$43,432 = total billed cost per year

Students Receiving Aid: 80%

Application:
early action: none
priority decision: 2/1
regular decision: 3/1

common app: no

Presidential Elite Scholarships
award	full tuition plus $10,000/year; renewable for 4 years; 8-10 offered each year.
eligibility	4.0+ GPA, 36+ ACT/ 1600+ SAT
application	additional scholarship application - available on website
deadline	application for admission must be completed by 12/15 to be considered for all scholarships.

National Alumni Association Crimson Scholarships
award	full tuition plus $3,500/year, $300 book grant; renewable for 4 years.
eligibility	3.8+ GPA, 32+ ACT/ 1490+ SAT, top 2% of class
application	additional scholarship application - available on website
deadline	application for admission must be completed by 12/15 to be considered for all scholarships.

Presidential Scholarship
award	$26,000/year; renewable for 4 years.
eligibility	3.5+ GPA, 32+ ACT/ 1420+ SAT
application	additional scholarship application - available on website
deadline	application for admission must be completed by 12/15 to be considered for all scholarships.

Several other in-state and out-of-state scholarships available at http://scholarships.ua.edu/types/

UA Scholarship
award	$20,000/year; renewable for 4 years.
eligibility	3.5+ GPA, 30-31+ ACT/ 1360-1410+ SAT
application	additional scholarship application - available on website
deadline	application for admission must be completed by 12/15 to be considered for all scholarships.

Foundation in Excellence Scholarship
award	$15,000/year; renewable for 4 years.
eligibility	3.5+ GPA, 29+ ACT/ 1330-1350+ SAT
application	additional scholarship application - available on website
deadline	application for admission must be completed by 12/15 to be considered for all scholarships.

Collegiate Scholarship
award	$8,000/year; renewable for 4 years.
eligibility	3.5+ GPA, 28+ ACT/ 1300-1320+ SAT
application	additional scholarship application - available on website
deadline	application for admission must be completed by 12/15 to be considered for all scholarships.

Capstone Scholarship
award	$6,000/year; renewable for 4 years.
eligibility	3.5+ GPA, 27+ ACT/ 1260-1290+ SAT
application	additional scholarship application - available on website
deadline	application for admission must be completed by 12/15 to be considered for all scholarships.

University of Alaska-Anchorage

Anchorage, Alaska   907-786-1480   www.uaa.alaska.edu

Basic Profile:
enrollment: 16,762 (public)
average ACT: n/a
average SAT: n/a
U.S. News ranking: 76 (regional west)
Student/Faculty Ratio: 12/1

Financial Information:
$22,530 = non-resident tuition (WUE = $9,540)
$11,878 = room/board
$1,046 = fees (WUE = $1,526)
$36,894 = total billed cost per year (WUE = $24,384)
Students Receiving Aid: 81%

Application:
rolling admission

UAA Administrative Scholarship
award   up to $11,000 per year; partial tuition for students accepted into the University Honors College.
eligibility   accepted into a Baccalaureate degree program and 3.2 GPA
application   online scholarship application, letter to Dean of Honors College

University of Arkansas-Fayetteville

Fayetteville, Arkansas   479-575-5346   www.uark.edu

Basic Profile:
enrollment: 27,194
average ACT: 23-28
average SAT: 1020-1240
U.S. News ranking: 133 (national)
Student/Faculty Ratio: 19/1

Financial Information:
$23,422 = tuition (non-resident)
$11,020 = room/board
$1,746 = fees
$36,188 = total billed cost per year
Students Receiving Aid: 81%

Application:
early action: 11/15
priority decision: 11/15
regular: 8/1

scholarship: 11/1

Non-Resident Tuition Award
award $10,600-$13,700
eligibility   minimum 3.3 GPA and 24 ACT or 1160 SAT
application   no additional application
deadline   application deadline

Chancellor's Scholarship, Chancellor's Community Scholarship, and the Silas Hunt Scholarship
award $5,000-$8,000 per year; renewable for 4 years; stipends for research and international travel.
eligibility   awarded to top candidates from the applicant pool
application   online application
deadline   apply and submit transcripts and test scores by 11/1

Honors College Fellowship
award $17,500 per year; renewable for 4 years; 70 awarded per year
eligibility   32 ACT or 1450 SAT and 3.8 high school GPA
application   complete fellowship application
deadline   apply and submit transcripts and test scores by 11/1

University of Connecticut

Storrs, Connecticut   860-486-2000   www.uconn.edu

Basic Profile:
enrollment: 27,721 (public)
average ACT: 26-31
average SAT: 1120-1410
U.S. News ranking: 56
Student/Faculty Ratio: 16/1

Financial Information:
$35,216 = tuition (non-resident)
$12,874 = room/board
$2,882 = fees
$50,972 = total billed cost per year
Students Receiving Aid: 79%

Application:
early action: 1/1 non-binding
regular decision: 1/15
*rolling admission
common app: no

Total billed cost per year does NOT include travel, books, or pizza money.

Academic Excellence Scholarship
award	varies
eligibility	top of graduating class, competitive SAT/ACT score and GPA (determined by Undergraduate Admissions Office.)
application	all applicants who apply for admission to U. Conn. are considered; no separate application is required.
deadline	priority given to students whose admission application is received by 12/1 (early action).

Leadership Scholarship
award	varies
eligibility	commitment to multicultural diversity and leadership, top of graduating class, competitive SAT/ACT score and GPA (determined by Undergraduate Admissions Office.)
application	all applicants who apply for admission to U. Conn. are considered; no separate application is required.
deadline	priority given to students whose admission application is received by 12/1 (early action).

UConn Award
award	varies
eligibility	top of graduating class, competitive SAT/ACT score and GPA (determined by Undergraduate Admissions Office.
application	all applicants who apply for admission to U. Conn. are considered; no separate application is required.
deadline	priority given to students whose admission application is received by 12/1 (early action).

University of Dallas
Irving, Texas   972-721-5000   www.udallas.edu

Basic Profile:
enrollment: 2,387 (private)
average ACT: 27
average SAT: 1260
U.S. News ranking: 13 (regional West)
Student/Faculty Ratio: 11/1

Financial Information:
$37,652 = tuition
$12,400 = room/board
$3,000 = fees
$53,052 = total billed cost per year
Students Receiving Aid: 98%

Application:
early action I: 11/1 non-binding
early action II: 12/1 non-binding
regular decision: 3/1
rolling deadline: 8/1
common app: yes (supplement)

Academic Achievement Award
award	$10,000-$30,000 to full tuition/year; renewable for 4 years; number awarded varies each year. University of Dallas is remarkably generous to National Merit Scholars.
eligibility	based on GPA and test scores—Scholarship Calculator available at http://www.udallas.edu/admissions/calculator.html
application	all applicants to the University of Dallas are considered; no separate application is required.
deadline	application for admission must be received by 1/15 (priority decision).

University of Denver
Denver, Colorado   303-871-2036   www.du.edu

Basic Profile:
enrollment: 11,797 (private)
average ACT: 25-31
average SAT: 1180-1340
U.S. News ranking: 87
Student/Faculty Ratio: 11/1

Financial Information:
$49,392 = tuition
$13,005 = room/board
$1,164 = fees
$63,561 = total billed cost per year
Students Receiving Aid: 85%

Application:
early action: 11/1 5
regular decision: 2/1
common app: yes

Merit-based Awards
award	$9,000-$23,000/year, renewable
eligibility	based on GPA and test scores
application	automatically considered upon application submission.

Total billed cost per year does NOT include travel, books, or pizza money.

D

University of Georgia

Athens, Georgia   706-542-3000   www.uga.edu

Basic Profile:
enrollment: 36,574 (public)
average ACT: 26-30
average SAT: 1400
U.S. News ranking: 54
Student/Faculty Ratio: 18/1

Financial Information (non-resident):
$30,392 = non-resident tuition and fees (GA residents = $11,818)
$10,060 = room/board
$40,452 = total billed cost per yr (GA residents = $21,878)

Students Receiving Aid: 95%

Application:
early action: 10/15 non-binding
regular decision: 1/16
common app: no

UGA Foundation Fellowship
award $12,000/year for in-state students + Zell Miller Scholarship ($9,552), $19,458/year for out-of-state students + Presidential waiver ($18,574), 18-22 scholarships awarded.
eligibility   3.9+ GPA, 32+ ACT/ 1470+ SAT, leadership
application   separate application is required and can be obtained from the Admissions Office
              or online at https://www.admissions.uga.edu/article/foundation-fellowship-part-i.html;
deadline   11/1

Bernard Ramsey Honor Scholarship
award $6,000/year for in-state students + Zell Miller Scholarship ($9,552), $9,880/year for out-of-state students + Presidential waiver ($18,574), 25-30 scholarships awarded.
eligibility   3.9+ GPA, 32+ ACT/ 1470+ SAT, leadership
application   only studetns who have applied for the Foundation Fellowship will be considered, separate application is required and can be obtained from the Admissions Office or online at https://www.admissions.uga.edu/article/foundation-fellowship-part-i.html;
deadline   11/1

Presidential Leadership Scholarship
award $3,000/year, renewable; out-of-state fees waiver; 40-45 scholarships awarded.
eligibility   academic merit, demonstrated leadership, extracurricular involvement, commitment to service.
application   all applicants to the University of Georgia are considered; no separate application is required.
deadline   11/1

Classic Scholars
award   waiver of out-of-state tuition and fees equal to half the differential between in-state and out-of-state costs.
eligibility   non-Georgia residents, 29+ ACT/ 1380+ SAT
application   all applicants to the University of Georgia are considered; no separate application is required.
deadline   12/15

Charter Scholarship
award   waiver of out-of-state tuition, additional $1,500 yearly stipend; renewable for 4 years; awarded to approximately 225-275 freshmen per year.
eligibility   academic merit, demonstrated leadership, extracurricular involvement, commitment to service.
application   all applicants to the University of Georgia are considered; no separate application is required.
deadline   12/15

University of Kansas

Lawrence, Kansas   785-864-2700   www.ku.edu

Basic Profile:
enrollment: 27,565 (public)
average ACT: 22-28
average SAT: n/a
U.S. News ranking: 115
Student/Faculty Ratio: 17/1

Financial Information:
$25,586 = non-resident tuition (KS residents = $9,818)
$9,152 = room/board
$1,006 = fees
$35,744 = total billed cost per year (KS residents = $19,976)
Students Receiving Aid: 83%

Application:
priority decision: 11/1 non-binding
regular decision: 2/1
*rolling admission
common app: no

Total billed cost per year does NOT include travel, books, or pizza money.

KU Excellence
award	$16,084/year; renewable for 4 years;
eligibility	academic merit; 3.5+ GPA, 30+ ACT/ 1390+ SAT
application	all applicants to the University of Kansas are considered; no separate application is required.
deadline	application for admission must be received by 11/1

KU Distinction
award	$13,580/year; renewable for 4 years;
eligibility	academic merit; 3.5+ GPA, 28+ ACT/ 1310+ SAT
application	all applicants to the University of Kansas are considered; no separate application is required.
deadline	application for admission must be received by 11/1

KU Achievement
award	$11,077/year; renewable for 4 years;
eligibility	academic merit; 3.75+ GPA, 24+ ACT/ 1160+ SAT
application	all applicants to the University of Kansas are considered; no separate application is required.
deadline	application for admission must be received by 11/1

University of Kentucky
Lexington, Kentucky   859-257-9000   www.uky.edu

Basic Profile:
enrollment: 29,781 (public)
average ACT: 22-28
average SAT: 1010-1250
U.S. News ranking: 133
Student/Faculty Ratio: 17/1

Financial Information:
$27,856 = non-resident tuition and fees (KY residents = $11,772)
$11,550 = room/board
$39,406 = total billed cost per year (KY residents = $23,322)

Students Receiving Aid: 94%

Application:
priority decision: 2/1
common app: yes

Otis A. Singletary Scholarship
award	full tuition, room & board, $10,000 housing stipend, renewable for four years.
eligibility	33+ ACT/ 1490+ SAT, 3.8+ GPA
application	no separate application is required, competitive academic scholarship section included on admission app.
deadline	application for admission must be received by 1/15

Presidential Scholarship
award	full tuition, renewable for four years
eligibility	31+ ACT/ 1420+ SAT, 3.5+ GPA
application	no separate application is required, competitive academic scholarship section included on admission app.
deadline	application for admission must be received by 1/15

Patterson Scholarship
award	full tuition, room & board, $10,000 housing stipend, renewable for four years.
eligibility	National Merit and Achievement Finalists, UK listed as #1 college choice.
application	no separate application is required
deadline	application for admission must be received by 2/1

Bluegrass Spirit Scholarship
award	$8,000, renewable for four years
eligibility	25 ACT or 1200 SAT and 3.0 unweighted GPA
application	no separate application is required, awarded automatically with acceptance.
deadline	application for admission must be received by 2/1

Total billed cost per year does NOT include travel, books, or pizza money.

University of Maine

Orono, Maine   207-581-1865   www.umaine.edu

Basic Profile:

enrollment: 11,219 (public)
average ACT: 21-26
average SAT: 960-1210
U.S. News ranking: 181
Student/Faculty Ratio: 16/1

Financial Information:

$30,970 = non-resident tuition and fees (ME residents = $11,170)
$10,418 = room/board
$41,388 = total billed cost per yr (ME residents = $21,588)

Students Receiving Aid: 95%

Application:

early action: 12/15
*rolling admission
common app: yes (supplement)

UMaine Flagship Match Program

This program that guarantees academically qualified, first-year students from New Hampshire, Massachusetts, Connecticut, Vermont, New Jersey, Pennsylvania, Illinois, Rhode Island, and California will pay the same tuition and fee rate as their home state's flagship institution.

Tier 1

award	$12,215 - $16,490
eligibility	minimum 3.0 GPA and 22+ ACT or 1120+ SAT. Residents of states outside of the Flagship Match program receive the flat scholarship amount of $13,200.
application	no separate application is required, awarded automatically with acceptance.
deadline	application for admission must be received by 2/1

Tier 2

award	$9,000
eligibility	2.9 or below GPA and 21 or below ACT or 1120 or below SAT
application	no separate application is required, awarded automatically with acceptance.
deadline	application for admission must be received by 2/1

University of Miami

Coral Gables, Florida   305-284-2211   www.miami.edu

Basic Profile:

enrollment: 16,825 (private)
average ACT: 28-32
average SAT: 1200-1390
U.S. News ranking: 46
Student/Faculty Ratio: 12/1

Financial Information:

$48,720 = tuition
$14,108 = room/board
$1,506 = fees
$64,334 = total billed cost per year
Students Receiving Aid: 85%

Application:

early action: 11/1 non-binding
early decision: 11/1 binding
regular decision: 1/1

common app: yes (supplement)

Stamps Family Foundation Scholarships

award	full cost of attendance plus stipend; renewable for 4 years; number awarded varies each year.
eligibility	4.0 GPA, top 5% of class, 34+ ACT/ 1500+ SAT
application	all applicants to the University of Miami are considered; no separate application is required.
deadline	application for admission must be submitted by 11/1.

Isaac Bashevis Singer Scholarships

award	full tuition; renewable for 4 years; awarded to approximately 20 freshmen per year.
eligibility	superior academic achievement, leadership, activities, service; top applicants in applicant pool.
application	all applicants to the University of Miami are considered; no separate application is required.
deadline	application for admission must be submitted by 11/1 or 1/1

Ronald A. Hammond Scholarships

award	full tuition; renewable for 4 years; approx. 30 awarded each year.
eligibility	3.3+ GPA, 28+ ACT/ 1250+ SAT
application	http://admissions.miami.edu/undergraduate/financial-aid/scholarships/ronald-a-hammond-scholarship/index.html
deadline	application for admission must be submitted by 11/1

Total billed cost per year does NOT include travel, books, or pizza money.

Presidents Scholarships

award	$18,000-$28,000/year; renewable for 4 years; number awarded varies each year.
eligibility	high grades and test scores
application	all applicants to the University of Miami are considered; no separate application is required.
deadline	application for admission must be submitted by 11/1 or 1/1

University of Mississippi

Oxford, Mississippi   662-915-7211   www.olemiss.edu

Basic Profile:

enrollment: 23,610 (public)
average ACT: 25
average SAT: 990-1200
U.S. News ranking: 145
Student/Faculty Ratio: 19/1

Financial Information:

$24,504 = non-resident tuition (MS residents = $8,550)
$10,696 = room/board
$100 = fees
$35,300 = total billed cost per yr (MS residents = $19,346)
Students Receiving Aid: 86%

Application:

rolling admission
common app: no

Academic Excellence Scholarships

a 3.0 GPA and a 32 ACT = $23k scholarship or full tuition paid (lower ACT scores reap lower, but still generous awards)

Stamps Scholarship

award	full cost of attendance plus $12,000 stipend; renewable for 4 years; number awarded varies each year.
eligibility	entering freshmen with exceptional academic and leadership records.
application	apply for admission to the University of Mississippi and complete online Special Programs & Scholarship Application.
deadline	1/5

Doris Raymond Honors Scholarship

award	$32,000 ($8,000 per year).
eligibility	entering freshmen selected to the Honors College.
application	apply for admission to the University of Mississippi and complete online Special Programs & Scholarship Application.
deadline	1/5

Harold Parker Memorial Scholarship

award	$32,000 ($8,000 per year).
eligibility	entering freshmen selected to the Honors College.
application	apply for admission to the University of Mississippi and complete online Special Programs & Scholarship Application.
deadline	1/5

Academic Excellence Scholarships

award	from $1,500 - $24,500 per year; may be renewed for up to 8 semesters.
eligibility	from 25 ACT+ and SAT 1130+; high school GPA 3.0+.
application	apply for admission to the University of Mississippi and complete online Special Programs & Scholarship Application.
deadline	1/5

Total billed cost per year does NOT include travel, books, or pizza money.

D

University of New Hampshire

Durham, New Hampshire   603-862-1360   www.unh.edu

Basic Profile:

enrollment: 15,351 (public)
average ACT: 22-27
average SAT: 1000-1210
U.S. News ranking: 103
Student/Faculty Ratio: 18/1

Financial Information:

$33,879 = non-resident tuition and fees (NH residents = $18,499)
$11,580 = room/board
$45,459 = total billed cost per yr (NH residents = $30,079)

Students Receiving Aid: 86%

Application:

early action: 11/15 non-binding
regular decision: 2/1
common app: yes (supplement)

Presidential Scholarship

award $7,000/year for in-state students, $10,000/year for out-of-state students; renewable for 4 years.
eligibility   academic achievement; top 10% of class, 29+ ACT/ 1390+ SAT
application   all applicants who apply for admission to UNH are considered; no separate application is required.
deadline   application for admission must be submitted by 12/1 (early action) or 2/1 (regular decision).

Dean's Scholarship

award $4,000/year for in-state students, $6,000/year for out-of-state students; renewable for 4 years.
eligibility   academic achievement; top 15% of class, 26+ ACT/ 1260+ SAT
application   all applicants who apply for admission to UNH are considered; no separate application is required.
deadline   application for admission must be submitted by 12/1 (early action) or 2/1 (regular decision).

Director's Scholarship

award $2,000/year for in-state students, $4,000/year for out-of-state students; renewable for 4 years.
eligibility   academic achievement; top 30% of class, 25+ ACT/ 1200+ SAT
application   all applicants who apply for admission to UNH are considered; no separate application is required.
deadline   application for admission must be submitted by 12/1 (early action) or 2/1 (regular decision).

University of North Carolina at Chapel Hill

Chapel Hill, North Carolina   919-966-2211   www.unc.edu

Basic Profile:

enrollment: 29,469 (public)
average ACT: 28-33
average SAT: 1270-1450
U.S. News ranking: 30
Student/Faculty Ratio: 13/1

Financial Information:

$34,938 = non-resident tuition and fees (NC residents = $8,910)
$11,190 = room/board
$46,128 = total billed cost per yr (NC residents = $20,100)

Students Receiving Aid: 66%

Application:

early notification: 11/1
regular notification: 3/1
common app: no

Robertson Scholars Program

award   full tuition, room and board, computer stipend; renewable for 4 years; awarded to
               approximately 18 freshmen per year; domestic and international summer experiences.
eligibility   academic distinction and intellectual curiosity, purposeful leadership, character and integrity.
application   separate application required found here: https://robertsonscholars.org/apply/high-school/; top
               applicants will be invited for an on-campus scholarship interview in early March.
deadline   11/15

Total billed cost per year does NOT include travel, books, or pizza money.

University of Notre Dame

Notre Dame, Indiana   574-631-5000   www.nd.edu

Basic Profile:

enrollment: 12,393 (private)
average ACT: 32-34
average SAT: 1350-1530
U.S. News ranking: 18
Student/Faculty Ratio: 10/1

Financial Information:

$53,391 = tuition and fees
$15,410 = room/board
$68,801 = total billed cost per year

Students Receiving Aid: 76%

Application:

regular decision: 1/1 binding
early action: 11/1
common app: yes

Stamps Scholars Program

award	full tuition and fees plus $12,000 enrichment fund; renewable for 4 years; five awarded each year.
eligibility	leadership, perseverance, scholarship, service, and innovation.
application	no separate application required
deadline	1/1

Hesburgh Yusko Scholars Program

award	$25,000/year, renewable for 4 years; four fully funded Summer Enrichment Experiences.
eligibility	counselor nomination, two letters of recommendation; academic accomplishment, moral character,
application	supplemental application found at http://hesburgh-yusko.nd.edu/applying-to-the-program/
deadline	11/15

Suzanna and Walter Scott Notre Dame Scholars Program

award	$25,000/year; renewable for 4 years; five awarded each year
eligibility	academic achievement, leadership, committed to service; top 3% of class
application	no separate application required
deadline	1/1

University of Oklahoma

Norman, Oklahoma   405-325-0311   www.ou.edu

Basic Profile:

enrollment: 31,176
average ACT: 26
average SAT: 1150-1380
U.S. News ranking: 97
Student/Faculty Ratio: 17/1

Financial Information:

$26,693 = non-resident tuition and fees (OK residents = $11,312)
$10,588 = room/board
$37,281 = total billed cost per yr (OK residents = $21,900)

Students Receiving Aid: 87%

Application:

scholarships: 2/1

Award of Excellence

award	$9,000 renewable for four years
eligibility	31 ACT or 1420 SAT and 3.75 GPA or top 10% of class rank
deadline	2/1

Distinguished Scholar

award	$8,000 renewable for four years
eligibility	29-30 ACT or 1350-1410 SAT and 3.75 GPA or top 10% of class rank
deadline	2/1

University Scholarship

award	$7,000 renewable for four years
eligibility	28 ACT or 1310 SAT and 3.5 GPA or top 10% of class rank
deadline	2/1

Academic Achievements

award	$6,000 renewable for four years
eligibility	26-27 ACT or 1240-1300 SAT and 3.5 GPA
deadline	2/1

Total billed cost per year does NOT include travel, books, or pizza money.

D

Non-Resident Merit Award

award	$4,000 renewable for four years
eligibility	24-25 ACT or 1160-1230 SAT and 3.5 GPA
deadline	2/1

Non-Resident Honor Award

award	$4,000 renewable for four years
eligibility	26 ACT or 1240 SAT and 3.25-3.49 GPA
deadline	2/1

University of the Pacific

Stockton, California   209-946-2285   www.pacific.edu

Basic Profile:

enrollment: 6,281 (private)
average ACT: 22-29
average SAT: 1010-1280
U.S. News ranking: 110
Student/Faculty Ratio: 12/1

Financial Information:

$47,480 = tuition
$13,082 = room/board
$684 = fees
$61,246 = total billed cost per year
Students Receiving Aid: 94%

Application:

early action: 11/15 non-binding
regular decision: 1/15
*rolling admission
common app: yes

Powell Scholars Program

award	$40,000/year; renewable for 4 years; stipends for research and international travel
eligibility	3.7+ GPA, 30+ ACT/ 1350+ SAT, leadership skills; on-campus interview
application	http://www.pacific.edu/About-Pacific/AdministrationOffices/Office-of-Financial-Aid/Types-of-Financial-Aid/Scholarships/Powell/Powell-Scholars-Application-Form.html
deadline	12/1

Regent's Scholarship

award	$20,000/year; renewable for 4 years; number awarded varies each year
eligibility	typical profile: 3.87 GPA, 1250 SAT/ 28 ACT
application	no separate application required
deadline	12/1

President's Scholarship

award	$16,000/year; renewable for 4 years; number awarded varies each year
eligibility	typical profile: 3.5 GPA, 1200 SAT/ 26 ACT
application	no separate application required
deadline	12/1

University of Rhode Island

Kingston, Rhode Island   401-874-1000   www.uri.edu

Basic Profile:

enrollment: 17,834 (public)
average ACT: 25
average SAT: 1182-1600
U.S. News ranking: 156
Student/Faculty Ratio: 17/1

Financial Information:

$30,862 = non-resident tuition & fees (RI residents = $14,138)
$12,528 = room/board
$43,390 = total billed cost per yr (RI residents = $26,666)

Students Receiving Aid: 93%

Application:

early action: 12/1 non-binding
regular decision: 2/1
*rolling admission
common app: no

Merit Scholarships

award	up to full tuition; renewable for 4 years; number awarded varies each year
eligibility	3.2+ GPA, 23+ ACT/ 1130+ SAT
application	all applicants who apply for admission to URI are considered; no separate application is required.
deadline	admission application must be submitted by 12/1 (early action) or 2/1 (regular decision)
notes	Nov. SAT and Oct. ACT are latest test scores considered. Committee consider single highest score for each section.

Total billed cost per year does NOT include travel, books, or pizza money.

University of Rochester

Rochester, New York   888-822-2256   www.rochester.edu

Basic Profile:

enrollment: 11,209 (private)
average ACT: 29-33
average SAT: 1280-1480
U.S. News ranking: 34
Student/Faculty Ratio: 10/1

Financial Information:

$52,974 = tuition
$15,938 = room/board
$952 = fees
$69,864 = total billed cost per year
Students Receiving Aid: 87%

Application:

early decision: 11/1 binding
regular decision: 1/5
common app: yes (supplement)

Rochester Merit Awards

award   range from $2,000 per year to full tuition.
eligibility   first-year and transfer students who demonstrate outstanding academic achievement and potential, regardless of financial circumstances.
application   all admitted undergraduate applicants are considered for merit scholarships.
deadline   3/15

University of the South (Sewanee)

Sewanee, Tennessee   931-598-1000   www.sewanee.edu

Basic Profile:

enrollment: 1,815 (private)
average ACT: 26-30
average SAT: 1150-1360
U.S. News ranking: 41 (liberal arts)
Student/Faculty Ratio: 10/1

Financial Information:

$44,848 = tuition
$12,880 = room/board
$272 = fees
$58,000 = total billed cost per yr (guaranteed for four years)
Students Receiving Aid: 85%

Application:

early decision I: 11/15 binding
early decision II: 1/15 binding
regular decision: 2/1
common app: yes (supplement)

Benedict Scholars

award   full tuition & fees, room & board; renewable for 4 years; awarded to 2 freshmen per year.
eligibility   academic excellence, intellectual promise, leadership ability, potential for service.
application   no separate application required
deadline   both the application for admission and scholarship application must be submitted by 11/15 or 12/1.

Wilkins Scholars

award $25,000/year; renewable for 4 years; awarded to approximately 100 freshmen per year.
eligibility   academic excellence, intellectual promise, leadership ability, potential for service.
application   no separate application required
deadline   both the application for admission and scholarship application must be submitted by 11/15 or 12/1.

Quintard, Fairbanks, and Otey Awards

award $5,000-$12,000/year; renewable for 4 years; number awarded varies.
eligibility   academic excellence, intellectual promise, leadership ability, potential for service.
application   no separate application required
deadline   both the application for admission and scholarship application must be submitted by 11/15 or 12/1.

Total billed cost per year does NOT include travel, books, or pizza money.

D

University of South Dakota

Vermillion, South Dakota   213-740-2311   www.usd.edu

877-269-6837

Basic Profile:

enrollment: 10,038 (public)
average ACT: 20-25
average SAT: 900-1130
U.S. News ranking: 223
Student/Faculty Ratio: 18/1

Financial Information:

$12,424 = non-resident tuition and fees (SD & IA = $9,060; MN = $9,388)
$7,846 = room/board
$20,270 = total billed cost per yr (SD & IA residents = $16,906; MN residents = $17,234)
USD is cheaper for non-residents than many public universities are for their actual in-state residents
Students Receiving Aid: 93%

Application:

early decision: n/a
regular decision: rolling
common app: no

George S. Mickelson Scholarship

award $10,000 per year; renewable for 4 years
eligibility   27+ ACT/ 1210+ SAT; on-campus interview
application   Academic Scholarship Application—generally available in October.
deadline   12/1

Coyote Commitment Scholarship

award   up to $3,500 per year; renewable for 4 years
eligibility   all first-time freshmen students
application   no separate application required
deadline   3/15

University of Southern California

Los Angeles, California   213-740-2311   www.usc.edu

Basic Profile:

enrollment: 43,871 (private)
average ACT: 30-33
average SAT: 1320-1480
U.S. News ranking: 21
Student/Faculty Ratio: 8/1

Financial Information:

$55,320 = tuition
$15,395 = room/board
$1,225 = fees
$71,940 = total billed cost per year
Students Receiving Aid: 61%

Application:

scholarship consideration: 12/1
regular decision: 1/15
common app: yes

Mork Family Scholarship

award   full tuition and $5,000 stipend; renewable for 4 years; awarded to 10 freshmen per year.
eligibility   academic excellence, SAT/ACT scores; top 1-2% of applicant pool.
application   all applicants who apply for admission to USC are considered; no separate application is required; finalists invited for an
               on-campus scholarship interview.
deadline   application for admission must be submitted by 12/1 (priority decision)

Stamps Leadership Scholarship

award   full tuition, $5,000 enrichment fund; renewable for 4 years; awarded to 5 freshmen per year.
eligibility   academic excellence, SAT/ACT scores; top 1-2% of applicant pool.
application   all applicants who apply for admission to USC are considered; no separate application is required; finalists invited for an
on-campus scholarship interview.
deadline   application for admission must be submitted by 12/1 (priority decision)

Trustee Scholarship

award   full tuition; renewable for 4 years; awarded to 100 freshmen per year.
eligibility   academic excellence
application   all applicants who apply for admission to USC are considered; no separate application is required.
deadline   application for admission must be submitted by 12/1 (priority decision)

Presidential Scholarship

award   1/2 tuition; renewable for 4 years; awarded to 200 freshmen per year
eligibility   academic excellence
application   all applicants who apply for admission to USC are considered; no separate application is required.
deadline   application for admission must be submitted by 12/1 (priority decision)

Total billed cost per year does NOT include travel, books, or pizza money.

University of Utah

Salt Lake City, Utah   801-581-8761   www.utah.edu

Basic Profile:
enrollment: 31,860 (public)
average ACT: 22-29
average SAT: 1140-1330
U.S. News ranking: 110
Student/Faculty Ratio: 16/1

Financial Information:
$26,298 = non-resident tuition and fees (UT resident = $8,382)
$10,314 = room/board
$36,612 = total billed cost per yr (UT residents = $18,696)

Students Receiving Aid: 78%

Application:
priority decision: 12/1
application deadline: 4/1
*rolling admission
common app: no

Non-Resident President's Scholarship
award	full tuition and fees, $750 stipend; renewable for 4 years.
eligibility	academic achievement, leadership abilities, activity involvement, personal accomplishments.
application	no separate application
deadline	both the application for admission and scholarship application must be submitted by 12/1.

Academic Excellence Scholarship
award:	full tuition renewable for a maximum of eight semesters provided students maintain 3.6 cumulative GPA
eligibility:	non-resident status, based on evaluation of GPA and ACT/SAT scores
application	no separate application required
deadline	12/1

Freshman Academic Achievement Award for Non-Residents
Award (non-renewable)	GPA	ACT	SAT
$6,000	3.0	26-27	1240-1300
$8,000	3.0	28-29	1310-1380
$10,000	3.0	30-32	1390-1480
$12,000	3.0	33-36	1490-1600
eligibility	non-resident, all states		
application	no separate application		
deadline	both the application for admission and scholarship application must be submitted by 12/1.		

University of Wisconsin-Platteville

Platteville, Wisconsin   608-342-1125   www.uwplatt.edu

Basic Profile:
enrollment: 8,945 (public)
average ACT: 22
average SAT: 1110
U.S. News ranking:
Student/Faculty Ratio: 22/1

Financial Information:
$15,393 = non-resident tuition and fees (WI residents = $7,543; MN=$8,423; tri-state = $12,243)
$7,070 = room/board
$22,463 = total billed cost per year (WI = $14,613; MN = $15,493; tri-state = $19,313)
94 (regional midwest)
Students Receiving Aid: 86%

Application:
rolling admission

Chancellor Scholarship
award	up to the cost of tuition and fees; renewable for 4 years;
eligibility	highly competitive scholarship program with a limited number of entering freshman recipients annually. Selected based upon demonstrated leadership in their school and community.
application	no separate application
deadline	12/31

University of Wyoming

Laramie, Wyoming   307-766-1121   www.uwyo.edu

Basic Profile:

enrollment: 12,648 (public)
average ACT: 21
average SAT: 980
U.S. News ranking: 181
Student/Faculty Ratio: 14/1

Financial Information:

$16,110 = non-resident tuition (WY residents =$4,020)
$10,320 = room/board
$1,560 = fees
$27,990 = total billed cost per yr (WY residents = $15,900)
Students Receiving Aid: 94%

Application:

early decision I: 11/1 binding
early decision II: 1/1 binding
regular decision: 1/1
common app: yes (supplement)

Rocky Mountain Scholars Award

award	$3,000 for 3.0 GPA & 21 ACT, renewable
	$6,000 for 3.0 GPA & 26 ACT, renewable
	$10,000 for 3.7 GPA & 27 ACT, renewable
	(see entire scholarship grid at uwyo.edu)
application	no separate application
deadline	confirmed by 5/1

Honors College Scholarship

award	$1,000 to $4,000; renewable for 4 years
eligibility	maintain a 3.25 GPA
application	honors application and essay
deadline	applications must be received by 2/1

Vanderbilt University

Nashville, Tennessee   615-322-7311   www.vanderbilt.edu

Basic Profile:

enrollment: 12,587 (private)
average ACT: 32-35
average SAT: 1430-1590
U.S. News ranking: 14
Student/Faculty Ratio: 8/1

Financial Information:

$46,500 = tuition
$15,584 = room/board
$2,029 = fees
$64,113 = total billed cost per year
Students Receiving Aid: 69%

Application:

early decision I: 11/1 binding
early decision II: 1/6 binding
regular decision: 1/6
common app: yes (supplement)

Ingram Scholarship

award	full tuition; summer stipends; renewable for 4 years
eligibility	academic merit, leadership, community service, on-campus interview, top 1% of applicants.
application	separate application is required: http://www.vanderbilt.edu/scholarships/application.php
deadline	both the application for admission and scholarship application must be submitted by 12/1.

Cornelius Vanderbilt Scholarship Program

award	full tuition; renewable for 4 years; one summer stipend.
eligibility	academic merit, leadership, community service, on-campus interview, top 1% of applicants.
application	separate application is required: http://www.vanderbilt.edu/scholarships/application.php
deadline	both the application for admission and scholarship application must be submitted by 12/15.

Chancellor's Scholars

award	up to full tuition; renewable for 4 years; one summer stipend
eligibility	exceptional academic accomplishments and intellectual promise, leadership; top 1% of applicants.
application	separate application is required: http://www.vanderbilt.edu/scholarships/application.php
deadline	application for admission must be submitted by 12/15

Several other specialty scholarships available at http://www.vanderbilt.edu/scholarships/additional.php

Total billed cost per year does NOT include travel, books, or pizza money.

Wabash College

Crawfordsville, Indiana   765-361-6100   www.wabash.edu

Basic Profile:

enrollment: 843 (men only)
average ACT: 22-28
average SAT: 1040-1250
U.S. News ranking: 65 (liberal arts)
Student/Faculty Ratio: 9/1

Financial Information:

$42,800 = tuition
$9,800 = room/board
$850 = fees
$53,450 = total billed cost per year
Students Receiving Aid: 99%

Application:

early decision: 10/15 binding
early action: 11/1 non-binding
regular decision: 1/15
*rolling admission
common app: yes

Top Ten Scholarships

award	$17,500/year; renewable for 4 years
eligibility	3.25+ GPA, top 10% of class, participate in the Top Ten Program in February
application	no separate application required

Top Twenty Scholarships

award	$15,000/year; renewable for 4 years
eligibility	top 20% of class, make a campus visit by mid-February
application	no separate application required

Wabash College Lilly Awards

award	tuition, fees, room & board; renewable for 4 years
eligibility	character, creativity; on-campus interview; at least one: 3.5+ GPA, top 20% of class, 25+ ACT/ 1720+ SAT
application	two recommendations, Lilly Award application found at http://www.wabash.edu/admissions/finances/lilly
deadline	applications due by 3/1, campus visit completed by 3/24.

Honor Scholarships

award	up to $40,000 per year; renewable for 4 years
eligibility	high performance on written application exams given at Wabash in March
application	all applicants who complete written scholarship exams are considered; no separate application is required.
deadline	application for admission must be submitted by 3/7; exams must be completed on campus in March.

Wake Forest University

Winston-Salem, North Carolina   336-758-5201   www.wfu.edu

Basic Profile:

enrollment: 7,968 (private)
average ACT: 27-31
average SAT: 1240-1400
U.S. News ranking: 27
Student/Faculty Ratio: 10/1

Financial Information:

$52,348 = tuition and fees
$12,657 = room/board
$65,005 = total billed cost per year

Students Receiving Aid: 48%

Application:

early decision: 11/15 binding
regular decision: 1/1
common app: yes (supplement)

Nancy Susan Reynolds Scholarship

award	full tuition, room & board, $3,400+ stipend; renewable for 4 years; up to 6 freshmen per year.
eligibility	excellent academic achievement, leadership abilities, activity involvement, personal accomplishments;
average rank:	top 1%, as well as holding leadership positions in the community.
application	no separate application; finalists invited for an on-campus scholarship interview in March.
deadline	both the application for admission and scholarship application must be submitted by 1/7.

Stamps Scholarship

award	full tuition, room & board, fees, $3,400+ stipend; renewable for 4 years; up to 6 freshmen per year.
eligibility	excellent academic achievement, leadership abilities, activity involvement, personal accomplishments;
average rank:	top 1%, as well as holding leadership positions in the community.
application	no separate application; finalists invited for an on-campus scholarship interview in March.
deadline	both the application for admission and scholarship application must be submitted by 1/7.

Guy T. Carswell Scholarship

award	full tuition, room and board, and $3,400+ stipend; renewable for 4 years; up to 6 awarded/year.
eligibility	outstanding academic promise, leadership, and talent.
application	no separate application; finalists invited for an on-campus scholarship interview.
deadline	both the application for admission and scholarship application must be submitted by 1/7.

Joseph G. Gordon Scholarship

award	full tuition, room and board, and $3,400+ stipend; renewable for 4 years; up to 7 awarded/year.
eligibility	outstanding academic promise, leadership, and talent; average rank: top 1%, average SAT: 1500+
application	no separate application; finalists invited for an on-campus scholarship interview.
deadline	both the application for admission and scholarship application must be submitted by 1/7.

Graylyn Scholarship

award	full tuition, fees, room & board, $3,400 stipend; renewable for 4 years; awarded to 1 freshman per year.
eligibility	academic excellence and leadership, average rank: top 1%, average SAT: 1500+.
application	no separate application; finalists invited for an on-campus scholarship interview in March.
deadline	both the application for admission and scholarship application must be submitted by 1/7.

Washburn University

Topeka, Kansas   785-670-1010   www.washburn.edu

Basic Profile:

enrollment: 6,636
average ACT: 22
average SAT: n/a
U.S. News ranking: 93 (regional midwest)
Student/Faculty Ratio: 12/1

Financial Information (non-residents):

$19,830 = tuition (KS residents = $8,760)
$8,555 = room/board
$55 = fees
$28,440 = total billed cost per yr (KS residents = $17,370)
Students Receiving Aid: 94%

Application:

priority decision: 2/15
application deadline: 8/1
* rolling admission
common app: no

Academic Merit Scholarships

award & eligibility   renewable for four years

ACT	GPA 3.0-3.20	3.21-3.40	3.41-3.60	3.61-3.80	3.81-4.0
21-22	$500	$750	$1,000	$1,250	$1,500
23-24	$750	$1,000	$1,250	$1,500	$2,000
25-26	$1000	$1,250	$1,500	$2,000	$2,500
27-28	$1250	$1,500	$2,000	$2,500	$3,000
29-30	$1500	$2,000	$2,500	$3,000	$3,500
31-32	$2000	$2,500	$3,000	$3,500	$4,000
33-34	$2500	$3,000	$3,500	$4,000	$4,500
35-36	$3000	$3,500	$4,000	$4,500	$5,000

application	no separate application
deadline	2/15

Several other specialized scholarships available at http://washburn.edu/admissions/paying-for-college/scholarship.html

Washington University in St. Louis

St. Louis, Missouri   314-935-6000   www.wustl.edu

Basic Profile:

enrollment: 15,032 (private)
average ACT: 32-24
average SAT: 1400-1550
U.S. News ranking: 18
Student/Faculty Ratio: 8/1

Financial Information:

$53,399 = tuition and fees
$16,440 = room/board
$69,839 = total billed cost per year

Students Receiving Aid: 54%

Application:

early decision I: 11/15 binding
regular decision: 1/15
common app: yes (supplement)

John B. Ervin Scholars Program

award	up to full tuition, $2,500 annual stipend; renewable for 4 years; number awarded varies each year.
eligibility	exceptional academic achievements & leadership abilities; commitment to service & diversity.
application	essay, letter of recommendation, finalists will be invited for an on-campus scholarship interview; separate application is required: http://admissions.wustl.edu/SiteCollectionDocuments/FL14_Scholarship_Application.pdf
deadline	1/5

Annika Rodriguez Scholars Program

award	up to full tuition, $2,500 annual stipend; renewable for 4 years; number awarded varies each year.
eligibility	exceptional academic achievements & leadership abilities; commitment to service & diversity.
application	essay, finalists will be invited for an on-campus scholarship interview; separate application is required: http://admissions.wustl.edu/SiteCollectionDocuments/FL14_Scholarship_Application.pdf
deadline	1/5

Danforth Scholars Program

award	up to full tuition; renewable for 4 years; up to four full-tuition scholarships awarded each year.
eligibility	exceptional academic achievements & leadership abilities; commitment to service & diversity.
application	nomination required, interview weekend, essay.
deadline	1/5

Several other specialized scholarships available at:
http://admissions.wustl.edu/scholarships-financial-aid/Freshman-Academic-Scholarship-Fellowship-Programs/Pages/default.aspx

Washington & Lee University

Lexington, Virginia   540-458-8710   www.wlu.edu

Basic Profile:

enrollment: 2,172 (private)
average ACT: 30-33
average SAT: 1310-1470
U.S. News ranking: 10 (liberal arts)
Student/Faculty Ratio: 8/1
The W&L Promise—free tuition to any undergraduate student from a family income below $75,000.

Financial Information:

$51,420 = tuition
$13,925 = room/board
$1,035 = fees
$66,380 = total billed cost per year
Students Receiving Aid: 63%

Application:

early decision I: 11/1 binding
early decision II: 1/1 binding
regular decision: 1/1

common app: yes (supplement)

Johnson Scholarship Program

award	full tuition, room & board; renewable for 4 years; approx. $7,000 stipend, awarded to 10% of incoming class.
eligibility	exceptional academic performance; unusual promise for leadership and service.
application	W&L's writing supplement, essay, SAT or ACT with Writing, three recommendations, interview recommended
deadline	12/1
notes	Applying for the Johnson Scholarship Program also places a student under consideration for several other merit-based scholarships that award up to full tuition. For details, see http://www.wlu.edu/johnson-program/the-johnson-scholarship/other-scholarship-opportunities

Westmont College

Santa Barbara, California   805-565-6200   www.westmont.edu

Basic Profile:

enrollment: 1,298 (private)
average ACT: 26
average SAT: 1200
U.S. News ranking: 96 (liberal arts)
Student/Faculty Ratio: 11/1

Financial Information:

$44,130 = tuition
$14,296 = room/board
$1,174 = fees
$59,600 = total billed cost per year
Students Receiving Aid: 98%

Application:

early action: 11/1 (non-binding)
regular decision: 2/15
common app: yes

Augustinian Scholarship
award	85% of tuition covered, renewable for four years
eligibility	Invitation only, based on holistic review of academic record. Approximately 60 scholarships are awarded each year.
renewal	Maintain full-time status of 12 credit hours per semester and maintain 3.25 GPA

President's Scholarship
award	$22,000 per year, renewable for four years
eligibility	31 ACT or 1420 SAT and 3.95 GPA.
renewal	Maintain full-time status of 12 credit hours per semester and maintain 3.25 GPA

Ruth Kerr Scholarship
award	$20,000 per year, renewable for four years
eligibility	29 ACT or 1350 SAT and 3.75 GPA.
renewal	Maintain full-time status of 12 credit hours per semester and maintain 3.0 GPA

Wallace L. Emerson Scholarship
award	$18,000 per year, renewable for four years
eligibility	24 ACT with 3.95 GPA to 31 ACT with 3.25 GPA. See full table on website.
renewal	Maintain full-time status of 12 credit hours per semester and maintain 3.0 GPA

Founders Scholarship
award	$15,000 per year, renewable for four years
eligibility	21 ACT with 3.95 GPA to 31 ACT with 3.00 GPA. See full table on website.
renewal	Maintain full-time status of 12 credit hours per semester and maintain 2.75 GPA

Warrior Academic Award
award	$12,000 per year, renewable for four years
eligibility	21 ACT with 3.75 GPA to 29 ACT with 3.0 GPA. See full table on website.
renewal	Maintain full-time status of 12 credit hours per semester and maintain 2.0 GPA

William Jewell College

Liberty, Missouri   816-781-7700   www.jewell.edu

Basic Profile:

enrollment: 1,090-1,200 (private)
average ACT: 22
average SAT: 1100
U.S. News ranking: 147 (liberal arts)
Student/Faculty Ratio: 10/1

Financial Information:

$33,500 = tuition
$9,930 = room/board
$900 = fees
$44,330 = total billed cost per year
Students Receiving Aid: 100%

Application:

priority date: 1/15
early decision: 11/1
common app: yes

*rolling admission

Oxbridge Scholarship
award	$26,000, awarded to 18-22 students who agree to study one of six Oxbridge majors
eligibility	mean ACT of 30 and class rank in the top 10%

Jewell Premier Scholarships

award	$20,000-$26,000; renewable for 4 years
eligibility	3.5+ GPA, 31+ ACT, essay, resume, Scholar Recognition Day in Feb. or March
application	no separate application
deadline	1/15

Academic Scholarships

award	$13,000-$18,000; renewable for 4 years
eligibility	3.4 GPA and 24 ACT or 1170 SAT sliding scale to 4.0 GPA and 30 ACT or 1400 SAT
application	no separate application
deadline	1/15

 Worcester Polytechnic Institute

Worcester, Mass.   508-831-5286   www.wpi.edu

Basic Profile:

enrollment: 6,573 (private)
average ACT: 27-32
average SAT: 1310-1480
U.S. News ranking: 116 (regional)
Student/Faculty Ratio: 18/1

Financial Information:

$49,860 = tuition
$15,644 = room/board
$870 = fees
$66,374 = total billed cost per year
Students Receiving Aid: 97%

Application:

early action I: 11/1 non-binding
early action II: 1/1 non-binding
regular decision: 2/1

Presidential Scholarship

award	$20,000 minimum; renewable for 4 years; number awarded varies each year
eligibility	exceptional academic performance, SAT/ACT scores; leadership, service, activities
application	all applicants to Worcester Poly Tech are considered; no separate application is required
deadline	admission application must be received by 11/15 (early action I),1/1 (early action II) or 2/1(reg. decision)

Several other specialized scholarships available at http://www.wpi.edu/admissions/undergraduate/apply/merits.

THE *OTC* PRIVATE SCHOLARSHIP DATABASE

Appendix E contains the most current information available at the time of printing. Items are subject to change.

		Award	Deadline	Eligibility	Requirements	Details of Requirement(s)	Website
A							
1	American Legion Oratorical Contest	varies by State	varies by state	HS student	speeches	Assigned Constitutional Issue	http://www.legion.org/ oratorical
3	Akash Kuruvilla Memorial Scholarship	$1,000	mid June	undergrads	750 word essay, 500 word personal statement, two letters of recommendation, and academic transcript	You must submit a 750 - word essay answering the following question: "What does the phrase 'The American Dream' mean to you, and how do you embody 'The American Dream'?"	https://www. akmscholarship.com/
4	American Fire Sprinkler Association Scholarship Program	$2,000	early April	HS senior	10 question open book quiz	use, benefits, or history of automatic fire sprinklers	www.afsa scholarship.org/
5	Distinguished Young Women Cash Scholarships & College- Granted Scholarships	varies by college	varies by state. Typically applicants enroll during the summer between sophomore and junior	-female -US citizen -have never been married -have never been pregnant	interview, fitness, self- expression, scholastics, talent	in addition to giving a possible speech, applicants must prepare a choreographed routine	http://distinguishedyw. org/scholarships/
6	America's National Teenager	$1,000-$1,0000	July	women ages 12-18	scholastic/ community service pageant	academics, onstage question, interview	http://nationalteen.com/ nationals-info/
7	Amy Writing Awards	$1,000-$10,000	mid Jan. may submit up to 10 articles	all students	must have published religious article in secular publication	article must have directly quoted the Bible and be published in a secular publication.	www.amyfound.org/ amy_writing_awards/ amy_writing_awards. html

		Award	Deadline	Eligibility	Requirements	Details of Requirement(s)	Website
8	youngARTS Program	$250-$10,000 and trophy	mid Oct.	age 15-18 or grades 10-12	varies by category	categories include cinematic arts, dance, design, jazz, music, photography, theater, visual arts, voice and writing	www.youngarts.org/apply
9	Ayn Rand Essay Contests	$30-$2,000	late March to Late April	HS students and undergrads	Essay- for big bucks.	8th-10th grade: 600-1200 words on Anthem; 11th-12th grade: 800-1600 words on Fountainhead ; 12th & undergrads: 800- 1600 words on Atlas Shrugged	https://www.aynrand.org/students/essay-contests
B							
10	BMI Student Composer Awards	$500-$5,000	early Feb.	citizen of Western Hemisphere country, under 28, studying music	submit original, unpublished musical score	classical tradition	bmi.com/foundation/program/bmi_student_compos er_awards/
12	Burger King/ McLamore Scholarship	$1,000-$50,000	mid Dec. - only first 50,000 applications processed	HS seniors, live in USA, Canada, or Puerto Rico, 2.5+ GPA, plan to be a full-time student	application, school nomination, scores, financial need	varies by year - see website	www.bkmclamore foundation.org/ WhatWeDo/ ScholarsProgram
C							
13	Canon Envirothon	$1,000-$5,000 for each team member	varies by location	HS students form five-member teams	teams compete in competition that stresses knowledge of forestry, soils, aquatics, wildlife, and current environmental issues		www.envirothon.org/
14	Coca-Cola Scholars Program	$1,000-$20,000	late Oct.	HS seniors, 3.0+ GPA	preliminary online application; additional applications for those that advance	academic achievement, extracurricular activities, community service, etc.	http://www.coca-colascholars foundation.org/ applicants/
15	Collegiate Inventors Competition	up to $30,000 ($10,000 for advisor)	mid Nov.	teams of/ or individual undergraduate and graduate students	original, working, and documented/ patented scientific innovations, essay	essay must describe key characteristics of invention	www.invent.org/ collegiate/
D							

		Award	Deadline	Eligibility	Requirements	Details of Requirement(s)	Website
16	Disaster Preparation Scholarship	$2,000	early May	HS and college students	video contest	You must create a video that shows how properly planning for a hurricane or other flood disaster can be a valuable tool and upload it to YouTube in order to be considered for this award.	https://waterdamage specialists.com/ scholarship/
17	Discover Student Loans Scholarship	$2,500	late Feb.	HS seniors	Application		https://www.discover. com/student-loans/ scholarships/award. html
18	Discovery Young Scientist Challenge	$500- approx. $25,000	mid April	grades 5-8	nomination based on participation in a science fair affiliated with Science Service	Submit a 1-2min. video on a scientific concept, selected from a given list	www.youngscientist challenge.com/
19	Teens for Jeans Scholarship	$500- $5,000	late Feb.	HS students	Upload a photo of the jeans you collect and donate to a local shelter		https://www. dosomething.org/us/ campaigns/teens-jeans
20	Donna Reed Performing Arts Scholarships	$625- $1,000	late April	HS seniors or undergrad artists in acting, vocal, or musical theater	video or audio tape audition in one of two categories	3 finalists give live performances	http://www.donnareed. org/html/templates/ dr_section.php?dr_ section=scholar
21	Dupont Challenge	$1,000- $5,000	late Jan.	grades 6-12	science essay	700-1000 words about a technological or scientific theory, development, or event	thechallenge.dupont. com/essay/
E							
22	Elie Wiesel Prize in Ethics	$500- $5,000	early Dec.	undergraduate juniors and seniors	essay	3000-4000 words on pressing ethical issue	www.eliewiesel foundation.org/ prizeinethics.aspx
23	Elks Americanism Essay Contest	$250- $1,000 savings bond	January	grades 5-8	essay of 300 words or fewer	essay should be of a patriotic nature	https://www.elks. org/programs/ americanism.cfm
24	Elks Most Valuable Student Competition	$4,000- $50,000	mid Nov., must take ACT or SAT before mid Nov.	HS seniors, possibly with demonstration of financial need	test scores, transcript, application, 2 recommendations, essay, scholarship, leadership, and financial need	< 500 words describing the role leadership has played in HS accomplishments, career aspirations, achieving life goals, and preparing for college	www.elks.org/enf
F							

		Award	Deadline	Eligibility	Requirements	Details of Requirement(s)	Website
25	Federal Junior Duck Stamp Conservation and Design Program	State: varies National: $200-$1,000	March or Jan. - varies according to	grades K-12	stamp design	9"x12" picture of a North American waterfowl	http://www.fws.gov/birds/education/junior-duck-stamp-conservation-program/junior-duck-stamp-contest-information.php
27	Fleet Reserve Association Americanism Essay Contest	$1,000-$5,000	Dec. 1	grades 7-12	essay, sponsored by branch of FRA of Ladies Auxiliary	<350 words on America/patriotism	http://www.fra.org/fra/Web/Web/Content/FRA_Scholarships.aspx
G							
28	Gates Millennium Scholars	amounts vary, average =	mid. Jan.	HS senior, minority background, financial need, 3.3+	school nomination package		www.gmsp.org
29	George S. and Stella M. Knight Historical Essay Contest (Sons of the American Revolution	$1,000-$5,000	late Dec.	9-12 grade	essay with 5 sources	800-1,200 words on the founding of our nation	https://www.sar.org/education/youth-contests-awards/george-s-stella-m-knight-essay-contest
30	Glamour 's Top Ten College Women	$3,000-$20,000	mid Sept.	undergrad female, junior	transcript, list of extracurricular activities, recommendations	<500 words on most meaningful achievements and their relation to future goals	http://www.glamour.com/images/inspired/2016/04/2017-cwoty-application.pdf
H							
31	Hearst Journalism Awards Program	$1,000-$10,000	vary by competition	undergraduates with less than one year professional journalism experience	requirements vary by category (print, writing, photojournalism, broadcast news, multimedia etc.		www.hearstfdn.org/
32	Hood Milk Sportsmanship Scholarship	$5,000	Mid March	HS student athletes across New England	Requires 3.0 GPA or higher	Students will be asked to write an essay explaining how they display sportsmanship and integrity on and off the field.	https://hood.com/scholarship
33	Horatio Alger Association Scholarships	$2,500-$22,000	late Oct.	HS seniors w/ involvement in community and school activities, 2.0+ GPA, and financial need (>$50k)	application and 4 short answer essays on the application		https://scholars.horatioalger.org/
34	Humane Studies Fellowships	up to $15,000	late Jan.	graduate students	1-3 recommendations, 2 essays (50-1000 words)	essay must outline proposed course of study (usually relates to free market	www.theihs.org/

		Award	Deadline	Eligibility	Requirements	Details of Requirement(s)	Website
I							
35	Intel Science and Engineering Fair (ISEF)	$500-$50,0000	mid May	HS students	participation in affiliated fairs with science fair project	categories cover a broad range of physical science, natural sciences, and mathematics	https://student.societyforscience.org/intel-isef-awards
J							
37	Jaycees Scholarships	$1,000	apps. may be requested until Feb.	HS seniors, undergrads, and grad. students, financial need	application		http://www.raleighjaycees.org/projects/Scholarship/
38	Joseph S. Rumbaugh Historical Oration Contest (Sons of the American Revolution scholarship)	$200-$5,000	varies	9th-12th grade	speech	five to six minutes on a person, event, or document of the Revolutionary War	https://www.sar.org/education/youth-contests-awards/joseph-s-rumbaugh-historical-oration-contest
39	Junior Achievement Scholarship Program	varies by program	varies by program	age varies by program, must be members of Junior Achievement	requirements vary by program (programs include: art, writing, education, engineering, and others)	all require ACT/SAT scores and a transcript	www.ja.org
40	Junior Science Humanities Symposium	$1,000-$12,000	varies by region	HS students	written report and oral presentation	any scientific field	www.jshs.org
L							
41	L. Ron Hubbard Writers and Illustrators of the Future	$500-$5,000	entries are judged every three months	any age	applicants submit original prose or illustration—no poetry; applicants must not have been previously published	prose must be under 17,000 words and be either fantasy, science fiction, or horror; illustrations must be science fiction or fantasy	www.writersofthefuture.com/
M							
42	Mensa Scholarships	Varies by locality	mid. Jan.	HS seniors and undergraduates	3 levels of competition; essays are judged by panels of 3	550 words about vocational and academic goals	http://www.mensafoundation.org/what-we-do/scholarships/us-scholarship-process/us-scholarship-application/
43	Morris K. Udall Scholarship	$7,000	early March	undergraduate sophomores and juniors who are committed to careers related to the environment or tribal public policy	B average, 3 recommendations, institutional nomination, application, essay, transcript	<800 words on a speech, legislative act, book, or public policy statement by either Morris K. Udall or Stewart L. Udall and its impact on your	http://www.udall.gov/ourPrograms/scholarship/scholarship.aspx

		Award	Deadline	Eligibility	Requirements	Details of Requirement(s)	Website
					N		
44	NACA Regional Council Student Leader Scholarship	varies by program	varies by program - first 75 applications for each scholarship are considered	undergrad and graduate students	applicants are expected to provide evidence of significant participation and leadership on campus	<100 word bio	https://www.naca.org/ Foundation/Pages/ Scholarships.aspx
45	National Beta Club Scholarship Program	$1,000-$15,000	mid Nov.	HS seniors who are active National Beta Club Members	nomination by local National Beta Club chapter, application	must exemplify clubs goals and submit SAT/ACT scores	https://www.betaclub.org/scholarship
46	National History Day	$250-$1,000	deadlines vary by state and category, national competition held in June	students grades 6-12	students participate in group or an individual paper, an exhibit, a performance, a documentary, or a web site	each year has a theme (past themes include: "Rights and Responsibilities," "Taking a Stand," and "Revolution, Reaction, Reform")	http://nhd.org/affiliates/
47	National Honor Society Scholarship	$1,500-$25,000	mid-late Jan.	HS seniors	NHS chapter nomination, transcript, application, 2 brief recommendations, essay	<300 words on a topic related to scholarship, service, character, or leadership	https://www.nhs.us/ students/the-nhs-scholarship
48	National Peace Essay Contest	$1,000-$10,000	mid March	HS students	essay	1,000 to 1250 words on a provided international affairs topic; past topics included human rights violations, war crimes, peacekeeping, intervention	http://www.usip.org/ AFSAEssayContest
49	National WWII Museum Essay Contest	$1,000	mid March	HS students	100 word essay	submit an essay answering the following question "How do you define a hero?"	http://www. nationalww2museum. org/learn/education/ for-students/essay-contests/
50	No Essay College Scholarship	$2,000	entries are chosen at the end of every month	HS seniors and undergraduate students	online application with a short about you		https://colleges.niche. com/scholarship/apply. aspx
51	NSHSS Foundation STEM Scholarship	$1,000	early April	HS seniors	available for students interested in studying science, technology, engineering, or mathematics	students must have above a 3.0 GPA	http://nshssfoundation. org/scholarships/

		Award	Deadline	Eligibility	Requirements	Details of Requirement(s)	Website
52	Children of Warriors National President's Scholarship	$2,000-$5,000	early March	HS seniors, must complete 50 hours of community service during HS years	descendent of veteran(s); financial need; application including <1000-word essay, character, scholastic	four letters of recommendation required - see application form for details, ACT/SAT scores and FAFSA required	www.legion-aux.org/Scholarships/
O							
53	Odenza Vacations Scholarship	$500	early June	ages 17-24	essay, minimum GPA of 2.5	Submit answer to the essay question, which can be found on the application page	http://odenzavacations scholarships.com/vacations/208/eligibility_odenza_vacations_college_scholarship.php
54	Olin L. Livesey Scholarship Fund	$250-$10,000 (according to need)	(according to need)	HS seniors, financial need	activity list, recommendations, transcript, financial need is a factor		no website; call at 909-648-6778
55	Optimist International CCDHH Scholarships	$2,500	varies by chapter	all HS students who are deaf or hard of hearing, enter through local Optimist Club	4-5 minutes project presented orally or through sign language	topic provided by organization (past topic has been "If I could change the world")	www.optimist.org/e/member/scholarships2.cfm
56	Optimist International Essay Contest	$2,500	late Feb.	HS students under 19, enter through local Optimist Club	essay 700-800 words on a provided topic	past topic: "I want to make a difference because…"	http://www.optimist.org/e/member/scholarships3.cfm
57	Optimist International Oratorical Contest	$1,000-$2,500	late March	HS students under 19, enter through local Optimist Club	speech	4-5 minutes, memorized, on a provided topic	http://www.optimist.org/e/member/scholarships4.cfm
P							
59	Profile in Courage Essay Contest	$500-$10,000	early Jan.	HS students	essay	< 1000 words to describe and analyze an act of political courage by a United States elected official that took place during or after 1956. The essay may concern an issue at the local, state, national, or intl level.	http://www.jfklibrary.org/Education/Profile-in-Courage-Essay-Contest.aspx
60	Prudential Spirit of Community Awards	$1,000-$5,000	early Nov.	grades 5-12	service project, verification from local administrator; application		spirit.prudential.com/view/page/soc/14830

		Award	Deadline	Eligibility	Requirements	Details of Requirement(s)	Website
R							
61	Radio and Television News Directors Association Scholarships	$1,000-$10,000	early May	undergrads (sophomores on up) with an interest in radio or television	varies by scholarship	resume, three sample of journalistic work, recommendation, and info about professional intentions; different awards may require minority status or financial need, reference	http://www.rtdna.org/content/scholarships
62	Religious Liberty Essay Scholarship Contest	$500-$2,000	early March	HS juniors or seniors	students submit an essay	800-1,200 word essay on the following topic "Should an elected official be able to opt out of certain job duties?"	
S							
63	Scholarship Points Scholarship	$1,000-$10,000	mid March	HS students	selection based on random drawing	Simply make an account on their website	https://www.scholarshippoints.com/free-college-scholarships/
64	Scholastic Art and Writing Awards	$1,000-$10,000	varies by category	grades 7-12	students submit work in any number of 15 Art, 10 Writing, and 7 special categories	varies by category	www.artandwriting.org/awards
65	Siemens Westinghouse Science & Technology Competition	$1,000-$100,000	late Sept.	HS students	individual or team research project	project must contribute to society and enhance the knowledge base of a particular discipline	https://www.siemens-foundation.org/programs/the-siemens-competition-in-math-science-technology/
66	Signet Classic Student Scholarship Essay Contest	$1,000	mid-April	HS juniors and seniors	2-3 page essay	classic literary work selected every year for essay topics	http://www.penguin.com/services-academic/essayhome/
67	Soroptimist Programs	$3,000-$10,000	deadlines vary (but before Dec.)	female, primary financial supporter for family, financial need	application, two references		www.soroptimist.org/whatwedo/programs.html
T							
68	Tesoro Youth Leadership Award	$2,500	late Feb.	HS seniors	essay under 500 words, transcript, resume, recommendation, and color headshot	topic such as "How have you exhibited values of integrity and respect in leadership and participation in school and community events	http://nshssfoundation.org/resources/tesoro-youth-leadership-awards/

		Award	Deadline	Eligibility	Requirements	Details of Requirement(s)	Website
69	Thermo Fisher Scientific Antibody Scholarship	$5,000-$10,000	late June	undergraduate students majoring in	complete online application with academic transcript		https://www.thermofisher.com/us/en/home/life-science/antibodies/thermo-fisher-scientific-antibody-scholarship-program.html
70	Toshiba/NSTA ExploraVision	$5,000-$10,000 and other prizes	late Jan.	grades K-12, students form 2-4 person teams	essay and website designs to explain your idea, Entry form, Bibliography	each team prepares a written description of a futuristic technology and five sample illustrations of potential web pages that would explain the technology	www.exploravision.org/
				U			
71	U.S. Bank Internet Scholarship Program	$5,000-$20,000	late May	HS students and undergraduates	selection based on random drawing		https://www.usbank.com/community/financial-education/scholarship.html
72	U.S. Foreign Service National High School Essay Contest	$1,250-$2,500, full tuition for a Semester at Sea voyage	mid March	HS students	essay	750-1000 words on a provided foreign affairs topic	www.afsa.org/essaycontest/
73	U.S. Senate Youth Program	$5,000-$10,000	state deadlines vary, but are before December (usually Sept.- Nov.)	HS juniors and seniors	application process varies by state, but is based on the student's activities and knowledge of government and politics		http://ussenateyouth.org/selection_process_qualify/
				V			
74	VFW Youth Essay Competition	$500-$5,000	early Nov.	grades 6-8	essay	300-400 words on a chosen theme; past themes have included "The America I bielive in"	https://www.vfw.org/PatriotsPen/
75	VFW Voice of Democracy	$1,000-$30,000, and other local, smaller scholarships	early Nov.	HS students	3-5 minute recorded essay	students write a patriotic essay and record themselves reading the essay and submit the tape	https://www.vfw.org/VOD/

E

		Award	Deadline	Eligibility	Requirements	Details of Requirement(s)	Website
W							
76	Washington Crossing Foundation Scholarships	$500-$5,000	mid Jan.	HS seniors who pursue a government career	transcript, test scores, recommendations, activity list, <300 word essay	discuss career goals and inspiration from Washington's crossing of the Delaware	www.gwcf.org
77	We the Students Scholarship	$5,000	Early Feb.	Students ages 14-19	500-800 word essay	Students write an essay on how the Founding Fathers believed in the sanctity and important of the individual liberties guaranteed in the Bill of Rights	https://www.billofrightsinstitute.org/engage/students-programs-events/scholarship/
Y							
78	Young American Patriotic Art Awards	$500-$10,000	late March	HS students	original artwork along with brief explanation of patriotism expressed in the art	specific size and subject requirements vary; accurate portrayal of the flag required (if used)	http://www.vfwauxiliary.org/programs-page/scholarships/
79	Young Naturalist Awards	$50-$2,500	early March	grades 7-12	essay judged on 70 point scale, must include photographs	word ranges vary from 500-3000 words depending on grade level; entrants choose between a narrative or an essay focusing on field-journal entries	www.amnh.org/learn-teach/young-naturalist-awards

NOTES

NOTES

OVERVIEW OF CANADIAN COLLEGES

Appendix F contains the most current information available at the time of printing. Items are subject to change.

(A STRONG U.S. DOLLAR MAKES CANADIAN COLLEGES EVEN MORE AFFORDABLE.)

ACADIA UNIVERSITY   *OTC* Recommended

Wolfville, Nova Scotia   902-585-1222   www.acadiau.ca

by the numbers…

3,411	total enrollment
$17,363 CAD	tuition
$10,900 CAD	room/board
$28,263 CAD	total

brief overview…

- International Students: 9%
- Full Time Students: 93%
- 1st-year residence spaces: 800
- Maclean's Guide Ranking: 2/21 (universities)
- Nearest major city: Halifax (350,000—1 hour drive)

BISHOP'S UNIVERSITY   *OTC* Recommended

Sherbrooke, Quebec   819-822-9600   www.ubishops.ca

by the numbers…

2,679	total enrollment
$6,815 CAD	tuition
$9,500 CAD	room/board
$26,315 CAD	total

brief overview…

- International Students: 6%
- Full Time Students: 99%
- 1st-year residence spaces: 685
- Maclean's Guide Ranking: 11/21 (universities)
- Nearest city: Sherbrooke (194,600),
- Nearest major city: Montreal (3,814,700—2 hour drive)

MCGILL UNIVERSITY   *OTC* Recommended

Montreal, Quebec   514-398-3910   www.mcgill.ca

by the numbers…

27,526	total enrollment
$16,816 CAD	tuition
$7,589 CAD	room/board
$2,828 CAD	fees
$27,232 CAD	total

brief overview…

- International Students: 23%
- Full Time Students: 82%
- 1st-year residence spaces: 3,060
- Maclean's Guide Ranking: 1/15 (medical doctoral)
- McGill is considered the "Harvard of Canada". It has a large population yet reasonable class sizes, and its perks include excellent academic programs, an internationally renowned reputation, and a beautiful campus in the heart of the historically rich, bilingual city of Montreal.

MOUNT ALLISON UNIVERSITY   *OTC* Recommended

Sackville, New Brunswick   506-364-2269   www.mta.ca

by the numbers...

2,422	total enrollment
$17,600 CAD	tuition
$10,073 CAD	room/board
$27,673 CAD	total

brief overview...

- International Students: 8%
- Full Time Students: 95%
- 1st-year residence spaces: 750
- Maclean's Guide Ranking: 1 (universities)
- Mount Allison may be an historic university (established in 1839) but the academic atmosphere is hardly obsolete, due to its lively local music scene and a host of student activities like film clubs, hockey, theatre and more.

ST. FRANCIS XAVIER UNIVERSITY   *OTC* Recommended

Antigonish, Nova Scotia   1-877-867-7839   www.stfx.ca

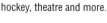

by the numbers...

4,662	total enrollment
$16,168 CAD	tuition
$11,632 CAD	room/board
$27,800 CAD	total

brief overview...

- International Students: 3.3%
- Full Time Students: 87.6%
- 1st-year residence spaces: 997
- Maclean's Guide Ranking: 1/21 (undergraduate)
- Maclean's Reputational Survey: 17/47
- St. Francis Xavier maintains a Jesuit tradition of academic excellence and community enrichment; it offers a small campus but encourages global thinking.

UNIVERSITY OF BRITISH COLUMBIA

Vancouver, British Columbia   604-822-3014   www.ubc.ca

by the numbers...

18,305	total enrollment
$37,680 CAD	tuition
$10,859 CAD	room/board
$48,539 CAD	total

brief overview...

- International Students: 14%
- Full Time Students: 70%
- 1st-year residence spaces: 5,694
- Maclean's Guide Ranking: 4/15 (medical doctoral)
- Nearest major city: Vancouver (2,328,000)

UNIVERSITY OF CALGARY

Calgary, Alberta   403-220-6645   www.ucalgary.ca

by the numbers...

30,878	total enrollment
$6,110 CAD	tuition
$8,705 CAD	room/board
$14,815	total

brief overview...

- International Students: 2%
- Full Time Students: 88%
- 1st-year residence spaces: 841
- Maclean's Guide Ranking: 7/15 (medical doctoral)
- Nearest major city: Calgary (1,230,000)

CARLETON UNIVERSITY

Ottawa, Ontario   613-520-7400   www.carleton.ca

by the numbers...

27,273	total enrollment
$12,380 CAD	tuition
$10,647 CAD	room/board
$23,027 CAD	total

brief overview...

- International Students: 10%
- Full Time Students: 85%
- 1st-year residence spaces: 2,800
- Maclean's Guide Ranking: 7/11 (comprehensive)

DALHOUSIE UNIVERSITY

Halifax, Nova Scotia   902-494-2450   www.dal.ca

by the numbers...

18,159	total enrollment
$19,020 CAD	tuition
$10,895 CAD	room/board
$29,915 CAD	total

brief overview...

- International Students: 6%
- Full Time Students: 86%
- 1st-year residence spaces: 2,595
- Maclean's Guide Ranking: 7/15 (medical doctoral)
- Nearest major city: Halifax (350,000)

UNIVERSITY OF GUELPH

Guelph, Ontario   519-821-2130   www.uoguelph.ca

by the numbers...

28,674	total enrollment
$22,090 CAD	tuition
$9,264 CAD	room/board
$31,354 CAD	total

brief overview...

- International Students: 2%
- Full Time Students: 91%
- 1st-year residence spaces: 4,100
- Maclean's Guide Ranking: 4/11 (comprehensive)
- Nearest city: Guelph (195,000); nearest major city: Toronto (5,623,500, 1½ hour drive)

UNIVERSITY OF MANITOBA

Winnipeg, Manitoba   204-474-8808   www.umanitoba.ca

by the numbers...

29,260	total enrollment
$13,615 CAD	tuition
$9,224 CAD	room/board
$22,839 CAD	total

brief overview...

- International Students: 4%
- Full Time Students: 81%
- 1st-year residence spaces: 765
- Maclean's Guide Ranking: 15/15 (medical doctoral)
- Nearest city: Winnipeg (742,400)

F

MEMORIAL UNIVERSITY OF NEWFOUNDLAND

St. John's, Newfoundland   709-737-4431   www.mun.ca

by the numbers...

17,581	total enrollment
$11,460 CAD	tuition
$8,814-$10,307 CAD	room/board
$21,767 CAD	total

brief overview...

-International Students: 3%
-Full Time Students: 81%
-1st-year residence spaces: 700
-Maclean's Guide Ranking: 5/11 (comprehensive)
-Nearest city: St. John's (175,000)

UNIVERSITY OF NEW BRUNSWICK

Fredericton, New Brunswick   506-453-4865   www.unb.ca

by the numbers...

10,438	total enrollment
$9,193 CAD	tuition
$9,750 CAD	room/board
$18,943 CAD	total

brief overview...

-International Students: 3%
-Full Time Students: 81%
-1st-year residence spaces: 1,732
-Maclean's Guide Ranking: 6/11 (comprehensive)
-Nearest city: Fredericton (50,535); nearest major city: St. John's, New Brunswick (126,600, 1½ hour drive)

QUEST UNIVERSITY

Squamish, BC   888-783-7808   www.questu.edu

by the numbers...

540	total enrollment
$35,000 CAD	tuition
$13,450 CAD	room/board
$48,450 CAD	total

SIMON FRASER UNIVERSITY

Burnaby, British Columbia   604-291-3995   www.sfu.ca

by the numbers...

29,652	total enrollment
$25,220 CAD	tuition
$10,064 CAD	room/board
$35,284 CAD	total

brief overview...

-International Students: 11%
-Full Time Students: 66%
-1st-year residence spaces: 727
-Maclean's Guide Ranking: 2/11 (comprehensive)
-Nearest city: Burnaby (essentially a suburb of Vancouver, population 2,328,000)

UNIVERSITY OF TORONTO

Toronto, Ontario   416-978-2190   www.utoronto.ca

by the numbers…

86,709	total enrollment
$45,690 CAD	tuition
$16,311 CAD	room/board
$62,001 CAD	total

brief overview…

- International Students: 14%
- Full Time Students: 88%
- 1st-year residence spaces: 5,153
- Maclean's Guide Ranking: 2/11 (medical doctoral)
- Nearest major city: Toronto (5,623,500)

UNIVERSITY OF VICTORIA

Victoria, British Columbia   250-721-8121   www.uvic.ca

by the numbers…

21,593	total enrollment
$21,675 CAD	tuition
$9,306 CAD	room/board
$30,981 CAD	total

brief overview…

- International Students: 4%
- Full Time Students: 75%
- 1st-year residence spaces: 2,070
- Maclean's Guide Ranking: 2/11 (comprehensive)
- Nearest city: Victoria (352,400)
- Victoria is often considered as one of the most beautiful and unique cities in Canada. It is about a two-hour ferry ride from Vancouver.

UNIVERSITY OF WATERLOO

Waterloo, Ontario   519-888-4567   www.uwaterloo.ca

by the numbers…

36,657	total enrollment
$31,170 CAD	tuition
$10,683 CAD	room/board
$41,853 CAD	total

brief overview…

- International Students: 10%
- Full Time Students: 92%
- 1st-year residence spaces: 5,548
- Maclean's Guide Ranking: 3/11 (comprehensive)
- Nearest city: Waterloo (97,475); nearest major city: Kitchener (489,100—15 minute drive).

WILFRID LAURIER UNIVERSITY

Waterloo, Ontario   519-884-0710   www.wlu.ca

by the numbers…

18,903	total enrollment
$28,350 CAD	tuition
$11,750 CAD	room/board
$40,100 CAD	total

brief overview…

- International Students: 1%
- Full Time Students: 84%
- 1st-year residence spaces: 3,418
- Maclean's Guide Ranking: 4/21 (undergraduate)
- Nearest city: Waterloo (97,475); nearest major city: Kitchener (489,100—15 minute drive).

UNIVERSITY OF WINDSOR

Windsor, Ontario   519-253-3000   www.uwindsor.ca

by the numbers...

15,574	total enrollment
$20,500 CAD	tuition
$7,500 CAD	room/board
$28,000 CAD	total

brief overview...

- International Students: 10%
- Full Time Students: 82%
- 1st-year residence spaces: 679
- Maclean's Guide Ranking: 8/11 (comprehensive)
- Nearest city: Windsor (331,500); nearest major city: Detroit, Michigan (15 minute drive).

YORK UNIVERSITY

Toronto, Ontario   416-736-5000   www.yorku.ca

by the numbers...

52,418	total enrollment
$24,587 CAD	tuition
$9,702 CAD	room/board
$34,289 CAD	total

brief overview...

- International Students: 5%
- Full Time Students: 82%
- 1st-year residence spaces: 1,340
- Maclean's Guide Ranking: 9/11 (comprehensive)
- Nearest major city: Toronto (5,623,500)

ART SCHOOLS IN CANADA • SPECIALTY COLLEGES

Prestigious Art Institutes in the United States can cost aspiring artists more than $50,000 a year, but the little known secret is that a comparable education can be obtained in Canada for a fraction of the price.

ALBERTA COLLEGE OF ART AND DESIGN

Calgary, Alberta   403-284-7617   www.acad.ca

by the numbers...

1,213	total enrollment
$14,935 CAD	tuition
$873 CAD	fees
$15,808 CAD	total

-No on-campus residency offered.

brief overview...

- The programs range from traditional majors, such as painting and drawing, to innovative degrees in digital media and design.
- Small class sizes; third and fourth year students are provided personal studio spaces; first year classes in- clude liberal studies and art history.

EMILY CARR UNIVERSITY OF ART AND DESIGN

Vancouver, British Columbia   1-800-832-7788   www.eciad.ca

by the numbers...

1,873	total enrollment
$15,966 CAD	tuition
$3,000 CAD	art supplies
$18,966 CAD	total

-No on-campus residency offered.

brief overview...

-Most Popular Majors: Animation, Communication Design, Industrial Design, Photography
-One common foundation year; third year students can take a semester at one of 65 other art institutes in North America, Europe, or Australia; fourth year studies usually include internships.

NOVA SCOTIA COLLEGE OF ART AND DESIGN

Halifax, Nova Scotia   1-888-444-5989   www.nscad.ca

by the numbers...

833	total enrollment
$19,170 CAD	tuition
$1,805 CAD	art supplies
$20,975 CAD	total

-No on-campus residency offered.

brief overview...

-Known as a world-class art institute, producing highly- employable graduates who go on to work in web and graphic design firms, film and television, illustration, and other fields of fine art.
-Also offers many internship opportunities for students.
-Most popular degrees: Ceramics, Film, Fine Art, Photography.

ONTARIO COLLEGE OF ART AND DESIGN

Toronto, Ontario   416-977-6000   www.ocad.ca

by the numbers...

3,431	total enrollment
$18,055 CAD	tuition
$2,500 CAD	art supplies
$20,555 CAD	total

brief overview...

-Highlights include an art program in Florence, Italy, and a recent campus-wide renovation program, which incorporates the brand new Sharp Centre for Design.
-Ontario is the oldest and largest of all Canada's Art Institutions.
-Most popular degrees: Advertising, Drawing and Painting, Graphic Design, Illustration.

MILITARY OPTIONS

College ROTC Background Information

ROTC programs were designed to augment the service academies in producing leaders and managers for the armed forces. Each branch of the service has a specific set of courses and training that officers must complete prior to joining. ROTC programs allow students to do this while completing their college education. Upon graduation, members are commissioned (certified) by the President of the United States to serve as a leader in active, reserve, or guard components of each branch.

ROTC Financial Benefits

Each branch of the service offers ROTC scholarships to eligible students. Eligibility criteria is listed by branch below. The table below lists the different scholarship levels.

Scholarship Type	Pays	Monthly Stipend	When Do I Apply?
4-Year National	Full Tuition, Books, and Fees	$200	Junior/Senior Year of HS
2- or 3-Year Scholarships	Full Tuition, Books, and Fees	$200	Freshman/Sophomore Year of College
College Program	N/A	$200	Freshman/Sophomore Year of College
Unit Scholarships	Full Tuition, Books, and Fees	$200	Freshman/Sophomore Year of College

Frequently Asked Questions about the ROTC

1. Am I obligated to the service if I join ROTC without a scholarship?

   No.

G

2. Am I obligated to the service if I receive an ROTC scholarship?

Yes and No.

- The NO part: You are not obligated until the first semester of your sophomore year if you have a four-year scholarship. This is commonly referred to as the freshman trial period.

- For two- and three-year scholarship winners, your obligation will occur upon completion of your services' respective summer training.

- College Program students have an obligation that normally begins after their junior year.

3. Can ROTC students be called to war while in college?

No. Only trained personnel are sent to combat. You can think of ROTC and your college education as a prolonged training period.

ROTC Branch Comparison

Can I choose my school?

Students that apply for Army ROTC scholarships can choose up to three schools. Scholarships are awarded based upon availability at the school of your choice. The Army does try to match the needs of the student in most cases, but the Army does have final say to which school you attend.

Naval ROTC grants the student the most flexibility in selecting schools. Students can attend any one of 67 host NROTC universities once they obtain a scholarship.

Air Force ROTC scholarships are distributed by major. You are free to choose any school as long as the school you want to attend offers AFROTC, and you choose an approved scholarship major.

Can I choose my major?

Yes, within limits, and you must complete one year of calculus and one year of calculus-based physics.

Minimum Test Requirements

ROTC scholarships are increasingly competitive. ACT scores at least in the mid to high 20s and SAT scores of at least 1250 are usually necessary for consideration.

*ROTC information was compiled from the U.S. Military's website and from recruitment literature.

Military Academies

School	Air Force Academy	Coast Guard Academy	Merchant Marine Academy	Military Academy	Naval Academy
Location	USAF Academy, CO	New London, CT	Kings Point, NY	West Point, NY	Annapolis, MD
Undergraduate Enrollment	4, 524	996	927	4,347	4,479
Admissions Office Contact	719-333-2520	800-883-8724	516-773-5391	914-938-4041	410-293-4361
Admissions Deadlines	1/31	3/1	3/1	2/28	1/31
percent of applicants accepted	19 percent	24 percent	28 percent	16 percent	14 percent
SAT Verbal	580-668	570-670	540-640	570-680	570-680
SAT Math	610-690	610-680	595-660	590-680	620-700
ACT Score	27-31	27-31	25-29	28	—
percent graduated in top 10 percent of class	50 percent	50 percent	18 percent	72 percent	54 percent
percent graduated in top 25 percent of class	81 percent	90 percent	23 percent	93 percent	81 percent

NOTES

ACKNOWLEDGMENTS

This book would not have been possible without our *OTC* staff, especially Makayla Stephens, Heidi Macy, Deb Selby, Joni Woodruff, and Pat Olson-McGee.

The staff at Concierge Publishing also provided invaluable support on our OnToCollege™ series: the *Platinum Guide*, *America's Most Affordable Colleges*, and the *College Counselor's Manual*.

NOTES

NOTES

Reaching Higher: The Simple Strategy to Transform America's K-12 Schools explains the driving force behind *OnToCollege*.™

If your goals are to increase scores and scholarships, to ensure every student gets into their best-fit college at the right price, and to create two- and four-year college graduates with minimal debt...

This is the book!

Order one for every staff member today!